WHEN I FELL FROM THE SKY

The True Story of One Woman's Miraculous Survival

WHEN I FELL FROM THE SKY
The True Story of One Woman's Miraculous Survival

BY JULIANE KOEPCKE

IN COLLABORATION WITH BEATE RYGIERT
TRANSLATED BY ROSS BENJAMIN

Title Town
PUBLISHING

WHEN I FELL FROM THE SKY

The True Story of One Woman's Miraculous Survival

Written by Juliane Koepcke
In Collaboration with Beate Rygiert
Translated by Ross Benjamin

TitleTown Publishing, LLC
P.O. Box 12093 Green Bay, WI 54307-12093
920.737.8051 | titletownpublishing.com

North American Editor: Stephanie Finnegan
Production Associate: Martin Lederman
Cover Design: Dale Fiorillo
Interior Layout and Design: Erika L. Block

PUBLISHER'S CATALOGING-IN-PUBLICATION DATA:

Koepcke, Juliane.

When I fell from the sky : the true story of one woman's miraculous survival / Juliane Koepcke ; in collaboration with Beate Rygiert ; translated by Ross Benjamin. 1st English ed. ~ Green Bay, Wis. : TitleTown Publishing, c2011.

p. ; cm.

ISBN: 978-0-9837547-0-1
Translation of: Als ich vom Himmel fiel : wie mir der Dschungel mein Leben zurückgab (Munich : Malik, 2011; 9783890293899).
Includes index.
Summary: Describes the 11-day ordeal faced by the 17-year old sole survivor of an airplane crash in the Peruvian jungle in 1971.

1. Koepcke, Juliane. 2. Airplane crash survival~Peru~Personal narratives. 3. Aircraft accidents~Peru~Personal narratives. I. Rygiert, Beate. II. Benjamin, Ross. III. Title: Als ich vom Himmel fiel.

TL553.9 .K6413 2011

363.1/248092~dc23   1110

Printed in the USA
first edition ♻ printed on recycled paper
10 9 8 7 6 5 4 3 2 1

For my mother, who dedicated her short life to the birds of Peru,
and who was torn much too soon from my side.

CONTENTS

She did not leave the airplane, the airplane left her.

—*Werner Herzog, director and producer*

He was the first person I saw, and it was as if an angel were coming toward me.

—Juliane Koepcke, *describing her rescuer in the* Wings of Hope *documentary*

Christmas Eve, 1971

The flight from Lima to Pucallpa takes only about an hour. On December 24, 1971, the first thirty minutes are perfectly normal. Our fellow passengers are in high spirits. Everyone is excited to celebrate Christmas at home. The luggage bins are stuffed with presents, and everyone is settled in for the flight. After about twenty minutes, we're served a small breakfast, which includes a sandwich and drink. Ten minutes later the stewardesses are cleaning up our areas.

Then, all of a sudden, we hit a storm front.

And this time it's completely different from anything I've experienced before. The pilot does not avoid the thunderstorm, but flies straight into the cauldron of hell. It turns to night around us, in broad daylight. Lightning is flashing feverishly from all directions.

At the same time an invisible power begins to shake our airplane as if it were a plaything. The people cry out as objects fall on their heads from the violently opened overhead compartments. Bags, flowers, packages, toys, wrapped gifts, jackets and clothing rain down hard on us; sandwich trays and bags soar through the air; half-finished drinks splatter on our heads and shoulders. Everyone is frightened, and I hear screams and cries.

A few weeks before that flight on Christmas Eve, 1971, I had gone on an eight-day trip with my whole class. We flew to Arequipa in the southern part of the country, and in a letter to my grandmother I wrote: *The flight was glorious!* At the end of the trip, the return flight to Lima was extremely turbulent, and many of my classmates felt physically ill. But I wasn't nervous at all. I even enjoyed the rocking. I was so naive that it didn't even occur to me that something could happen.

My mother, however, doesn't like to fly. She often says: "It's totally unnatural that such a bird made of metal takes off into the air." As an ornithologist, she sees this from a different standpoint than other people do. On one of her flights to the United States, she already had an experience that gave her a huge scare, when an engine malfunctioned. Even though nothing happened and the plane was still able to land safely with one engine, she was sweating.

"Hopefully, this goes all right," my mother says. I can feel her nervousness, while I myself am still pretty calm.

Then I suddenly see a blinding white light over the right wing. I don't know whether it's a flash of lightning striking there or an explosion. I lose all sense of time. I can't tell whether all this lasts minutes or only a fraction of a second: I'm blinded by that blazing light.

With a jolt, the tip of the airplane falls steeply downward. Even though I'm in a window seat all the way in the back, I can see the whole aisle to the cockpit, which is below me. The physical laws have been suspended; it's like an earthquake. No, it is worse. Because now we're racing downward. We're falling. People are screaming in panic, shrill cries for help; the roar of the plummeting turbines, which I will hear again and again in my dreams, engulfs me.

And there, over everything, clear as glass, I hear my mother saying quite calmly: "Now it's all over."

Today I know that at that moment she already grasped what would happen.

I, on the other hand, grasp nothing at all.

An intense astonishment comes over me, because now my ears, my head—no, I myself am completely filled with the deep roar of the plane, while its nose slants almost vertically downward. We're plummeting. But this nosedive, too, I experience as if it lasted no longer than the blink of an eye. From one moment to the next, the people's screams go silent. It's as if the roar of the turbines has been erased.

My mother is no longer at my side and I'm no longer in the airplane. I'm still strapped into my seat, but I'm alone.

At an altitude of about ten thousand feet, I'm alone.

And I'm falling, slicing through the sky . . . about 2 miles above the earth.

1 My New Life

A view into the canopy of the rain forest of Panguana, 2010. This is the type of canopy that broke my fall through the sky. (Photo courtesy of Juliane (Koepcke) Diller)

Many people wonder how I still manage to get on airplanes, for I am one of the few who have survived a plane crash from a great height. It was a catastrophe that occurred nearly ten thousand feet over the Peruvian rain forest. But that's not all: After the crash I struggled for eleven days on my own through the jungle. At that time, when I fell from the sky, I was just seventeen years old.

Today I'm fifty-six. A good age for looking back. A good time to confront old, unhealed wounds and to share with other people my memories, which are just as fresh and alive after all these years. The crash, of which I was the sole survivor, shaped the rest of my life, pointed it in a new direction and led me to where I am today. Back then, newspapers all over the world were full of my story. Among them there were many half-truths and reports that had little to do with the actual events. Because of them, people still approach me to this day and ask about the crash. Everyone in Germany and Peru seems to know my story, and yet scarcely anyone has a genuine idea of what really happened back then.

Of course, it's not so simple to understand that after eleven days fighting to survive in the "green hell of the jungle," I still love the rain forest. The truth is: For me it was never a "green hell." When I plunged to earth from such a great height, the forest saved my life. Without the leaves of trees and bushes cushioning my fall, I never could have survived the impact on the ground. When I was unconscious, it screened me from the tropical sun. And later it helped me find my way out of the untouched wilderness back to civilization.

Had I been a pure city child, I never would have made it back to life. It was my good fortune that I had already spent a few years of my young life in the "jungle." (Nowadays the term "rain forest" is preferred to "jungle," but we used the words interchangeably back then.) In 1968, my parents had realized their dream and founded a biological research station in the middle of the Peruvian rain forest. At the time, I was fourteen years old and less than thrilled about leaving behind my friends in Lima and moving with my parents, our dog and parakeet, the whole kit and caboodle, into the "middle of nowhere." In any case that's how I imagined it back then, even though my parents had taken me from an early age along on their expeditions.

The move to the jungle was a real adventure. On our arrival, I immediately fell in love with that life, as simple and modest as it might have been. For almost two years I lived in Panguana, as my parents had christened the research station after a native bird. In addition to being taught by them, I went to the school of the jungle. There I got to know its rules, its laws and its inhabitants. I became acquainted with the plant life, explored the world of animals. Not for nothing was I the daughter of two well-known zoologists: My mother, Maria Koepcke, was Peru's leading ornithologist, and my father, Hans-Wilhelm Koepcke, was the author of an important comprehensive work on the life-forms of the animal and plant world. In Panguana, the jungle became my home, and there I learned which dangers loom in it and which don't. I was familiar with the rules of conduct with which a person can survive in this extreme environment. As a child, my senses were already sharpened for the incredible wonders contained by this habitat, which leads in biodiversity worldwide. Yes, I was already learning to love the jungle back then.

Those eleven days far from settlements in the middle of the tropical rain forest, eleven days during which I didn't hear a human voice and didn't know where I was, those extraordinary days have made my attachment still deeper. At that time I formed a bond with the jungle, which decisively influenced my later life, and it continues to do so today. I learned early that we're afraid only of things we don't know. Human beings have a tendency to destroy everything that frightens them, even if they cannot begin to conceive of its worth. During my lonely journey back to civilization, I was often afraid, but never of the jungle. It wasn't its fault that I landed in it. Nature is always the same, whether we're there or not, it doesn't matter to it. But we—this, too, I experienced firsthand during those eleven days—cannot survive without it.

All this is reason enough for me to devote my life to the preservation of this unique ecosystem. With Panguana, my parents left me an inheritance that I have accepted with all my heart. And today I'm taking their work there into a critical new phase: Panguana, larger than ever, is to be declared a nature reserve. Not only is this the fulfillment of my father's dream, which he spent decades fighting for, but it is also a valuable contribution to the preservation of the Amazon Rain Forest. Not least of all, this can help prevent global climate catastrophe. The rain forest is not only full of wonders, most of which we don't even know yet—its preservation as the green lung of the earth is also crucial for the continued existence of an extremely young species on this planet: human beings.

The year 2011 is the fortieth anniversary of the 1971 airplane disaster. Over all these years, much has been written about my "accident," as I call the crash. Countless newspaper pages have been filled with what people take to be "Juliane's story." From time to time there were good articles among them, but unfortunately also many that had little do with the truth. There was a time when the media attention almost overwhelmed me. To protect myself, I remained silent for years, rejected every interview and withdrew completely. But now the time has come to break my silence and tell how it really was. That's why I am now sitting at the Munich Airport on packed suitcases to begin a journey that will be important to me for two reasons: to achieve the goal of establishing Panguana as a nature reserve, and to face my past. Past, present and future are thus meaningfully intertwined. What happened to me back then and the question of why I, of all people, was the only survivor spared in the LANSA disaster—now all this finally takes on a deeper meaning.

And then I'm sitting on the airplane. Yes, people wonder with amazement how I manage to get on airplanes time and again. I manage it with willpower and discipline. I manage it because I have to if I want to return to the rain forest. But it's hard.

The airplane starts moving; we take off; we rise; we plunge deep into the dense cloud cover in the sky over Munich. I look out the window, and suddenly I see . . .

2 A Childhood Among Animals

My favorite pet, a tinamou named Polsterchen (Little Pillow) because of its soft plumage, 1967. (Photo courtesy of Juliane (Koepcke) Diller)

. . . those impenetrable black clouds and flashes of lightning. We've hit a heavy thunderstorm, and the pilot flies straight into the seething cauldron. The airplane turns into the plaything of the hurricane. Baggage and gifts wrapped for Christmas, flowers and toys fall down on us from overhead compartments. The airplane plunges directly into deep air pockets and then rises rapidly again. The people scream with fear. And suddenly there's that blinding flash over the right wing of the airplane. . . .

I take a deep breath. Above me the sign turns off; I can unfasten my seat belt. We're just beyond Munich, and our airplane has reached its cruising altitude. After a layover in Madrid, my husband, Erich Diller, and I will board the plane to Lima. Then there are still twelve hours ahead of me, twelve hours of extreme tension about six miles above the ground. Over Portugal, we will leave the mainland behind and cross the Atlantic.

If I want to return to the country where I was born, I have no other choice. Even in the age of the low-budget flight, a trip around half the globe is no picnic. I'm entering not only another continent, but also another time zone, climate and season. When it's spring at home, autumn is beginning in Peru. And even within Peru, I experience two different climate zones: the temperate one in Lima and the tropical one in the rain forest. But above all, each trip for me is a journey into the past. For in Peru, I came into the world; in Peru, I grew up; and in Peru, the event occurred that would change my life from the ground up. I was in a plane crash, survived by some miracle for several days completely on my own in the middle of the jungle and found my way back to other people. Back then, my life was given to me a second time. It was like a second birth. Only this time my mother lost her life.

7

My mother often told me how happy she was when she was pregnant with me. My parents conducted their intensive research together and loved their work more than anything. They had met as doctoral students in Kiel, and because it was difficult for passionate biologists to find a suitable position in postwar Germany, my father decided to immigrate to a country with a high, as yet unexplored, biodiversity. His then-fiancée, Maria von Mikulicz-Radecki, was excited about the plan and followed him after receiving her doctorate, which was unheard of at that time for an unmarried young woman. My grandfather was not at all pleased that my mother went on the long journey all by herself. But once she got something into her head, she could no longer be dissuaded from it. (Incidentally, my husband claims that I inherited that from her.)

In the cathedral of the Miraflores District in Lima, they were married soon after their arrival in the New World. My mother was disappointed that as a Catholic she was wed to my father, who was a Protestant, not on the main altar but in a small adjacent chapel. At that time interdenominational marriages were in the minority, and the Catholic priest tried hard to influence my mother to lead my father to the "true faith." This insistence annoyed my mother so much that she stopped attending the Catholic service and also decided after my birth to baptize me as a Protestant.

At the time my parents got married, my mother still didn't speak any Spanish, so she couldn't follow the wedding ceremony. At one point it became strangely silent in the church, and then the priest said: "*Señora*, you have to say *sí* now."

And "*sí*"–"yes"–both of them said from the bottom of their hearts. Not only to each other, but also to the kind of life they wanted to lead together. From their small apartment they soon moved into a larger house, which belonged to friends, and here I was born. Later they founded a few blocks away the "Humboldt House," well known at the time in researcher circles, in which they sublet rooms to scientists passing through from all over the world. They divided their private area of the house simply with curtains. The Humboldt House in Miraflores would go down in history as the meeting place and base station of notable scientists.

Even though both of them were devoted to their work with heart and soul, I was absolutely a wanted child. My father was hoping for a girl, and when I entered the world in 1954, on a Sunday at seven o'clock in the evening, in the Clínica Delgado in the Miraflores District of Lima, his wish came true. I was born prematurely in the eighth month of my mother's pregnancy and first had to go into the incubator. Perhaps it was a good omen that my parents decided to give me the name Juliane. It means "the cheerful one"—I find that the name suits me well.

At that time my father's mother and his sister, Cordula, were also living with us in Peru. My grandmother wanted to spend a few years in the country to which two of her sons had immigrated. For after my father had settled down here, Joachim, his younger brother, decided in 1951 to build a life here too. He worked as an administrator on various large haciendas in the north of the country. One of them was even as large as Belgium. My parents visited Uncle Joachim several times there in Taulís, which was an exceptionally interesting area for them as zoologists. Because the Andes are relatively low there, at about 6,500 feet, an unusual flora and fauna exchange takes place between the east and west side of the mountain range, and my parents discovered some new animal species there. But completely unexpectedly, while my grandmother and aunt were making their departure plans in Germany, my uncle Joachim had a deadly accident in Taulís. Having just been perfectly healthy, he died within less than two hours from spasms. To this day it remains unresolved whether he fell victim to tetanus or might have been poisoned by opium farmers he was onto.

But his mother and sister had already severed all ties at home and now decided to come, anyway. So I had the good fortune of having not only my father and mother, but also my grandmother and aunt around during the first years of my childhood. The two of them remained in Peru for six years. My aunt worked for a time as the editor in chief of the *Peruvian Post*, a German newspaper in Lima. Then they returned to their native country, my aunt because of better professional opportunities and my grandmother for health reasons, and probably also because she was homesick for Germany.

I grew up with both languages, Spanish and German. The latter was spoken at home, and it was really important to my parents that I learned their mother tongue perfectly. By no means was that a given. Some of my schoolmates of German descent had only an imperfect mastery of the language of their ancestors. I spoke Spanish with my Peruvian friends, with our housemaid and later also in school. My parents had first really learned the language in Peru, and even though they were proficient in it, a few mistakes would always creep in. But Peruvians are polite people; when it was necessary to point out an error, they always did so as gently as possible.

One day, when I was already almost grown up, I realized that my father used the formal mode of address with me in Spanish. I told him: "You can't do that. I'm your daughter!" But he became really embarrassed and confessed to me that he had never properly learned the informal mode. He was a very formal person, had few close friends and, thus, used the polite form of address without exception.

In Lima, I attended the German-Peruvian Alexander von Humboldt School. Instruction was mostly in German, but the military regime at the time placed value on subjects like history and regional geography being taught in Spanish. I remember my school days as very pleasant, even though my Peruvian schoolmates came from much better circles. No wonder, because you had to pay tuition, which the poorer families couldn't afford. When you finished school, there was a mandatory trip, which in Peru was called the "Viaje de Promoción." I took part in it, but there was to be no "Abitur," as the German university entrance exam is called, for me. A German delegation would have come specifically to test us, but a flight over the Andes would change everything.

When I came home from school, I was always surrounded by animals. As an ornithologist, my mother was constantly bringing birds home that had been injured or shot and that we nursed back to health. For a while tinamous were her main object of study. This family of birds outwardly displays similarities with partridges, but is not otherwise related to them. They occur only in South and Central America. It is funny to compare their behavior with South American machismo. For among tinamous the females are in charge: They have several males at once, who have a lot of work to do. They build the nest, have to brood the eggs and raise the young, while the female defends the turf. That caused problems with the breeding: If a male wanted to leave the nest to eat something, the female would promptly chase it back onto the eggs. Incidentally, they were brown as chocolate and shiny as porcelain.

Sometimes we also raised hatched chicks. We fed them carefully with the dropper. They liked a mixture of hard-boiled egg, ground meat and vitamin formula best. My mother had a real knack for this: Not once did a chick she was raising die. I was responsible for naming the creatures. I came up with the wildest things: A large lizard I christened Krokodeckchen (a combination of the German *"Krokodil"* and *"Eidechschen,"* the diminutive for a lizard; in English, it might have been something like Crocolizzy), and my three tinamous I named Piups (an imitation of its call when it was frightened), Polsterchen (Little Pillow, because of its soft plumage, which I loved to pet and which it often ruffled) and Kastanienäuglein (Little Chestnut Eye, because of its beautiful chestnut brown eyes).

These animals originally come from a magical landscape. It's called Lomas de Lachay and is a fog desert area on the Pacific Coast. An extremely dry desert, the Atacama, runs through parts of Peru. Because out on the ocean, the cold Humboldt Current flows by, a dense fog cover forms, known as *"garúa,"* which provides astonishingly lush vegetation at particular points where it meets the Andean slopes. In the middle of the desert, you thus encounter in those places vibrantly colorful islands of plants. My parents took me there with them a few times. This blooming oasis in the middle of the brown desert monotony appeared to me on each visit as a true wonder. And that's where our tinamous came from.

A multicolored parrot named Tobias also lived with us, whom I called "Bio" even before I learned to speak. Bio had already been in the house before my birth and at first couldn't stand me, because he was jealous. When as a small child I approached him, shouting "Bio, Bio," full of excitement, he would peck at me, until he finally had to accept me. Tobias was a very smart parrot, who didn't like it at all when his cage was soiled. When he had to go, he let out a certain sound. That was a sign for us to take Tobias out of the cage and bring him to the toilet. Yes, to the regular toilet for people! We held him above the bowl and—plop!—he did his business. When Tobias one day suffered a heart attack, my mother cured him with Italian Cinzano. That revived his circulation, and is it any surprise: From that day on, he was a fan of this aperitif. Whenever guests came, Tobias waddled over and wanted to have his sip too.

In a letter to a friend in Germany, my mother wrote of my great enthusiasm for the jungle when she took me with her for the first time to the Río Pachitea, which would later become so important for my life. At the time I was only five years old:

She copes amazingly well with any situation, such as sleeping in a tent or in a sleeping bag on a rubber mattress, whether on the beach or on a boat. For her, these are all interesting things. And you have to imagine the atmosphere on the Río Pachitea: the dim morning or evening with dense fog, the calls of the howler monkeys, the river silvery green, close to the boat the high wall of the dark jungle, from which the many-voiced concert of the crickets and cicadas sounds. You feel as if you're really in primordial nature. Juliane was probably most excited about the blooming trees and the diversity and beautiful shapes of the leaves. She has already collected a herbarium. . . .

When I was nine years old, the Belgian animal catcher Charles Cordier visited us with his wife and his menagerie. Cordier was commissioned by famous zoological gardens all over the world to trap specimens of particular animal species. He had an extremely intelligent gray parrot named Kazuco, who could speak more outstandingly than I ever witnessed a parrot speak before or since. There was also the boxer Böcki and the owl Skadi, who was allowed to fly around the bathroom at night. Monsieur Cordier released mice for the owl to catch. Sometimes it also attacked Daddy's shaving brush, because it looked so similar. Kazuco, the gray parrot from the Congo, greeted you in the morning with "Good morning" and in the evening with "Good evening." I was extremely fascinated by the clever little guy, who could also say "Böcki, sit!" And the boxer would actually sit down. Kazuco picked up sounds and sentences incredibly quickly. During the days in the Humboldt House, he learned to say: "Lima has two million people." I loved to stroke his magnificent gray-shaded plumage. Once he bit my finger hard—to this day I have a scar. Unfortunately, our Tobias died that same year of pneumonia.

I myself became seriously ill the next year—during summer vacation, of all times! I got scarlet fever, which really alarmed my parents, for my father's youngest sister had died of that illness at the same age. I was always so small, thin and frail, and so the whole family heaved a sigh of relief when after several weeks I was back on my feet and could take care of my animals again.

From an early age I was also totally enthusiastic about dogs. At the age of three I already got a spaniel. I loved Ajax dearly. Unfortunately, we had to give him away, because he needed more space to run around in than was possible in the city, and he constantly ravaged our garden. How sad I was then!

I was all the more blissful when a long-cherished wish of mine finally came true at the age of nine: We went to the animal shelter, where Lobo was already waiting for me. Lobo was a gorgeous German shepherd mix. He later came with us when we moved from Lima into the jungle to Panguana. He lived to the ripe old age of eighteen.

Some birds even came to us on their own, just as if word had gotten around that they would have it good with us. One day a gigantic Andean blackbird fluttered in, and, of course, it stayed too. My parents had visitors that day, American ornithologists from Berkeley, who immediately gave it the right name. They named the blackbird Professor because of its yellow-rimmed eyes, which gave it a bespectacled, intelligent look. Besides the Professor—whom I, however, called Franziska—we also had a yellow-crowned Amazon and a sunbittern. Those are indescribably beautiful birds. When they spread their wings, a colorful fan opens in the spectrum of dazzling earth colors. Later, in the jungle of Panguana, I benefited from my early experiences. When Indians brought me fig parrots, which they had taken from the nests when the birds were very small, I managed to raise them. In the manner of the indigenous people, I prechewed bananas and stuck the mush into their beaks. In this way they became amazingly tame.

There were also rare birds near Lima, in an inaccessible cove right by the sea. My parents liked to go there. While they pursued their observations, I played on the beach and often got sunburn. Which is no wonder, for Lima is only a few degrees of latitude from the equator. In any case my dermatologist still says today: "Your back has definitely seen too much sun." How right he is! In those days people were still carefree about sunbathing. It was similar with fleas. We always carried a spray can of DDT—that would be unthinkable today!

On this beach lived tiny crabs, which were called *"muy-muy."* "Muy" is the Spanish word for "many." The doubling of the word says something about the way they would appear. Sometimes they covered the whole beach, along the shoreline, and if you wanted to go in the water, you had to walk over them barefoot. That felt really strange! But I was a girl who knew no fear and no disgust for the excesses of nature, and I ran as fast as I could over them and then plunged into the water.

Back when my father finally arrived in Lima after an odyssey that lasted years, he had in his pocket a letter of recommendation to the daughter of an admiral who was acquainted with my maternal grandfather. When he showed up, completely ragged, at that door, they at first didn't even want to let him in. The letter of recommendation, however, opened not only the door for him, but also the hearts of these people, who later became my godparents. So it was that along with our home—the Humboldt House—my godfather's house became one of my favorite places in Lima. My godfather and his family were German too and made a fortune in Peru in the cotton and paper trade. When my mother arrived in Lima, these faithful friends even organized my parents' wedding. Up to the age of fourteen, I often spent vacations there. I loved that house, built in Bauhaus style, with its magical garden, swimming pool and goldfish pond, in which I learned to swim. In this garden I also sometimes let my tinamous, which I always brought along in a cage, run free. To this day I can see myself walking down the street from the Humboldt House to the coast, the cage with Little Pillow and Little Chestnut Eye in one hand and my bag in the other. The house is in a prime location on the steep coast that descends from the city to the Pacific. At the time there were nothing but such villas in that area. Those who lived there could afford a large staff. But my parents lived much more simply and preferred it that way. It was important to them to remain "down-to-earth." But many of my schoolmates grew up with servants. If they had to sneeze, some of them immediately called for their maid so she would bring them a handkerchief and a glass of water.

What a shock it was when on one of my later visits, I returned to the area and all around my godfather's house high-rises had sprouted up out of the ground like gigantic mushrooms! How minutely the actually sizeable and capacious house now cowers in the shadows of those architectural giants! All the other villas were torn down in the meantime, sold by their earlier owners for large sums. Only my godfather's daughter steadfastly refused to do the same. She didn't even change her position when an amusement park was built in the immediate vicinity. And so her house is a persistent witness from the years of my childhood, a sign of continuity in the changing times.

Today my parents' house, the Humboldt House, is gone too. As in every metropolis in the world, the neighborhoods of Lima often change more rapidly than one would wish. The streets of my childhood are still quiet and safe—but when I first discovered that the house had disappeared, a great sadness came over me. That happens when it becomes a certainty that from now on all you have left are memories: how the Humboldt House was often full of scientists, whether ornithologists, geologists or cactus researchers. They came from all over, from Switzerland, Germany, the United States, Australia. Each of the three guest rooms had its own bathroom, and for all the visiting researchers there was a gigantic shared study, a library and a communal kitchen. The explorers received support from the German Foreign Office and the German Ibero-America Foundation founded in 1955, and my father usually secured a sort of grant through the Peruvian ministry of agriculture for the on-site costs. When the scientists then went on their expeditions, they could store their things with us. When they returned, they always had a lot to tell and show. That was a glorious time for me.

But my parents experienced how fragile this happiness was when they planned a two-month trip to the jungle less than half a year after my birth. I stayed behind, well taken care of by my aunt and my grandmother. But only eight days after their departure, an accident occurred in the mountain rain forest on the eastern slope of the Andes. A truck hurled a fallen telephone power line through the air with incredible speed and, unfortunately, it knocked down both my parents and injured them seriously. My father suffered numerous cuts and a concussion, and broke a collarbone and a rib. My mother initially lay unconscious, bleeding heavily. It turned out that she'd suffered a skull fracture. She was bedridden for many weeks and recovered only slowly. Later she had no memory of the accident and the time that followed, and she had lost her sense of smell and, partially, taste. All her life she was plagued by frequent headaches. But once she had recovered, that didn't prevent her from pursuing her research work again. "It would have been much worse," she would say, "if I couldn't see anymore."

As soon as it was possible, my parents took me with them on their expeditions. Often we went to the sparse mountain forest of Zárate, on the western side of the Andes. It was a very remote, still completely unexplored forest with numerous new animal species. Here my mother discovered an entirely new bird genus and named it "Zaratornis." Because it was a previously unknown vegetation zone, my parents also found here many new plants and even trees, which created a stir among experts. I still remember those excursions clearly: First we drove a great distance in the car; then we climbed the mountain on foot—I can still feel today the weight of my small backpack. We couldn't make the climb in one day, so we had to spend a night on the mountainside under the open sky. Once we arrived up in the forest, we would then camp, usually for about a week. My parents kept secret the entrance to this forest, to protect it from plunderers. I loved those excursions and could occupy myself for hours in nature, as little as I still was.

I was just two years old when my father set out on a much farther journey: He had to return to Kiel and hold a few mandatory lectures in order to qualify as a university professor. He departed on December 27, 1956, on the ship *Bärenstein* and reached Bremen on January 25, 1957. Because of formal difficulties in Kiel—above all, because he didn't live in Germany—he ultimately gave his professorial-qualification lecture in July at the university in Hamburg. Here he immediately went on leave for a few years under the condition that he would hold lectures after his return. He wrote his *"Habilitationsschrift,"* the postdoctoral dissertation required for a professorship in Germany, on the ecology and biogeography of the forests on the western side of the Peruvian Andes.

As if Europe didn't want to let him out of its clutches this time, his return journey to Peru proved extremely difficult: First he intended to depart from La Rochelle on the *Reina del Pacífico*, which was delayed. After a long wait he found out that the ship had hit a coral reef and had to be repaired in England. So he traveled back to Paris to book a new passage, only to learn to his horror that all the ships were already booked up until the end of the year. By chance he was able to get on the *Luciana*, which left from Cannes. But the *Luciana* only made it as far as the Canary Islands, having suffered a serious mechanical breakdown on the way. So he had to look for a new passage and found it on a ship named *Ascania*, which brought him to Venezuela, where he didn't arrive until September 7. And from there he had to conquer the remaining three thousand miles to Lima on the land route via Bogotá and Quito. This odyssey must have seemed to my father like a déjà vu of his first journey to Peru! But there will be more on that later.

I hadn't seen my father for nine months—no wonder I at first called him "Uncle Daddy" after his return!

Another person who is inextricably connected to my childhood is Alida, our former maid. She belongs to the black minority in Peru and was eighteen years old when she came to us. I was five. At that time I was very thin and never wanted to eat. Late in the afternoon I could still be seen strolling through the garden with something in my mouth, and most of the time it was the leftovers from lunch. Today Alida is pushing seventy, and whenever I'm in Lima, we see each other. We always have a lot to talk about. We swap recipes, and at some point we turn to the past.

"Do you remember," I ask her, "when a poisonous snake escaped from that German scientist? Fortunately, you didn't know it was poisonous."

"Yes," she replies, rolling her eyes, "but I was the one who discovered its trail in the garden! At the last moment your father caught it and had it brought to the crazy guy on the ship."

We remember how she allowed me to roast marshmallows with my schoolmates over candle flames, and how none other than Alwin Rahmel, a very close friend of our family—a German businessman who has lived in Peru for over fifty years, has known me since I was born and lends his help and support to this day—persuaded me in a restaurant to order a *quadril*.

"You had no idea it was a gigantic steak," Alida recalls, laughing. "Then it was served and it was bigger than you."

When I couldn't sleep because I was afraid of the Tunshi—or Tunchi, as it's sometimes spelled—a legendary Peruvian bird from the jungle, Alida would comfort me.

"Tunshis only live in the jungle," she said. "Here in Lima, there's no Tunshi, far and wide."

She could not have suspected that we would actually move into that jungle a few years later. But I never saw Tunshis. However, when I was not even five years old, I did see an angry bull.

At that time we once again took an excursion into the rain forest. There lived Peter Wyrwich, a German cattle rancher who lent my parents a hand, and now and then caught specific birds and mammals at the behest of the natural history museum. When we visited, I romped around with Peter Jr., his son. We had to stick our little noses into everything, whether it was machines or the animals in their stables. I never played with dolls, anyway, and was always much more interested in technical things.

"Come on," Peter said self-confidently one day, pulling me into the stable, "now I'll show you how to milk the cow."

Though this "cow" was, in fact, a young bull, neither Peter nor I had any idea that there's a small but important difference between female and male animals. When Peter pulled hard on the thing on the bull that he took for the udder, it reacted extremely crossly. The bull kicked me in the head and I went flying across the stable. That's just the way it is: If you grow up with animals, you sometimes have to be able to take things as they come.

If you have zoologists for parents, it's also better not to get the creeps too easily: Once my parents bought a gigantic shark at the market, in whose stomach there was a human hand! It probably came from a victim of the prison island out on the sea, which, like Alcatraz, was notoriously escapeproof. Anyone who tried would end up in a strong current pulling him irresistibly out into the open sea: It was said that no one had ever made it to the mainland. The shark, however, was not a man-eater, and the hand was undoubtedly consumed only after the man's death. Later this shark—without its contents—could be admired in the museum.

As long as I wasn't in school yet, my parents took me with them most afternoons to the museum. There, in the huge halls with their tall double doors and the many specimens of Peruvian animals and plants, I wandered around. Sometimes I would get a little scared, especially from the mummies on display, until these strange things became a part of my life like everything else.

Then, all of a sudden, I was told: We're going to Germany. That was in the summer of 1960. I was five years old and now I would be going for the first time to the country of my ancestors. Actually, all three of us wanted to travel across the Atlantic, but someone had to look after the Humboldt House and its guests. My mother wanted to meet well-known colleagues in Europe and compare findings with them, and since I couldn't stay alone with my father for five months, she simply took me with her. I was really excited, because the journey promised to be thrilling. First we took a roaring propeller plane to Guayaquil in Ecuador. From there we went on a banana freighter named *Penthelicon* via the Panama Canal toward Hamburg. I watched the bananas being loaded at the port—gigantic still-green bunches. If one of them had even the smallest yellow spot, they were just thrown into the water and fished out again by natives who circled the steamer in their dugout canoes. That really made an impression on me, because at home food was never just thrown out like that.

Along with the fruit that was loaded, animals came on board: lizards, huge spiders and snakes. I think I was the only person who found that so great. The crew was not at all thrilled about it! While my mother was still polishing her lecture in the cabin, I explored the ship, getting on some of the seamen's nerves. In the Atlantic, we saw whales and flying fish, and I stood at the railing and was really impressed. And I was impressed again, later, after our arrival in Berlin. There lived my maternal grandparents and my aunts and uncles. There was snow! And double-decker buses! And crows, at the sight of which, to the amusement of our fellow travelers, I said: "Mommy, look at the vultures! They're so little here!" All these things were new to me, and I was fascinated.

During those weeks my mother took trips to Paris, Basel and Warsaw to meet colleagues and work at the famous museums there, for they had interesting bird skins—that is, prepared stuffed birds—from Peru in their collections. When she went on those trips, she left me with relatives. And then Christmas was approaching; and to my great horror, I had to participate in a musical as an angel, even though I fought tooth and nail against it. I was a shy child, and then suddenly I was standing on a stage with golden wings and everyone found me "cute"!

I saw my aunt Cordula again, who was now working as a writer in Kiel—and who was aghast that I knew all the animals only by their Latin names. When I saw an owl in a picture book, I said: "Oh, an *Otus*." At that, my aunt turned indignantly to my mother and said: "Really, Maria, you can't do that with the little one." But those were the times before the animals were given German names; most of which my parents didn't like, anyhow, because they found them unsuitable or misleading.

For my mother this was the last time she saw her father. He died unexpectedly six years later, when I was eleven years old. I will never forget how shaken I was when my mother closed herself in her room for hours and wept heartrendingly. Only after she explained to me why she was so sad did I calm down again. In my young life there was nothing worse than seeing my mother cry.

She was a kind and gentle person and often had to offset my father's irascible character. Even though she was married not only to him, but also to science, she was interested in many other subjects. As mentioned above, she was among the leading ornithologists in South America, and to achieve that required a great deal of commitment and a certain willingness to sacrifice. My mother had those qualities. I once experienced something with her that I never forgot. We were in the jungle and observed a sunbittern in its nest, while countless mosquitoes swarmed around us. I wanted to swipe at them, but then that so rare and shy bird would surely have flown away. My mother whispered to me very softly: "You must not move now, even if you get stung." And so we remained in the cloud of mosquitoes without making a sound for a quarter of an hour. My mother also said: "If you want to be a biologist, you have to learn to sacrifice." This sentence encapsulates really well what our research work consists of. She and my father complemented each other perfectly—after she died, he was never the same. Then he was only half. For me, too, it was unspeakably hard, because my mother was simply torn from us much too soon. There were still so many conversations for us to have, which would never come to pass.

Suddenly we hit turbulence. That's not good for me, not good at all. For even though I have my fear of another plane crash pretty well under control, the shaking that seizes our plane now, high over the Atlantic, immediately brings back those images. The nightmare of every airplane passenger returns: the roaring of the turbines, which I hear in my dreams to this day. And that blinding light over one of the wings. The voice of my mother, which says . . .

3 What I Learned About Life From My Father

My father exploring the rain forest of Panguana, 1968.
(Photo courtesy of Juliane (Koepcke) Diller)

. . . *"Now it's all over!"* My mother says that quite calmly, almost tonelessly.

I feel for my husband's hand next to me and force myself to return to the present. That's never easy when I'm overcome by memories. Is it really my husband's hand I'm holding? Or is it my mother's hand?

"Don't worry," I say to my husband. "It's only a bit of turbulence, nothing more."

Then we look at each other and can't help laughing. For it's clear to us, of course: I'm the one who's more scared than he is. But it's easier for me to give him the courage that I lost for a moment. "Thanks for comforting me," my husband says, squeezing my hand. Of everything I love so much about him, his wonderful sense of humor is sometimes the most important.

And then the turbulence calms down. The airplane moves very peacefully through the air, and I take several deep breaths.

Phew, that roller-coaster ride went right to my core.

"Look," says my husband, pointing out the window. "The coast of Brazil! We've reached the South American continent!"

And I'm already distracted and look out the window. I always want a window seat; that didn't change after the crash. On the contrary, when I can see what lies below me, I'm somewhat calmer. And from that point on, I don't come out of my astonishment, even though I've already experienced this flight so many times. The apparent endlessness of the Atlantic gives way to the same apparent endlessness of the Amazon Rain Forest. And today the visibility is so good that you can see clearly different twists and turns of the rivers glittering in the sun. Apart from that, the monotony of the jungle resembles the monotony of the waves. Even the color is almost the same, a washed-out green from this height. When I fell from the sky, the

23

approaching treetops looked like heads of broccoli, densely packed. But right now I don't want to think about that.

Instead, I tell my husband how much time and effort it cost my father to get to Peru after the end of the Second World War. When we groan because our backs hurt and our legs become heavy after the twelve-hour flight, that's nothing at all in comparison to what my father took on back then. And if he hadn't set out for a new world, my life certainly would have gone completely differently.

It all began in 1947. My father was a young, ambitious biologist seeking to achieve pioneering work in the field of ecology and zoogeography, and was therefore interested in lands with the highest possible biodiversity. South America was a possibility, but also Sri Lanka. Practical-minded as he was, he wrote a letter to the university in Lima—in German, because he had not yet mastered Spanish. Did they have any use for a young zoologist with a doctorate? He wrote a similar letter to Ecuador. That was two years after the war's end. A whole year later he actually received a reply from the natural history museum in Lima, to which his letter had been forwarded. The reply was as simple as his question had been: Yes, he could come. They had a position for him.

It was a letter with consequences. Travel in postwar Europe was a difficult matter, above all for Germans. There were no passports, so it was impossible to receive a visa. Though my father had the longed-for job in Lima, he had no idea how he would get there. His university girlfriend, Maria, who would later become my mother, shared his enthusiasm for research and definitely wanted to accompany him. To my grandmother she said resolutely: "I'm going to marry this man. Him or no one!" At the end of 1947, the two of them got engaged. When my father received the invitation to Peru, it was a foregone conclusion for both of them that he should accept the offer. Maria would simply follow him later, as soon as she got her doctorate.

With the letter from Lima in his pocket, my father proceeded to the German branch of a South American bank, where he was advised to travel to Genoa and embark there. There were shipowners who would take German emigrants with them for free. So my father decided to try this. In the middle of winter, he went to Mittenwald, where he soon learned that he could enter Italy only illegally. On his first attempt to climb over the Austrian border

24

fence, he took a bad fall and had to be brought to the hospital in Innsbruck. Once he recovered, he didn't let that prevent him from making a second attempt. This time he sensibly crawled under the fence. Then he traversed the Alps, walking and hitchhiking, and reached Genoa in an adventurous way. How great was his disappointment when he found out at the port that a steamer had just cast off for South America. No one knew when the next would arrive. There were no timetables in those confusing times in the aftermath of the war. My father was not a person who was content to wait. He traveled on to Rome, where he managed to get a Red Cross passport, which was issued by the Vatican. This, he was told, would make his journey considerably easier. But Rome was full of Germans who had already been waiting for weeks and months to get to South America. My father learned that the chances were better in Naples, so he headed south on foot. On the way he was arrested and was put in a notorious prison camp. Under the pretext of checking his papers, the Italians held him there for several months. A group of fellow prisoners eventually tried to persuade him to escape. In particular, a North African young man raved to him about his native land and urged him to come along. Even though my father was a man of action, he didn't get drawn into that. And that was a good thing: Anyone who broke out was rapidly caught again and harshly punished. But then a miracle occurred—about which he told me fondly and often. He prayed all the time for the Lord to make the walls that enclosed him collapse. And that's exactly what happened: In a night of heavy rain, the wall of the camp simply crumbled next to him, and he was able to escape. Of course, his pursuers were right on his heels, but he was smarter than they were. Instead of running away as far as he could, he hid in a bush very close to the camp. He covered himself with ferns and stayed there for a night and a day. Only when the search for him was aborted as fruitless did he continue his escape. Of course, he was now much more careful and trekked mainly at night. During the day he hid or knocked on the doors of farmhouses, where he was taken in hospitably most of the time. One time, however, he came to the house of a bird hunter. He and his wife were particularly friendly and shared their meal with him. For that reason he gave the signora his last object of value, a brooch. But when he wanted to continue on his journey, the bird hunter said he would never find the way on his own, and it would be better if he came with him. En route my father realized that the man intended to betray him, and he just barely managed to get himself to safety.

But that adventure was far from the end of his odyssey. In Naples, too, there was no ship, and so he continued on his way to Sicily. In Trapani, there were indeed fishing cutters at anchor. My father didn't hesitate to speak to all the owners, but none were willing to ferry him to Africa.

I think many people would have lost heart by now. But my father was cut from a different cloth. He told himself that if he had found no ship in Italy to bring him to South America, then he would find one in Spain. So he trekked back up the entire Italian boot and headed north from Genoa toward France. When he finally reached the border city of San Remo, he was told that it was completely impossible to cross the border. It was still one big minefield, but my father was much too resolute to let these dangers deter him.

On a dark night he crossed the mountains at the border and walked on toward Nice. There, for the first time in a long while, he was picked up by a car. In Aix-en-Provence, he got out and right at the next gas station asked the driver of an expensive car whether he could give him a lift. He refused categorically when he heard my father was a German. Only once the cashier put in a good word for him did the man take pity and give him a lift, after all. It turned out that the driver was Jewish, which cast his initial refusal in a different light. When he heard my father's story, he even gave him 150 francs. That was very largehearted, because at that time anyone found at a checkpoint with less than one hundred francs was arrested as a vagabond. "Someone who has come as far as you have," said the man in parting, "will make it to South America too."

But it didn't look that way at all. When my father arrived in Marseille, he didn't find a ship there either. Rumor had it that every four or five months a South America–bound steamer left from Portbou. But my father didn't want to wait that long. He decided to follow his original plan and tramp to Spain.

Again he heard that this was impossible: This time the Pyrenees were said to be the end of the line. In comparison to this mountain range, people said, the Alps were a walk in the park. Again my father was undaunted. He followed the rocky course of a stream higher and higher, until he felt from the wind that a Mediterranean mountain climate surrounded him. He'd done it! He was in Spain.

There, however, he had to be especially circumspect. Supporters of the dictator Francisco Franco didn't think twice before putting illegal foreigners into their notorious camps. Once again, my father hid during the day and only walked at night.

But in Barcelona, too, there were no ships departing for South America, and so my father headed for central Spain, always keeping his distance from the cities, staying as close as possible to the mountains. At one point, as he was resting under a carob tree in a completely remote area, a storm began to gather. Dogs howled in the distance, and more and more of them joined in. It took a little while before my father realized that these were wolves, but people posed more danger to him than wild animals did.

In Córdoba, the small amount of baggage he still had was stolen. He immediately continued on his way to Seville. There he received for the first time a sign that his dream of reaching Peru might become a reality, after all. Shortly before my father's departure from Germany, my mother's family gave him some advice: In Lima, there was a connection to the daughter of an admiral friend. He should get in touch with her if he ever arrived in the city. Now he received a letter of recommendation from a German family in Seville, also addressed to the admiral's daughter. Two recommendations to one and the same person—something simply had to come of that!

Given the enormous distances my father had covered up to that point, the journey from Seville to Cádiz was a stone's throw. From there, ships were supposed to leave for Peru. But once again, he arrived just a few days too late. A ship had just started for Lima with Germans on board. In his despair my father told everyone about his situation. A supporter of General Franco's then connected him to an organization that helped Germans leaving Europe for political reasons. That was not at all the case with my father. Perhaps he would have grasped at this straw, if it had not quickly turned out to be a waste of time and effort. There were many empty promises, but no actions. And there were constantly new rumors. In a town named San Fernando, he now heard, a ship would be casting off for Uruguay in a short time. That would at least be South America, so my father hurried to the small port town. There he met a mason who also wanted to cross the Atlantic. Together they found the ship. It was a salt ship, and it really was about to depart. The two of them didn't think twice before stowing away on board. They made their way to the cargo hold, tied handkerchiefs over their faces, jumped into the salt and burrowed into it as well as they could. After an endless odyssey my father was finally aboard a ship heading for South America—as an illegal passenger, buried in several tons of salt.

For four days they stuck it out. Rough seas caused the ship to roll and pitch; the sun burned down; the salt penetrated all their pores; unbearable thirst tormented them—and finally the mason panicked. He wanted only one thing: out! My father figured out that the ship must have been only just level with the Canary Islands and implored his fellow traveler to pull himself together a little bit longer. Just one more day! But his companion no longer had the strength for that. So they revealed themselves and were promptly arrested. When the ship reached Tenerife, they were put in prison in its capital, Santa Cruz. Now my father faced the threat of transport back to Spain and a long internment in a camp there. However, he would get lucky. After fourteen days of detention, he was suddenly released and swiftly found passage on a ship bound for Recife in Brazil. There he went ashore a few weeks later.

Finally he was in South America—even though he was on the wrong side of the broadest part of the continent. But still: "Columbus cannot have rejoiced more than I did upon setting foot in America," my father said. By now, he already had been on the move for a year. How could he have suspected that it would take almost just as long to reach the capital of Peru?

And yet his plan was quite simple: As an experienced walker, he should be able to conquer the three thousand miles to Peru, he thought. Part of the journey he could even cover by train. Of course, everyone told him once again that it was utterly impossible to traverse Brazil in this way. And, of course, my father didn't let that deter him one bit. He set off, at first through endless plantation landscapes full of sugarcane and bananas. Then came the Caatinga, a four-hundred-mile-wide thornbush savanna, which he had to cross on foot.

Whenever he came to villages, he was an attraction. And my father was quickly infected by the Brazilians' enjoyment of life. "It was always fun," he recounted later. After another five-hundred-mile trek, he finally reached central Brazil. When he later looked back on this enormous feat of walking, he remarked: "On good days I walked twenty-five miles. On worse days it was around twenty."

Looking down on this vast expanse today from my window seat, I can scarcely imagine how it was possible for my father to cover that distance on foot. Now we are flying over the Amazon, near Manaus. The river, with its many branching veins, shimmers majestically in the sun. We can see clearly its chocolate brown water; shortly thereafter we are flying over black-water rivers—one of which, the largest, must be the Río Negro.

My father walked, unwaveringly focused on his goal, and that was Lima. And he wasn't just hiking—he trekked and observed at the same time! He already knew the wildlife of South America from his studies. But here, on remote paths through savanna and jungle, he could observe the way of life of many species unknown to him. He studied their predator-prey behavior, discovered competing species and even found time to keep a diary on all this. He had no trouble handling the heat.

In the meantime he had gotten very brown; and with the large straw hat on his head, he barely stuck out anymore in many villages. Only when he came to solitary farms did he often cause panic. If their husbands weren't at home, the women dropped everything and fled into the jungle. Still, he was taken in hospitably most of the time. And my father enjoyed his newly won freedom: As opposed to traveling in the war-ravaged European countries, here he didn't have to hide all the time.

"I hung my hammock wherever I wanted," he later enthused about his long march. He often penetrated forests that no one had ever entered before. Occasionally he was then overcome by something like doubt about whether it was really a good idea to expose himself to these dangers. However, my father never lost his confidence in himself. When people asked him where he was headed, he answered: "To Peru." Most of them had never heard of such a land.

And finally the day came: On May 15, 1950, the birthday of his fiancée, Maria von Mikulicz-Radecki, he reached the border of Peru. And as if that coincidence was not enough: Exactly one and a half years had passed since he had taken leave of my mother on November 15, 1948. From the border he was able to fly on a military plane to Lima. But I'm certain that my father would not have been deterred from crossing on foot the rest of the jungle, as well as the endless ice of the Andes.

Three years after he had inquired about a job, two years after he had received the reply from the natural history museum in Lima, my father entered the office of the stunned director there. His answer was succinct: The job was unfortunately no longer available. And so a new odyssey began for my father, that of finding work in the Promised Land. The Guano Company, which earned a lot of money with fertilizer made of bird excrement from boobies, cormorants, pelicans and penguins, was a potential employer. But when my father introduced himself there, they had no use for him. Then he met the dean of the University of San Marcos, who proposed to him after some back-and-forth to manage the fish section of the natural history museum, and asked what my father wanted to be paid. Probably my father had never thought about that over all the years of his long journey, for he mentioned a ridiculously small sum. And while my mother was crossing to Lima on the South Pacific steamer *Amerigo Vespucci*, my father started his first job in Peru for a meager salary. No sooner had my mother arrived than she, too, was hired to work in the museum and later took over the ornithology department. Shortly thereafter they were married: In Miraflores, a particularly beautiful district of Lima, they said "yes" to each other on June 24, 1950, the solstice, the day after my father's thirty-sixth birthday.

I often think of my father's long, arduous odyssey when I find myself in danger of becoming a little dispirited. Or when the old fears from the time of my crash are about to overcome me. Then his story is an illustration for me that it pays not to let things get you down. Not military posts, not missed boats, not mountain ranges that must be crossed, not thousands of miles to be covered on foot. "When we have really resolved to achieve something," my father once said, "we succeed. We only have to want it, Juliane."

He was right. After the crash, I wanted to survive, and I did the nearly impossible. After that, can you face anything worse?

Oh yes, you can. Every challenge presents itself as completely new. Just like anyone else, it always costs me enormous strength to translate what I want into action. Today I want with all my might for Panguana not only to remain in existence but also to be given a new form. I want my father's wish to come true for this area, in expanded form, to be declared a nature reserve. That's why I'm sitting on this airplane; that's why I'm overcoming my fears. And now, after many hours, the moment has almost come. The land of my childhood is already below me. We have just flown over the border between

Brazil and Peru. My heart pounds harder. Only about another hour. Already the jungle is giving way to the first ridges of the Andes. Once they're behind us, the plane will begin its final descent toward Lima. Then this long flight, too, will come to a good end, thank God.

My father shooting photos in the forest of Panguana, 1970.
(Photo courtesy of Juliane (Koepcke) Diller)

4 My Life in Two Worlds

An adventurous trip to Panguana: we crossed a damaged bridge in a four-wheel-drive Toyota vehicle, 2006. (Photo courtesy of Juliane (Koepcke) Diller)

I heave a sigh of relief. Did it again. Just through passport control, to the baggage claim, and then I'm looking into familiar faces and being fervently embraced. Alwin Rahmel, a longtime friend of our family, insisted this time on personally picking my husband and me up at the airport.

On the drive to our hotel, I take in the city: Lima is lively, colorful and a little bit louder each year. That was already the case in the past; yet, in comparison to those days, Lima today is scarcely recognizable. Granted, years before my birth, my father already wrote to my mother, before she came to Lima, *This city can certainly not be called beautiful,* and yet in my childhood it had a charm all its own. In those days there was scarcely a building in the whole city that was higher than four stories. In Spanish Colonial style they were lined up, side by side, surrounded by trees. Now each time I arrive, I find new oversized luxury buildings with the insignia of banks, car dealerships, casinos and hotels along the street in the city center. They differ starkly from the cozy neighborhoods that made up the city of my childhood. There are places and areas I scarcely recognize. Here the road system was changed; there a new highway was built. I don't think everything new is bad. For example, the separate bus lane in the middle between two roads I find very practical. Trees have even been planted along it, even if they're currently still small and their later magnificence is only vaguely discernible.

Yes, Lima's streets are busy. One *"hora punta,"* as rush hour is called here, merges seamlessly into the next. Even though so much has changed, I feel as if I'm coming home. I look around and bombard our friend with my questions. What have I missed during all the time I was in Germany?

Peru remains a country full of contrasts. That's how it was in the past, and little has changed in that respect to this day. Back then, I was among the privileged children, without being aware of it. If someone had asked me whether there are poor neighborhoods in Lima, I would have indignantly denied it. Today I am aware that my parents and I, even though they attached a great deal of importance to living modestly, were among the rich. My world was Miraflores. That was where my godparents lived, and it remains today one of the better areas of Lima. Meanwhile, I also know that in those districts farthest from the ocean, the ones that ascend the slopes to the Cordillera Negra, many people live in slums. It is for that reason that it always strikes me as a little anachronistic when some of my old schoolmates in Lima say: "How can you stand it in Germany? You don't even have staff there." I wince at such statements, because they ignore the other half of Peru, the extreme poverty that exists alongside this wealth.

Alwin Rahmel tells me about that too, and about the progress of his charitable work in the slums of Lima. Children often don't get even one meal a day there if they aren't lucky enough to be at one of the free meals of the Lima childcare organization. Yes, Peru is a country full of contrasts. And I love it the way it is. I'm proud of my ability as a German and Peruvian to unite both worlds. Germany is the country in which I live—and where I'm also really happy to be. But I'm bound to Peru with my heart. In Germany, I love that things generally work better. In Peru, I like the music, the warmth and the humor of the people. And I love Peruvian cuisine.

On this first evening we visit my favorite restaurant. We're warmly welcomed, as if we were here just last week, and for a moment I even imagine that's the case. Everything is the same as always. My life in Germany merges seamlessly into my Peruvian existence, like one half of a zipper into the other. I order *papa a la huancaína*, which I'm mad about. It is potatoes in a spicy cheese sauce. How often I've tried to cook this in Munich; but because the right cheese and the yellow Ají peppers for the sauce are simply not available in Germany, it doesn't work out so well. *It just tastes better here*, I admit to myself with a sigh, and let the sauce melt on my tongue. In Peru, there are around four thousand different known kinds of potatoes. They come in white, yellow, red, brown, purple and all the shades in between. My husband chooses a *chupe*, one of the delicious stews that efficiently warm you up, because this evening it's also perceptibly chilly in Lima. Once, many years ago, I read an article in a German magazine headlined FIRST-RATE CLIMATE IN LIMA, but I was afraid that the editor fell under the spell of the triple rhyme in German, PRIMA KLIMA IN LIMA, for the Lima climate is anything but first-rate. Most days of the year, the sky is overcast, it's often foggy, and at times the damp coolness creeps into your bones. That's due to the Humboldt Current flowing past, nearby, coming cold from the Antarctic to meet the otherwise warm sea, thus ensuring a fair amount of "steam."

The different landscape forms are also extreme in this country: The desert runs from north to south along the coast; it is followed by the Andes, with their mighty mountain ranges and high plateaus; and finally, on their east side, the Amazon Rain Forest. As a result of the great difference between the coast and rain forest, our suitcases always contain two sorts of clothing: warmer clothes for Lima and midsummer clothes for the rain forest.

The different habitats of the coast, mountains and rain forest each hold very particular flora and fauna, which I often had the opportunity to marvel at on my trips into the jungle with my parents. Yes, and these journeys lasting several days from Lima over the Andes into the rain forest are among my most wonderful and richest childhood memories:

In Lima, we would usually take a bus run by the company "La Perla de los Andes." The baggage would be tied to the roof, and then a few boys would climb up, whose job was to make sure during the entire drive over the mountains that nothing fell down or got stolen. The baggage guards working for the competing company, León de Huánuco, might have been better, because that bus line was famous for its reliability. But I was not yet at an age where that concerned me. I would look out the window, for shortly after leaving Lima, you already began rapidly gaining altitude. Still, the trip took over eight hours before you reached the Ticlio mountain pass. Its elevation is 15,800 feet, and yet it's still the lowest pass of the central and southern Andes! For most passengers, that was high enough—if you couldn't hold it together, you suffered terribly from altitude sickness. Once, sitting next to me, there was a woman in an advanced stage of pregnancy who continually had to vomit.

The higher you get, the sparser the already scanty vegetation becomes. Still, there are frequent villages to which the road snakes upward in endless switchbacks. On the Ticlio, there's snow on the ground all year; and very close to the pass, though it's hard to believe, there's actually a town. It's called La Oroya, and it is occupied by miners. It is a bleak place, a collection of miserable huts with colored corrugated metal roofs. During the day it's cold, and at night it's still colder, in a way that goes straight into your bones. No wonder the Indians of the High Andes always wear heavy clothing. When it's possible, they sleep with kith and kin and all the livestock in a single room. And ornithologists even find hummingbirds up there that go into a torpor at night, a sort of nocturnal hibernation, by lowering their metabolism in order to protect themselves from the icy cold. Somewhat lower down you come across Peruvian pepper trees growing wild, on which what we know as pink peppercorn thrives, as well as other sparse trees. Only once you've crossed the Ticlio does the vegetation gradually return. Your gaze is drawn downward into the river valleys, which are green and fertile.

It's a long journey: First you go over the Cordillera Negra, which is covered with lichens and algae, giving the mountains a dark color. Then comes the next mountain range, the Cordillera Blanca. Farther in the north of Peru, glorious snow-covered twenty-thousand-foot peaks rise from it, and it connects to the Altiplano, an extensive high plain with the Puna grassland, covered with a prickly yellow plant. Here there are some gorgeous lakes, which at certain times are populated by flamingoes. The colors of this bird went into the Peruvian national flag. According to the legend that my mother told me, José San Martín, when he proclaimed the republic of Peru, was at one point lying on the beach and resting. Then he saw a flamingo above him, and the red and white of the bird inspired the colors of the flag. The coat of arms also depicts the vicuña, a wild variety of camel. Its wool is even finer and softer than baby alpaca and was once reserved for the Inca kings. Next to the vicuña is a picture of a quina tree, which symbolizes Peru's rich flora. There's also a cornucopia with coins pouring from it. Ultimately, from all its mineral resources, Peru is among the richest countries in the world.

After the Ticlio, we would soon reach the Altiplano, and then hours would pass at an altitude between thirteen and sixteen thousand feet. Here, too, you come upon at most a mining town, where copper, wolfram, bismuth and silver are mined. Finally we would be going downhill again and would soon stop off in Huánuco, an old Spanish colonial city in one of the most fertile river valleys. It lies at an elevation of about six thousand feet—so by Andean standards on the lower end of the spectrum.

On my first trips we would always spend the night near here, for the road toward Tingo María became so narrow that it could be used only in one-way traffic. Spending the night meant you stayed in the bus, or else it could drive on without you.

Next comes a stretch of land known as the Cordillera Azul. It's densely wooded and hence gives off a bluish shimmer from a distance. By the time you finally reach Tingo María—well, then another eight-hour bus ride to Pucallpa lies ahead of you.

On the way my mother would always tell me which birds could be found where: In the cloud forest of the Cordillera Azul, right at the water divide La Divisoria, there were the glorious orange-red cocks of the rock. On a hill outside of Tingo María, in a cave called the Cueva de las Lechuzas, dwelled oilbirds, known in Peru as *guácharos*. They were nightjars, my mother taught me, which orient themselves in the dark with a primitive echolocation and whose body fat finds a use as lamp oil—hence their name. For the next couple hundred miles, I then had something to think about.

Two days and a night after setting off in Lima, we would finally reach Pucallpa, at the time a real small pioneer town. It was surrounded by farmland, and the farmland, in turn, by jungle. Here we could stock up on everything we would need in the jungle: basic foodstuffs like sugar, lard, oil and flour. After that, to get to Tournavista, the next leg of our journey, there were only two possibilities: either a boat or an off-road vehicle over wild paths through the forest. That was also only possible during the dry season. Otherwise, the roads turned into mud holes. Most of the time we would take the boat. On the Ucayali it would bring us to the mouth of the Río Pachitea. From there we would head upriver to Tournavista. The Texan family Le Tourneau gave this jungle village its name. Here we would spend the night with acquaintances, sleeping on the floor, and then look for a new boat for the continuation of our journey. To this day everything in the jungle is transported via the rivers—people, animals, baggage, all sorts of cargo. For two more days we would chug upriver.

At night we would sleep wrapped in wool blankets on a sandbank, and the next morning the journey would continue. Not until evening on the second day did we come to the mouth of the Yuyapichis, where Panguana is. The river's name comes from the old Inca language Quechua and means "lying river," because it can sometimes be so deceptive. At a given moment it may seem to be a tranquil, leisurely little river, but within a few hours, it can turn into a raging torrent—depending on the precipitation in the nearby

Sira Mountain Range, where the Yuyapichis originates.

On our journey there we would go through notorious rapids, in which you could capsize if the boatman wasn't experienced. During the whole trip, my mother never closed even one eye. She didn't want to miss anything, and there really was plenty to see: Once a brocket deer swam through the river, then caimans, a type of South American alligator, and snakes again. My mother kept pointing into the water and saying things like: "Look, Juliane. There's a bushmaster—one of the most poisonous snakes in the world. They're very aggressive. You have to be on your guard against them."

Then the mouth of the Yuyapichis would finally come into view. Here we went ashore and had to make our way through three more miles of untouched primary rain forest. It was a nasty path, full of climbing plants that were almost as high as I was tall. The ground consisted of deep mud or slippery laterite, which in heavy rain took on the traction of a sheet of ice. Once we'd gotten through this area—a week after the departure from Lima—we would finally reach the Yuyapichis again, on the other side of which was Panguana. My mother would blow a police whistle, and my father would come across with the dugout canoe to pick us up. Welcome home!

But I'm getting away from myself. My thoughts are jumping off course from my story again. For they revolve incessantly around Panguana, the research station my parents would found in 1968, which became my home for many years. As I look over the park in Miraflores, tired, full and happy to finally be here, as I go over our schedule for the next two days with Alwin and my husband, which couldn't be tighter—numerous visits to the authorities are on the agenda, a meeting with our lawyer to finally bring our cause a decisive step forward—as we savor a dessert on the house, my thoughts revolve around Panguana. And I admit: As much as I enjoy being in Lima, I can't wait to be in my beloved jungle again.

No. For me it was and is no green hell. It is part of me like my love of my husband, like the rhythms of *cumbia*, which are in my blood, like the scars that I still have from the plane crash. The jungle is the reason I get on airplanes again and again, and for it I'm even willing to grapple with the authorities.

The Peruvian word for bureaucracy is *"burocracia,"* and many say with a smile: *"burrocracia"*–which contains the Spanish word *"burro,"* the "ass." And that's no accident. Here in the Andean country, an apathy sometimes prevails that can drive many a European crazy. I'm almost afraid I'll be confronted with it on this trip too. With my goal of having Panguana declared a nature reserve, I ultimately have a great deal to sort out with officials and authorities. I speak about that with our friend Alwin Rahmel. As always he helps me fight my way through the only "jungle" I truly sometimes fear: that of the *burrocracia.*

Finally we get going. We're tired from the long journey. We still have to get used to the time difference.

When we arrive at the hotel, Alwin suddenly pauses.

"Did you notice that?" he asks me.

My husband and I look at each other questioningly. What does Alwin mean?

"That was a small earth tremor."

Right. An almost imperceptible jolt. Then everything's the same as before. It was as if there was a tear in time for a tiny moment.

"But that was nothing at all," Alwin immediately reassures me.

But I've been used to it from an early age. For on the Peruvian coast two tectonic plates grind against each other, and as a result there are constantly recurring earthquakes. Such a quake is a frightening experience. First you hear a sound that cannot be integrated into our realm of experience. "The earth grumbles," we say, and it can scarcely be put better than that. When it then begins to tremble, you become disoriented. That's because our senses cannot cope with this suspension of the established physical rules. Repeated earthquakes and seaquakes beset other South American countries too. Just recently Peru's neighboring country Chile was hit hard by one.

I remember well two particularly violent quakes. One took place in 1967, when I was thirteen years old. I was home alone and cleaning my box of watercolors when it began. First there was an intense vertical movement, the ground rose and sank, juddering under my feet. That was already alarming enough. But then the earth went into lurching movements, the ground virtually swung sideways, and that was especially terrible. People panicked; I heard them running and screaming in the street, and I was tempted to do the same. I realized that I was alone. To be confronted with this force of nature all on my own was really a special experience. Instead of running in the street, I reminded myself of what my parents had impressed on me for such situations: It was better to stay in the house and get under a door frame. There, where the ceiling is supported, you're much safer than in the open street, where a roof tile or a collapsing wall might strike you dead. That quake had a magnitude of 6.8 and lasted for quite a while. Luckily, not much happened in our area, and I escaped with no more than a scare.

When I was between the ages of eight and twelve, my parents went on several expeditions to Yungay, a small town in one of the most beautiful areas of the Cordillera Blanca, and they often took me with them. We camped in a famous valley named Callejón de Huaylas. I can still remember well the ice-cold water of the glacial lake in which I had to wash myself and the glorious colors of the sunset on the snow-covered slopes of the nearby twenty-thousand-foot mountains. There were massive rocks in bizarre formations, and among them was one that I especially liked. It looked like a gigantic matchbox set upright, so I named it the "matchbox rock." There were plants growing on top of it, and that made a strong impression on me.

In 1970, this area was beset by a powerful natural disaster. A 7-magnitude earthquake caused a large piece of the glacier to break off. It fell toward the valley into the lake, which burst its banks. Gigantic mudslides completely submerged several towns. In the small town of Yungay, only the tops of the palms on the Plaza de Armas jutted out of the desert of mud. All the residents were buried under the avalanches, except one school class and its teacher, who had been on an excursion to the higher-up cemetery at the time of the disaster. When the earthquake occurred, my parents and I were already living in Panguana, far away in the jungle, and even there it could still be felt perceptibly enough that the birds flew up in fright from the trees. Ten years later I would go to that area with fellow students, and one of the towns was still completely buried.

We say good-bye to Alwin, who clearly regrets having reminded me of the dangers of an earthquake. A short time later I see the familiar signs in the hotel that indicate the places where you should stay in case of a tremor. For anyone who lives in Peru, this phenomenon, too, becomes part of everyday life.

I, too, grew up with the fact that nothing is really safe, not even the solid ground under your own feet. And I find that this knowledge helps me again and again to keep a cool head even in difficult situations. Maybe that's another reason I survived the nightmare after the plane crash, because from an early age I was used to the fact that unusual things could happen—whether it was a poisonous snake creeping through the garden in the city of Lima, or waking up in the middle of the night to find the bed wobbling as if evil spirits were shaking it.

Fortunately, that is not the case tonight. Tired, we sink into our pillows. How happy I am to be back here. And yet I wouldn't like to live here all the time. I enjoy being at home in both worlds, even if it's difficult at times and I occasionally almost burst with longing for the country I'm not in at the moment.

But all this is balanced by the chance to expand my own horizon constantly. I don't mean only the wealth of experience. No, I'm speaking of the inner, emotional horizon. I was always someone who preferred to gather information firsthand. And that's only possible on-site, in close contact with people who live there. I think that benefits my work in Germany too. I feel privileged to be able to work in the Bavarian State Collection of Zoology. I value my colleagues. We are more than a community of scientists; we are like a family. I can justifiably say: I'm very content with my life. Isn't that strange? After everything that's happened? When I actually shouldn't even be here? My mother's last words still ring in my ears. The memory comes over me everywhere, without warning, on an airplane, in an elevator, in a dream. Then I hear my mother say: "Now . . .

5 How I Became a Jungle Girl

The vegetation is impenetrable near the riverside, 2010.
(Photo courtesy of Juliane (Koepcke) Diller)

. . . it's all over!" With a jolt the tip of the airplane falls steeply downward. Even though I'm in a window seat all the way in the back, I can see the whole aisle to the cockpit, which is below me. The physical laws have been suspended; it's like an earthquake. No, it is worse. Because now we're racing downward. We're falling. People are screaming in panic, shrill cries for help; the roar of the plummeting turbines, which I will hear again and again in my dreams, engulfs me. And there, over everything, clear as glass, my mother's voice: "Now it's all over!"

Everything would have turned out differently if my parents hadn't decided to relocate their workplace from the city of Lima to the middle of the jungle. They wanted to study on-site the diversity of the flora and fauna in the Amazon Rain Forest, which at the time was practically unknown. They wanted to live for five years in immediate proximity to their research field. And at some point thereafter they wanted to return to Germany.

I was fourteen when my parents put this plan into action. At the time I was less than thrilled by the idea of living in the jungle from that point on. I imagined sitting all day in the gloom under tall trees, whose dense canopy of leaves didn't let through a single ray of sunlight. I thought wistfully of leaving behind all my schoolmates in Lima. They all looked at me pityingly, for none of them could imagine living in the middle of the jungle. Most of them had never even set foot in it. Not that I was afraid—I knew the jungle already from excursions with my parents. But to take trips there and to move there with the whole kit and caboodle are not the same thing. At the age of fourteen you have other things in mind besides living in the wild.

Our departure was delayed. My father had been working for several years on a major and ambitious project, a multivolume work on the life-

43

forms of animals and plants, which he was determined to finish before the move to the jungle. My mother, who was fantastic at drawing, a master at sketching animals perfectly in any movement, would contribute the six hundred illustrations for it. They both worked feverishly. That was all right with me; I was in no hurry to leave. But we had already given up the Humboldt House and had to move for a few months into a small, expensive temporary apartment directly over a loud thoroughfare until we could finally get going.

So it turned into a long good-bye from the city, which wore on my parents' nerves. Above all my father was completely beat, and his mood often tense.

The closing down of the Humboldt House, in which my parents had lived for about twenty years all told, was a prolonged task. How much stuff had amassed in the course of time! In my parents' large study, all kinds of things were sorted out for weeks—no, months. Some things were thrown out, and what they wanted to keep was packed. No less than two hundred boxes were filled in this way. But, of course, my parents were far from able or willing to take everything with them into the jungle. So they developed an elaborate system to determine what they would store or loan, and where it would go.

I still remember well those weeks full of feverish activity. Alongside their usual work, my parents packed cartons. My father built one box after another; my mother made detailed lists of their contents. "Without these lists," she said to me often, "we're lost, Juliane. It's the only way we'll ever find anything again."

In December 1967, the first moving van drove to the museum, which my parents were lending furniture for a guest room and where they were permitted to store a lot of boxes. At my request we celebrated our last Christmas in the Humboldt House in an almost-empty dwelling. Only the living room remained for us, where we exchanged gifts under an especially beautiful Christmas tree. We filled my godfather's cellar with some of our boxes, and another family with whom we were friendly also offered to store about fifty cartons for us. And still, the small temporary apartment was completely full.

And, as is often the case with such a big step, our actual departure would be delayed for another half a year. There were so many things my parents still had to straighten out, so many projects to complete. Finally, all our remaining baggage, along with Lobo and my parakeet, Florian, was packed on the bed of a rented truck, and on July 9, 1968, the journey began.

I sat with my German shepherd on the truck bed under a blanket and watched as we gained altitude, and Lima, my friends, my schoolmates, Alida and my godparents—along with all my childhood memories—were left behind for good. I sensed that this would be a decisive break in my life, but I was too young to fathom what it really meant. In my veins flowed the same adventurous blood as in my parents'. Now that all the hustle and bustle of moving out and packing up was finally over, I was looking forward to what lay ahead of me: first of all the trip, about which I already knew that it would take many days.

Upward we went on curvy roads, which were occasionally so narrow that we had to worry more than once that the truck, along with its heavy load, would slide off the edge over the abyss. When evening came, we were already in the High Andes, not far from the Ticlio Pass, and here we all spent the night on the truck at an altitude of about thirteen thousand feet. In a letter to my grandmother and my aunt, I later wrote: *It was pretty cold. Lobo sat on the truck and was really frightened. Florian (my parakeet) wasn't doing especially well. He got seasick from the rocking of the truck, and there were times I thought he would die.* He was probably suffering not only from seasickness, but also from altitude sickness.

On the second day we crossed the Ticlio Pass, and the journey went on over several passes to Tingo María. Here the road conditions got worse and worse, and they didn't get any better when the rain started pelting down. Eventually we couldn't go on anymore, for a road construction machine stuck in the mud blocked our way. We weren't the only ones. Behind us more trucks were jammed up, and we had no choice but to park and spend the night right there. I still remember well how worried my parents were, for the constant rain could easily cause landslides. We had to be afraid of either sliding down the mountain ourselves, along with the road, or having an avalanche come down on our heads. Luckily, neither of those things occurred, and the next morning the road construction machine was successfully pulled out of the mud. The road was unobstructed again. That day we made it to just outside of Pucallpa, and so we were already in the middle of the rain forest. From here to Tournavista was another day's journey, and there our trip came to a temporary end.

In Tournavista, a village that was part of a large cattle farm, the friendly community provided us with a large room in a former school. We stacked our boxes against the wall up to the ceiling. Here we stayed for about a month. My parents finished their final work on their books and then planned how to proceed.

For where exactly in the jungle we were going to live was still not at all clear. My parents had heard of a spot on the bank of the Yuyapichis where there were said to be a few dilapidated huts, and my father wanted to take a look at them. My mother and I stayed behind in Tournavista, while he set off on his important mission to find the right place for our home.

On the bank of the Río Pachitea, at the mouth of the smaller Yuyapichis River, he asked for a boat and two able men who could paddle him up and down the river. And that's how he found "Moro."

Moro's actual name is Carlos Aquiles Vásquez Módena, but no one calls him that. Everyone knows him as Moro. It would prove to be a fortunate coincidence that he crossed paths with my father so early on. Over the years Moro has become the beating heart of Panguana, without whom the research station would not exist today. Back then, Moro, just twenty years old, and his friend Nelson took my father around by boat on several rivers in the Amazon Basin. They are small and large channels that run in wide curves through the jungle. If you don't know your way around, then in a short time you're hopelessly lost. At that time there were still no boats with outboard motors on the narrower rivers, and people relied on poles and paddles to make it upriver and over the rapids. Moro and his friend brought my father to the mouth of the Río Negro at the upper reaches of the Yuyapichis. They were on the lookout for an untouched area that could be reached by boat.

At Purma Alta, they went ashore and hiked downriver, until they came to a few Indian huts. These were the dwellings that my parents had heard about. Apart from four Panguana tinamous bathing in the dust in the shade of the huts, the place seemed to be deserted. My father said: "This is the right place!" A name was at his fingertips: Panguana—after the tinamous. My father and Moro explored the forest, and they liked what they found. The habitat abounded with animals, above all birds, butterflies and other insects. You might say it was a dream come true for any serious researcher. Due to the exertions of the long march to Peru, my father at that time suffered constant back pains. When Moro noticed that, he offered to help bring the baggage here from Tournavista. Naturally, my father agreed. That's how Moro and his family would come to occupy an important place in our lives.

In Tournavista, my mother and I were waiting expectantly to find out what news my father would bring us from his scouting expedition through the jungle. Where would I spend the next several years? To what remote place were my parents taking me? And then my father returned and reported: "I've found the right place. I've even already given it a name."

"And what's it called?" my mother asked.

"Panguana. What do you think of that?"

Of course, my mother was excited. She bombarded my father with questions. Where exactly was the place? What was the state of the huts? What animal species had he seen? Soon the two of them were absorbed in a lively conversation. I sighed. Once again they were in agreement, as always. Only I was worried. The place was secluded, that much I had already understood. And it would again take several days before we finally arrived there. I tried to figure out how many days' journey would then separate me from Lima. At the time I could not have imagined that I would take that journey so many times over all these years.

Soon we set off. The trip on the Río Pachitea took three days. One night we slept on a sandbank, and the second on the boat. There were several rapids, and one almost capsized us shortly before our destination. Finally we reached the mouth of the Yuyapichis, where we could spend the night with Moro's grandparents on their *"fundo"*—what cattle ranches are called in Amazonian Peru. The next day, when we finally arrived at the dilapidated huts after a grueling march through dense primary forest, my despondency turned immediately into excitement! Panguana wasn't gloomy at all! It was gorgeous, an idyll on the river with trees that bloomed blazing red. There were mango, guava and citrus fruits, and over everything a glorious 150-foot-tall lupuna tree, also known as a kapok, which is still the emblem of the research station today.

From the beginning I really liked being in Panguana. On the very first day, I met Moro. I think he was rather surprised at the massive amount of boxes and suitcases we had with us. It took months before we were able to bring everything, little by little, from Tournavista. Now the meticulous lists proved to be a blessing. As we unpacked, it turned out that we had only the bare necessities in clothing, but all the more equipment for research. Moro told me later that the people in the area were actually a bit put off that a few gringos showed up there just to explore the forest. He, too, was skeptical at first. But after my mother showed him her books and drawings and explained the scientific significance of the forest to him, he was fired with enthusiasm. Moro later told me, again and again, how my father's knowledge especially impressed him.

"If a bird whistled anywhere," he said, "he knew better than we natives what species it belonged to." My father's discipline also really impressed him.

"When he said he would be down by the river at eight o'clock in the morning, he was there *at eight o'clock,*" Moro emphasized. "Not a minute earlier and not a minute later. In each hand he carried a suitcase, so that he could keep his balance walking on swampy paths. But once he actually came five minutes late. That had never happened before, and he apologized immediately for it. '*Señor,*' I asked, 'what happened?' for he arrived with only one rubber boot. It had rained hard, the river was high, and one of his boots had gotten stuck in the muddy riverbed. That had cost him time he hadn't factored in. The boot was important to him. Luckily, it could be saved later during the dry season."

To this day we still enjoy laughing about this anecdote.

Besides Moro, there were also other locals, and Germans too, who helped us. Christian Stapelfeld, from Tournavista, and Lionel Díaz repeatedly arranged a boat for us and helped bring our belongings, little by little, to Panguana. Nicolás Lukasevich Lozano, known as "Cuto," whose mother came from Iquitos and whose father was Russian, also had large motorboats that ran on the river. Today he still lives in Puerto Inca. Back then, among other things, he transported the mail. My mother often traveled with him to Pucallpa and back. Then there was Ricardo Dávila, who was rumored to have many women and to have killed people. He was a gold seeker on the Río Negro. And, of course, we met and came to love Grandma Módena, Moro's grandmother, and Doña Josefa Schuler, who came from Pozuzo, a town that had been founded by Rhinelanders and South Tiroleans. Her husband, Don Vittorio Módena, was born in Trient. The two of them ran a beautiful farm with their family directly above the mouth of the Yuyapichis, where it flows into the Río Pachitea. This was where we always went ashore to start on our arduous march to Panguana.

How I loved to stop off at Doña Josefa Schuler's! She made the best bread in the whole jungle, which was called *"pan alemán,"* due to its origins, even though some ingredients—plantains and corn—were not exactly typically German. She woke up at four in the morning to bake this slightly sweet bread, and I loved its aroma and its extraordinary taste. Whenever we stopped by, we were warmly welcomed. Once, Doña Josefa offered my parents a whole loaf. To my horror they declined, and said they couldn't possibly accept it. I anxiously followed the back-and-forth; and when the bread, wrapped in a cloth, finally ended up in our bags, after all, I heaved a sigh of relief. At Doña Josefa's, there was also another delicacy: sweet cream, which she skimmed from the milk of her cows, a rarity in those hot temperatures. I can still see myself sitting in front of a plate of fried bananas covered in cream! Later my mother caught the bread-baking virus. In the jungle metropolis of Pucallpa, she got hold of sourdough, which on the homeward journey burst the plastic bag in which it was packed due to the intense warmth. In our jungle camp we attended to it daily, and so we got sourdough bread, which was baked first under a baking lid, then on a Primus burner and later, when we were set up better, on a two-flame kerosene stove.

When I talk to Moro these days, the changes in the rain forest repeatedly become clear to me. Back then, tilled fields were always far away from the farms and from Panguana. Today they've gotten dangerously close. Which is another reason to have Panguana declared a nature reserve. But the climate has changed too: These days it's much hotter than it used to be. Then Moro laughs and says I can't take part in all the work anymore the way I did back then as a young woman. He reminds me how I helped with the corn harvest, breaking the ears, grating the kernels. I was always there for the slaughter too. I quickly became a "jungle child," and I was just as content there as my parents.

Friends who came to visit us always reminded me of that later: "We never saw a married couple," they say, "as completely happy as your parents there in the jungle." For many it was simply unbelievable that two people could harmonize so perfectly with each other and find their life so fulfilling—and under such restricted conditions. But we didn't see it that way; what was missing in comfort was easily made up for by the wealth of nature around us. For my parents it was probably really the Shangri-la, which others seek all their lives and never find: heaven on earth, a place of peace and harmony, remote and sublimely beautiful. My parents had discovered it for themselves and found their happiness there: Panguana, the paradise on the Río Yuyapichis.

And me? I loved the *selva* (as the rain forest is called in South America). But I looked forward to each visit to the city, where it was always too loud and too busy for my parents. I could go to the movies with my friends again or drink a milk shake with them in my favorite bar—and when we then returned, I was happy to be the "jungle girl" once more. That included: living under one roof with vampire bats, avoiding the caimans in the Yuyapichis, poling across the river with the dugout canoe, carefully shaking out the rubber boots in the morning in case a poisonous spider should have made itself comfortable in them and watching out for the many snakes, because the forest back then reached right up to the houses. What my parents taught me at that time about living in the wild later saved my life.

In our early days in the jungle, our hut had no walls. The house stood on stilts, not only because of insects and snakes but also so that it would not be flooded during the rainy season. Soon we had walls put in, which were made of palm wood planks, as is common in native huts. Everything was bound together with lianas, and the roof was covered with palm branches. There were two rooms, a larger one for my parents and a small one for me, along with a sort of porch, on which we ate and worked. At first, we slept in sleeping bags and on air mattresses on the floor, which was made of the hard, thick bark of a palm. Later we slept on normal bed frames with mattresses—but with mosquito nets, for there were many spiders and at night insects could drop from the roof.

The food was quite simple. In addition to the basic provisions and canned goods that we purchased in Pucallpa and the bread my mother baked, we bought rice, beans and corn from the neighbors. We also got fish and meat from them—the latter when they slaughtered pigs or killed game, such as agoutis and pacas, which are South American rodents, and brocket deer and peccaries. Sometimes we fished for ourselves in the Río Yuyapichis. In a small area of Panguana, there was a grove with bananas, pineapples, guavas, avocadoes, mangoes, lemons, grapefruits and papayas—though, of course, it did not bear fruit year round. We also had manioc and pepper plants.

We prepared the food on a log fire or kerosene stove. There was no refrigerator, so we had to preserve meat by smoking or salting it. We had no electricity because a generator would have been too loud and scared away the animals. When it got dark, we lived by candles and flashlights. Though we also had a bright Petromax oil lamp, we rarely lit it, because its glow attracted too many insects, which would buzz around us in clouds so that we could scarcely breathe.

For us, this life was not as uncomfortable as it might seem. And we did not view it as permanent, but rather as a long but ultimately temporary research stay. For entertainment we listened to the news or music on our battery-powered radio. You could connect a record player to the radio, and sometimes we would put on classical concerts and symphonies by Mozart and Beethoven, which my parents really loved. In the evening we would often play cards and various board games together or read by candlelight. My parents were fond of telling me about earlier days and about their travels, and my mother made up wonderful animal stories for me.

With the neighbors we had casual but pleasant relations. They were mostly white settlers or mestizos. The natives living upriver, who belonged to the Asháninka people, also paid us occasional visits. I did not spend much time with the other children in the vicinity, because they were all much younger than I was. On top of that, the families lived far apart, and the path to the small village of Yuyapichis was endlessly long at the time and nearly impassable. We almost never went there. So I had no playmates, and yet I didn't really miss that because my days were so full.

We had a regular daily routine. At six o'clock in the morning, we went into the forest, often even before breakfast, for that was when the most was going on for an ornithologist. That is the hour of the antbirds, which follow the army ants on their marches through the country, because they eat the insects flushed by the ants. My parents had made observation paths everywhere, which they kept clear of leaves in an arduous Sisyphean task so that we could walk on them soundlessly. That's also how I learned to lay out a system of paths with a folding ruler and compass, to orient myself in the dense jungle, determine water divides and use old Indian paths as shortcuts. As Theseus once found his way in the labyrinth with the help of Ariadne's thread, I got used to scratching markings into trees with the bushwhacker so as to find my way back out of the jungle.

I also learned to recognize each bird from nothing but its call. With a tape recorder, antique by today's standards but state-of-the-art for the time, we made recordings that were later transferred to audiocassettes. Sometimes I got to hold the large parabolic mirror that reflected and enhanced the sounds for the microphone. With it we also recorded insects or frog calls. In general, the chorus of frogs in the jungle is an experience for the senses: Sometimes it's so loud that you can no longer understand your own words. That's the case in November and December, when all the frogs lay their spawn and tadpoles hatch in great multitudes. The ponds rise, seeming themselves to be a living creature. And when the South American bullfrog, the *hualo*, begins to croak, then everyone knows: The rainy season is coming. It doesn't matter what the meteorologists forecast; the *hualo* knows better. You can rely 100 percent on its call. Of course, there are also dry-season frogs, which can only be heard at that time of year. These animals have a sense for what's coming and don't need a weather chart.

Though I already had my own pets from an early age in Lima, it was clear that in the jungle we would get more. In the very first year of my stay in Panguana, neighbors gave me two very young blackbirds that had fallen out of their nest. I named them Pinxi and Punki and fed them with the dropper. The two funny birds grew on me, and I was really sad when Pinxi died one day. I rejoiced all the more when I got a "new Pinxi" for Christmas in 1970, as I wrote joyfully to my grandmother in Germany.

Around that time Moro gave me a little agouti, a New World rodent related to the guinea pig. I usually kept it in a cage, but, of course, I also let it run free outside now and then. It had become tame and always came back to me. On one of these occasions, a marten caught it in the evening and injured it badly. I was able to scare the marten away and take the poor agouti into my care. Soon, though, we realized that the internal wounds were too severe for it to survive. Before it could suffer too much, my mother put it out of its misery. She did this when it was necessary, in her distinctive way, at once sympathetic and professional. Sometimes this affected her really deeply, and I saw tears in her eyes.

Yes, the jungle was my teacher, as much as my parents were. They instructed me with discipline every morning. I was still legally required to attend school, and got the material from a friend in Lima by mail—even though it sometimes didn't arrive for weeks or months. My parents followed it. They were always after me to do things for school and not run off into the forest all the time. My father was really good at math, and I was really bad. So he decided one day: "Something must have gone wrong at the beginning. Let's start again from scratch." How thrilled I was! But he was right, and because he was really good at explaining it, it soon sank in. Suddenly my grades shot up. But I much preferred reading to algebra. I devoured any halfway-interesting reading material, so that my parents had to ration my reading. After all, every single book had to cover a great distance before I could hold it in my hands. I still remember well a thin-paper edition of *Quo Vadis*, of which I was only permitted to read fifty pages a day. That was hard!

The school of the jungle, the books, but above all my parents' teaching prepared me for what I want to achieve today: to save Panguana permanently from the encroachments of civilization. But that is only possible in Lima. Luckily, I also know my way around the city, and have been learning how to navigate the *burrocracia*.

In those days, too, the arm of the authorities reached all the way to our jungle station. After one and a half years, the educational authorities indicated their reservations about my being permitted to take the graduation exams without having sat at a regular school desk for the three decisive years. Even if I could pass all the tests without a hitch, it was no help: In March 1970, I had to go back to Lima and attend my old school there again.

Yes, by that time I thought of going back as something I "had" to do. That shows how much things can change. But when it was clear that the authorities would not relent, I looked forward to the chance to be with my friends again. After all, I wouldn't lose Panguana—I would return to it on all my breaks. In the meantime there were more and more airlines that flew to Pucallpa, so the strenuous journey over the Andes had become unnecessary.

Everything seemed very simple. No one suspected then what would happen one day. . . .

Despite the big time difference, my husband and I wake up the next morning and feel refreshed and well rested. A glance out the window and I'm in an even better mood than before, for today the sun can be detected in Lima's sky, an unusually friendly reception for this city. We enjoy breakfast, and then things get under way. In front of the hotel, we hail a taxi to our first meeting with the lawyer, whom I asked on my last visit to press ahead with the formalities for the acquisition of new land for Panguana.

Last year it became clear that as a Peruvian I could certainly purchase property in this country. But since by Peruvian law, one's spouse must also sign the contract of sale and is recorded in the land title register, we ran—once again—into a completely unforeseen problem. Because my husband is a German citizen, that's not possible. And if it's not possible, then I can't buy property.

"What?" I asked with consternation, but also combativeness. "That can't be. There must be some solution."

Yes, there is one. But the path to it leads through numerous offices. And today, fresh and well rested, we forge ahead slowly but tenaciously on this path. From the lawyer we continue on to all sorts of agencies, where we are sent from one office to the next. Each time we can calculate by those waiting in front of us how long it's going to take this time. But I'm tough, and this is ultimately what I've come here for. Desk by desk I work my way toward the goal, getting together the necessary papers and stamps on them to turn Panguana into a nature reserve. No one can stop me; not even the new official, wearing fashionable glasses, who was not yet sitting at this desk half a year ago, and who threatens to have the whole matter reviewed all over again, which would set me back years. With patience, the necessary assertiveness and expertise, combined with friendliness and persistence, I manage to convince this young woman too. And in this way the day and the next morning go by; at which point, sighing and satisfied, we can finally turn our back on the authorities for the first time.

One of our more pleasurable destinations today is the natural history museum, where my parents worked for so many years and where I still have old friends from that time, colleagues of my parents, who receive me warmly and help me however they can. Today the halls no longer seem as gigantic to me as they did when I was a child. Isn't it strange how rooms have the habit of shrinking when we get older?

In the meantime the biology department of a university in Lima has been named after my mother. My parents are still renowned figures here, and will most likely remain so.

"But you're famous," Alwin tries to tease me on the way to our last dinner before our departure into the *selva*. "If you'd allow it, the airport tomorrow morning would be full of journalists."

"No way," I snap at him. I'm fed up with those appearances. It's enough that the taxi driver this morning didn't take his eye off me in the rearview mirror and finally said, "I know you from somewhere, *señora*. First I thought you were Evita Perón. But now I know it: Aren't you Juliana? The one who survived the plane crash?" In Peru, I am always called Juliana—which the Peruvians spell with an *a* at the end, though my name is actually spelled the German way, with an *e* at the end. Even complete strangers know me by my first name, for I have become a sort of symbol among them because of my survival story.

Yes, today people still remember this story well, which I tried to forget for so many years. Once I might have cut short the conversation, but today I answer amiably and patiently. I've had to learn to deal with this sort of fame. Today I'm willing to confront my story. Here in Lima, it's always catching up to me, anyhow. Not least of all when I meet my friends from those days, and this evening we have dinner plans with Edith.

Whenever we see each other, I feel as if we separated only yesterday. So much binds us, and yet we lead two such fundamentally different lives. Yes, that was already the case back then, for Edith never visited me in Panguana, neither during our school days nor in the decades since. But that doesn't matter at all, just as I also have friends in Munich who have never been to Peru, or just as Moro so rarely comes out of his jungle. When I see Edith, my husband knows he can safely spend the next two hours talking to her husband, for we have "women's conversations," just as we used to do as teenagers. In Lima, we also always like to visit my close friend Gaby, who during my early days in Panguana regularly informed me how far they had come in school in Lima, so that I wouldn't miss the connection to my class.

Back then, after almost two years in the jungle, I was able to return to my old class without a problem, thanks to Gaby's help. To my teacher's surprise, my grades had actually improved, most of all in math. At first I lived in a room at the home of our longtime family doctor, with whom my parents were friendly. But when his daughter returned from abroad, and the room was being used, I moved into Edith's grandparents' apartment on the second floor of her parents' house. I'd have liked best, of course, to move back into the Humboldt House, which I thought of as my home, but that was unfortunately not possible. The Humboldt House no longer existed as an institution for traveling scientists, and the house now had other residents.

At first my friends said: "Juliane, why are you walking so strangely?" That's when I realized that in the jungle I had grown accustomed to always lifting my feet up sharply from the ground, to avoid tripping over a root or anything else. We laughed, and I broke the habit. At that point I was already learning to live in different worlds, and I enjoyed it. Those worlds could not have been more distinct from each other. In Panguana, we went to the river to wash; we slept in open Indian huts; food was cooked on simple kerosene flames. In Lima, on the other hand, I experienced all the comforts and conveniences of city life.

My remaining one and a half years in Lima were a wonderful, lighthearted time, which I spent with my peers. Despite my jungle experience I was a schoolgirl, like all the rest. I was one of them, and I liked that. In Panguana, I was almost exclusively with my parents; here I was with kids my age. I was a completely normal teenager, didn't worry all that much, spent my vacations in Panguana and the school days with my classmates in Lima.

On the first Christmas break after my return to Lima, I flew for the very first time by myself on an airplane from Lima to Pucallpa. That had also been the plan for Christmas in 1971. I was seventeen and had just graduated from Peruvian school. That was after eleventh grade, comparable to a German secondary-school diploma, which did not qualify you to attend university. Of course, I wanted to continue going to school and take the German Abitur, the university entrance exam.

As chance would have it, my mother already came to Lima in November, because she had some matters to attend to in the capital. She would have liked best to fly back to Pucallpa on the day before Christmas Eve to be with my father as soon as possible. Despite the flight from Lima to Pucallpa, which saved us a lot of time, the trip still took several days, depending on the water level of the rivers, on the roads and on how fast you found a boat.

56

"Shouldn't we fly earlier?" she asked me. "After all, you don't have classes anymore."

I made an alarmed face. For on December 23, the graduation ceremony took place, and on the evening before that, there was the first really big and important celebration of my life: the *"Fiesta de Promoción,"* the graduation ball. For weeks I had been saving earnings from German private tutoring sessions for my first long dress. It had an elegant blue pattern, puffy sleeves and was a little bit low-cut. I already had an escort too, the relative of a schoolmate. In those days you didn't go to such an occasion without a dinner partner. Not all my schoolmates wanted to take the Abitur, and so the graduation festivities were incredibly important for me; it was a good-bye to many of my friends. I was a girl who hadn't had too many social highlights in her youth, and so I implored my mother to let me take part in this celebration and attend the graduation on December 23. Of course, she understood.

"All right," she said, "then we'll fly on the twenty-fourth."

My mother tried to get a flight on the reliable Faucett airline, but they were all booked. The only other airline that flew to Pucallpa that day was LANSA, the Líneas Aéreas Nacionales S.A., which had already lost two planes in crashes. There was a saying that went: *"LANSA se lanza de panza,"* which roughly means: "LANSA lands on its belly." My father had specifically urged my mother not to fly with that airline. But the alternative would have been waiting another day, or even two. And my mother didn't have the patience for that.

"Ah," she said, "not every plane's going to crash."

And so she booked two seats for us on that plane. What we didn't know: It was the last airplane that LANSA even had. All the others had crashed already. One had even had an entire school class on board. Only a copilot had survived that crash with serious injuries. . . .

On the evening of our second day in Lima, my husband and I pack our suitcases once again. Yes, I admit, I'm excited. Full of anticipation for Panguana, I can hardly wait to finally be there again. I'm looking forward to the forest, the animals in it, the familiar sounds, the smell, the climate. Even though your blouse clings to your body from the first moment to the last, and all you do is sweat from morning to night. Even though the way there is still taxing, it's no comparison to what we used to have to do to get there. But mingled with my anticipation is also another feeling, and I know that it will never leave me, above all not before a flight from Lima to Pucallpa, the very route that would change my life so decisively. If it's never easy for me to board a plane, repeating this particular flight is the hardest. But I'll pull myself together. Colleagues accompanying us to Panguana to pursue their research work there joke sometimes that there's probably almost no safer way to fly than with me. For it's considered extremely improbable for one and the same person to crash twice. I can give examples, however, where that was indeed the case. But I don't want to think about that today.

The next morning the alarm goes off early. Just like that day, our flight is scheduled for seven o'clock. While we rush to get ready and are driven to the airport, it all comes back. It's four o'clock in the morning, and just like that day I don't feel well rested at all. As if I were seventeen again, I doze, thinking of the school festivities, the graduation ball. I didn't have the slightest idea how much that day would change my life. . . .

With my mother, in a canoe, on the Río Yuyapichis, 1969.
(Photo courtesy of Juliane (Koepcke) Diller)

6 The Crash

No escape: emergency exit from the wreckage of the LANSA plane at the crash site, 1998. (Photo courtesy of Juliane (Koepcke) Diller)

When we arrive at the airport early in the morning on December 24, 1971, it's packed. Several flights were canceled the day before, so now hundreds of people crowd around the counters, everyone anxious to get home in time for Christmas. There's chaos in the terminal. We got up so early, and now suddenly we have to wait. For a while it's not even certain whether our plane will fly to Pucallpa at all or instead head south to Cuzco. I'm really annoyed about this.

Also in the crowd, jostling for boarding passes, is the filmmaker Werner Herzog, who has already been trying indignantly for twenty-four hours to get seats for him and his film crew on a plane to Pucallpa, for his flight the previous day was canceled too. He has to get to the jungle to shoot scenes for his movie *Aguirre, the Wrath of God*. He puts up a fight to be able to fly in our plane, and he is really angry when he cannot. In all the commotion I take no notice of him. Only many years later will he tell me that we might even have directly encountered each other that day. Standing in line, I do notice two good-looking, cheerful boys about my age, speaking American English, with whom we exchange a few words. They explain that they live near Pucallpa in Yarinacocha, where a group of American linguists has been studying the language of the jungle Indians for years. Like my mother and me, they manage to get seats on the packed plane.

Finally, when it's already after eleven o'clock in the morning, our flight is called. And when we ultimately see the plane, we find it magnificent. It's a turboprop built by the company Lockheed, model L-188A Electra; in my eyes it looks as good as new. However, it's far from it, as we'll later find out. This type of airplane was actually designed for use in desert regions and had already been taken out of service in the United States for years. Because it has trouble withstanding turbulence—for its wings were, unlike those of other airliners, fastened firmly to the fuselage—a turboprop could not be less

61

suited for a flight over the Andes. No, it was not new, but assembled entirely from spare parts of other airplanes. Of course, we didn't know that at the time.

Its name is *Mateo Pumacahua*, and that strikes me as memorable, for it's the name of a national hero, who fought for Peru's independence and was ultimately quartered by the Spaniards. The two young Americans and I make jokes about the name, one of them saying: "Well, we'd better hope the plane isn't quartered too."

In the airplane we take our seats. Everything is completely normal. My mother and I sit in the second-to-last row, number 19. I sit by the window as always, seat F. From here I can see the right wing of the plane. It's a three-seat bench, my mother sits in the middle, and a thickset man takes the aisle seat and falls asleep on the spot.

My mother doesn't like to fly. She often says: "It's totally unnatural that such a bird made of metal takes off into the air." As an ornithologist, she sees this from a different standpoint than other people do. On one of her flights to the United States, she already had an experience that gave her a huge scare, when an engine malfunctioned. Even though nothing happened and the plane was still able to land safely with one engine, she was sweating blood.

And there was another incident that made her suspicious of flying. We had an acquaintance in Cuzco who refused to fly no matter what. "No," he said, "I don't fly, and that's that." For years he had always gone by land, wherever he traveled. He stuck to that; until one day, for some reason, he had to fly, after all. And that very plane crashed. For my mother that was a sort of omen.

Still, she flew often, especially from Lima to the jungle, as soon as that was possible, for in the end you were saving yourself so many hours of travel. Earlier, before there were regular airlines, we occasionally even took propeller planes over the Andes. Since those planes fly at a low altitude, it's always really turbulent, and even I sometimes felt queasy. A few weeks before that flight on Christmas Eve, 1971, I had gone on an eight-day trip with my whole class, the traditional *Viaje de Promoción*. We flew to Arequipa in the southern part of the country, and in a letter to my grandmother I wrote: *The flight was glorious!* Among other places, we visited Puno, Lake Titicaca and Machu Picchu, and from Cuzco we flew back to Lima. That flight was extremely turbulent, and many of my classmates didn't feel good. But I wasn't nervous at all. I even enjoyed the rocking. I was so naive that it didn't even occur to me that something could happen.

Today everything is quiet at the airport. My husband and I check in without a problem at the airline Star Peru. After that, we have breakfast calmly and unhurriedly at one of the new coffee shops. I try to act as if this flight were one of many. And in a way it is too. Then it's time to board. As always I sit on the right by the window. Who knows, we might have beautiful weather over the Andes today. The sun hasn't risen yet, and there's no telling from the chronically overcast Lima sky how things will look over the *cordilleras*.

It turns out that we got dream weather for this trip: The mountains are completely cloudless; the summits and glaciers gleam in the rising sun; the massive ridges and vast plateaus of the Andes appear first in pastel and then in shining colors. This spectacle lasts about twenty minutes, and then the mountain slopes in the east descend to the endless rain forest, which is already part of the Amazon region. Soon we'll reach the spot where it happened. . . .

The flight from Lima to Pucallpa takes only about an hour. On December 24, 1971, the first thirty minutes are—just like today—perfectly normal. Our fellow passengers are in high spirits. Everyone is excited to celebrate Christmas at home. After about twenty minutes, we're served a small breakfast of a sandwich and a drink, just as we are today. Ten minutes later the stewardesses already begin to clean up. And then, all of a sudden, we hit a storm front.

And this time it's completely different from anything I've experienced before. The pilot does not avoid the thunderstorm, but flies straight into the cauldron of hell. It turns to night around us, in broad daylight. Lightning is flashing incessantly from all directions. At the same time an invisible power begins to shake our airplane as if it were a plaything. The people cry out as objects fall on their heads from the open overhead compartments. Bags, flowers, packages, toys, wrapped gifts, jackets and clothing rain down hard on us; sandwich trays and bags soar through the air; half-finished drinks pour on heads and shoulders. The people are frightened; they scream and start to cry.

"Hopefully, this goes all right," my mother says. I can feel her nervousness, while I myself am still pretty calm. Yes, I begin to worry, but I simply can't imagine that . . .

Then I suddenly see a blinding white light over the right wing. I don't know whether it's a flash of lightning striking there or an explosion. I lose all sense of time. I can't tell whether all this lasts minutes or only a fraction of a second: I'm blinded by that blazing light; while at the same time, I hear my mother saying quite calmly: "Now it's all over."

Today I know that at that moment she already grasped what would happen. I, on the other hand, grasp nothing at all. An intense astonishment comes over me, because now my ears, my head—no, I myself am completely filled with the deep roar of the plane, while its nose slants almost vertically downward. We're plummeting. But this nosedive, too, I experience as if it lasted no longer than the blink of an eye. From one moment to the next, the people's screams go silent. It's as if the roar of the turbines has been erased. My mother is no longer at my side and I'm no longer in the airplane. I'm still strapped into my seat, but I'm alone.

Alone. At an altitude of about ten thousand feet, I'm alone. And I'm falling.

In contrast to the noise just a moment ago, the sounds of my free fall are downright quiet. I hear the rushing of the air, which fills my ears. Today I'm not certain whether I remained conscious without interruption, probably not. Presumably, the nosedive in the plane lasted much longer—according to technical calculations, even ten minutes. Only after a few weeks am I able to remember it at all. First I experience it in my nightmares, until the memory returns. And to this day, I still don't know how I could suddenly be outside the airplane.

In his text "Wings of Hope" in the book *Voyages into Hell*, Werner Herzog wrote, . . . *she did not leave the airplane, the airplane left her,* and that captures it exactly. I hung strapped into the seat, and around me was nothing. There has been much speculation about what exactly happened. Most likely, the airplane simply broke into many pieces after the lightning struck. We probably sat at one of the breaking points, and invisible forces hurled me out in the seat, into the middle of the raging elements. How exactly that happened, and what happened to my mother, I will never learn.

But I remember falling. I'm falling, and the seat belt squeezes my belly so tight that it hurts and I can't breathe. At that moment it becomes crystal clear to me what is happening. In my ears is the roar of the air, through which I'm moving downward. Before I can even feel fear, I lose consciousness again. The next thing I remember is hanging upside down while the jungle comes toward me with slowly spinning movements. No, it's not coming toward me; I'm falling toward it. The treetops, green as grass, densely packed, remind me of heads of broccoli. The images are blurred. I see everything as if through a fog. Then deep night surrounds me again.

I dream. . . .

It's always the same dream. Actually, it's two, which are interwoven; as in a kaleidoscope, I shift in my sleep from one into the other. In the first of these dreams, I'm racing furiously at a low height through a dark space, incessantly racing along the wall without hitting it. There's a roaring, humming sound in my ears, as if I myself were equipped with an engine. In the second dream I have the urgent need to wash myself because I feel completely filthy. I feel like my whole body is sticky and covered with mud, and I desperately have to bathe. And then I think in my dream: *But that's easy. All you have to do is get up. Just get up and go to the bathtub. It's not that far.* And at the moment I make the decision to get up in the dream, I wake up. I realize that I'm underneath my seat. My seat belt is unfastened, so I must have already been awake at some point. I've also apparently crawled still deeper under the sheltering back of the three-seat bench. I lay there almost like an embryo for the rest of the day and a whole night, until the next morning. I am completely soaked, covered with mud and dirt, for it must have been pouring rain for a day and a night.

I open my eyes, and it's immediately clear to me what has happened: I was in a plane crash and am now in the middle of the jungle. I will never forget the image I saw when I opened my eyes: the crowns of the jungle giants suffused with golden light, which makes everything green glow in many shades. This sight will remain burned into my memory for all time, like a painting. Those first impressions already show me a forest like the one I know from Panguana. I don't feel fear, but a boundless feeling of abandonment. And with excessive clarity I become aware that I'm alone. My mother, who was just sitting next to me, is gone. Her seat is empty. There's also no trace of the heavy man who fell asleep immediately after takeoff.

I try to stand up, but I can't. Everything immediately goes black before my eyes. I probably have a severe concussion. I feel helpless and utterly alone.

Instinctively, I look at my gold confirmation watch. It's still working. I can hear its soft ticking, but I find it hard to read the clock. I can't see straight. After a while I realize that my left eye is swollen completely shut. And through the other eye, I can see only as if through a narrow slit. On top of that, my glasses have disappeared. Since I was fourteen, I've worn glasses, even though I don't especially like them. Now they're gone. Still, I finally manage to read the time. It's nine o'clock. Going by the position of the sun, it's morning. I feel dizzy again, and I lie back exhausted on the rain forest floor.

What I don't know: The largest search operation in the history of Peruvian air travel has begun. Since the previous afternoon, all Pucallpa has been in extreme excitement. The city center was completely deserted in the afternoon and evening of December 24, because the people besieged the airport and even the runways. After the LANSA plane had disappeared from the radar screen from one moment to the next, shortly after it had sent a last radio message near Oyón, about fifteen minutes away from Pucallpa, it was gone without a trace. Contradictory information confuses and worries the family members. The hope that the plane made an emergency landing somewhere else is abruptly dashed. Eventually they can no longer close their eyes to the fact that the plane is missing, by all indications has crashed in the severe storm, the impact of which was felt all the way to Pucallpa. Heinrich Maulhardt, a friend of our family who was going to pick up my mother and me from the airport, is also among the people waiting. Now he has the difficult job of sending my father the bad news in the distant and inaccessible jungle.

After a while I try again to stand up. Somehow I get on my knees, but then everything goes black again and I feel so dizzy that I immediately lie back down. I try again and again, and eventually I succeed. Now I discover the injuries I've sustained: My right collarbone feels strange. I touch it, and it's clearly broken. The two ends have been pushed on top of each other and are not piercing through the skin, and it doesn't hurt at all. Then I find a gash on my left calf, perhaps one and a half inches long and deep, which looks like a canyon, jagged, as if it had been cut by a rough metal edge. But what's strange is that it's not bleeding at all.

And then, all of a sudden, I feel anew the absence of other people. No one is there, I know it. Not my mother either. But why? She was sitting next to me! I get down on all fours and crawl around. Search for her. Call her name. But only the voices of the jungle answer me.

7 Alone in the Jungle

Caña brava, *a giant reed, which covers the mouth of the small creek that I followed, where I later showed the rescue team the way back to the crash site, 2010. (Photo courtesy of Juliane (Koepcke) Diller)*

Later the residents of Puerto Inca, a rain forest city only about twelve miles as the crow flies from the spot where I found myself on the ground after the crash, told me that there had been a terrible storm with extremely powerful winds that day. There are people who claim to have heard an airplane circling over the city and then disappearing in the direction of the jungle. Had the pilot considered making an emergency landing in Puerto Inca? I doubt it. For the wreckage was found pretty much exactly on the route the airplane normally took. So the pilot did not deviate off course.

From Werner Herzog, I later learned of the conversations recorded in the cockpit shortly before the crash, for even the black box was eventually found among the wreckage. The pilots chatted about the upcoming Christmas celebration, about their children and families and how they hoped to return to Lima as quickly as possible. Apparently, the deadly thunderstorm had surprised them as much as it had us passengers. The airplane had already begun its final descent toward Pucallpa. I don't know, of course, whether the pilots had a choice, but in any case they steered the plane directly into the storm.

There was also a woodcutter in the rain forest during the crash, and he said he heard a loud bang, like an explosion. Later, when the rescue teams are searching for the crashed plane, he will report that to the commander in charge. But they won't believe him. Too many leads from the population that turned out to be false have made the search teams mistrustful. Is it fate that this very woodcutter, named Don Marcio, will later play a decisive role in my rescue?

What has most preoccupied me since then, and apparently others too, is the question of how in the world I could survive my plunge from an altitude of nearly two miles with such mild injuries. Even though it would later turn out that I was far more seriously wounded than I perceived after waking up, my injuries were laughable in comparison to the severity of my fall. Besides my collarbone I had broken nothing, and even my flesh wounds were manageable. How could that be? Was it a miracle? Or is there a rational explanation for it?

In conversation with Werner Herzog, I later thought about three possible explanations, and probably I owe my survival to a combination of all three:

First of all, it is known that in particularly extensive thunderclouds there are powerful updrafts, which drive everything upward and could conceivably catch and possibly even whirl aloft a falling person. Such updrafts could have cushioned my fall. It was true, after all, that during the brief interval when I was conscious I felt as if the rain forest were coming toward me in circles.

So I assume that I was simply spinning, just as a maple seed spins as it falls. And the three-seat bench, to one end of which I was fastened by my seat belt, could have worked above me like the little wing on the maple seed that is responsible for this spinning, slowing my fall. On top of that, a man who was involved in recovering the corpses told me that only one very well-preserved seat bench was found, and indeed in a place in the forest over which the giant trees were connected by a dense network of lianas. Perhaps that was "my" seat? Certainly, this tangle of lianas could have cushioned and slowed my plunge. Probably it even ensured that the three-seat bench ended up back under me so that I then fell through the lianas and tree branches as in a boat and landed relatively gently on the rain forest floor. For if I had hit one of the treetops unprotected, I would definitely not have survived the impact.

All that makes sense. And yet something remains. Something inexplicable. A great wonder. Many people have asked me since, how did it come about that I didn't die of pure fear during my free fall? The truth is: Strangely, I felt no fear at all. Even as I was plummeting and, fully conscious, saw the jungle whirling under me, I was completely aware of what was happening to me. Perhaps my conscious moments were too brief for me even to become frightened, but I think it's much more likely that we bear within us a sort of built-in safeguard, which protects us in such extreme moments from going mad with fear or even dying. My experience is: When you are in the midst of a terrible event—and the more horrible it is, the more this is true—you simply let go. The terror comes afterward, as in the tale of the rider who crosses a lake, realizes only after he has safely reached the other side how thin the ice was over which he drove his horse, and drops dead.

On December 25, 1971, as I awake from my long blackout in the middle of the jungle, I'm still in the midst of the event. Even though I'm fully aware that I've fallen out of the airplane, the serious concussion and probably also the deep shock keep me from simply going crazy. On top of that, my parents showed me from an early age that with calm and methodical thinking you could master almost any situation in which you end up in nature. And that's the case now too.

I don't doubt that I will somehow get out of this jungle. My parents already took me with them into the *selva* when I was a child, and we always came out safe and sound. Now I just have to find my mother. But how will I do that? I still feel as if I'm packed in cotton.

For someone who has never been in the rain forest before, it can definitely appear threatening. Then it seems like a wall through which green-filtered light falls, with countless shadows varying in thickness. The crowns of the trees are at a dizzying height, making anyone down on the jungle floor feel like a tiny creature. Everything is filled with life, and yet an untrained eye only rarely actually catches sight of a larger animal. There's scurrying, rustling, fluttering, buzzing, gurgling, clicking, whistling and snarling. For many of the noises, there aren't even words—and that's often much more frightening than when all the creatures can be seen. Frogs and birds make the most incredible sounds. If you aren't familiar with them, you often can't ascribe them to these animals, and to some people they might even seem malicious and menacing. And then there's the enormous dampness. Even when it's not raining, moisture drips down on you constantly, especially in the early-morning hours. The smells of the rain forest are unusual too; often it smells of musty rottenness, of the plants that intertwine and ramble, grow and decay. In these tendrils snakes can sit, poisonous ones and harmless ones, perfectly camouflaged. Often you mistake one for a branch, and don't even notice it. If you then see it after all, many people are seized with a natural, instinctive terror, which paralyzes them or drives them to flee wildly.

And, of course, there is a tremendous abundance of the most diverse insects. They are the true rulers of the jungle. Grasshoppers, bugs, ants, beetles and butterflies in the most magnificent colors. And many mosquitoes that like to suck human blood, as well as flies, which lay their eggs under the skin or in wounds. Stingless wild bees, which don't do anything to you, do, however, like to land in hordes on human skin or cling to your hair, as if stuck to it with glue.

In the rain forest after the crash, I encountered all this. But my advantage was: I had lived long enough in the jungle to become acquainted with it. My parents were zoologists, and there was almost nothing they hadn't shown me. I only had to find access to all this knowledge in my concussion-fogged head. Because now it was no longer just something I happened to pick up in passing. Now this knowledge was necessary for my survival.

That's also why to this day I still get invited to discussions, to television interviews, even to survival trainings. The most frequently asked question is: "What should you do if you're in an accident in the jungle?"

I'm familiar with the Peruvian rain forest, perhaps the Amazon too, but that's as far as it goes. What should you do to survive in the jungle? Unfortunately, that's impossible to say in general. Jungles have the peculiarity of being extremely different from one another. Each rain forest is governed by its own laws. Whenever an airplane crashes somewhere, my telephone won't stop ringing. Fate has apparently made me into an expert on surviving airplane disasters, and so I have to answer questions time and again. When a young woman disappeared in the jungle in the Congo a few years ago, a journalist asked me: "What would you advise her? How should she conduct herself?"

I had to give a disappointing answer: "I've never been in the Congo. I'd have to see on the ground first how things look there, what animals there are, what plants. Every jungle is different." Besides that, it's not in my nature to tell other people how they should conduct themselves. I would be the last person to tell this young woman what to do. I know all too well from my own experience that every situation demands new decisions.

That reporter then twisted my words and wrote that I'd said that if you're stranded in the jungle in the Congo, you're hopelessly lost. That's what often makes me so angry with journalists.

Then there was the twelve-year-old girl who was the sole survivor of a Yemeni plane that crashed in July 2009 near the Comoros Islands. She was able to cling to a piece of wreckage in the waves and had to make it through the whole night in the ocean, which I imagine as a terrible ordeal. Many people saw parallels to my story, because she, too, lost her mother in the crash. But that's where the similarities end. "What would you advise this girl for her life from this point on?" I was asked. In reply, I had to admit that despite my fate I'm an entirely normal person and don't feel called upon to tell complete strangers how they should now live their lives, just because both of us survived a plane crash. This sort of question bothers me, because I believe no one is entitled to give someone else sage advice.

But there also have been funny experiences. For example, a journalist from the *Süddeutsche Zeitung* once called and asked for an interview. He said on the telephone: "You'll also get a purple orchid as a gift from me."

"That's really nice of you," I replied, "but you don't have to do that. Where did you get such an idea, in the first place?"

He answered: "Well, you like purple orchids so much. I read that on the Internet."

And indeed: A young journalist had visited me at my workplace, where there happened to be such plants. In her article she wrote that I seemed to take refuge behind purple orchids and other plants. Sometimes I'm amazed at the imagination of press people.

Now and then, there are also interview questions about other topics, such as the future of Panguana, which I personally find much more exciting. But most of the time, it's always only about "that one thing." Almost everything in my life seems to have to do with the crash; that event has led me so decisively down particular paths.

My husband jolts me out of my thoughts.

"Here," he says, looking at his wristwatch, "here's where it must have happened."

I look down at the sea of treetops. Somewhere down there I landed in the jungle. Here is where I spent eleven days searching unwaveringly for a way out of the wilderness. It always fills me with astonishment that I'm still in the world, when all the others had to depart their lives. . . .

When I'm finally standing somewhat steadily on my two legs, I look around. There's nothing here besides my seat. I shout. No answer. I look up. Up above, beyond the dense treetops, the sun is shining. The thick green canopy of the jungle is completely intact. If an airplane crashed here a few hours ago, then it must have cut a swath! But there's no trace of that, far and wide.

I realize I have only one shoe on, a white sandal, open in the back and closed in the front, which I was also wearing on the day of my graduation ceremony. I keep this sandal on, even though later many people will say how ridiculous that was, and they will ask me why I didn't discard this single sandal, for you can't walk well with one shoe. But I keep it on, because without my glasses I can't see well, and this way at least one of my feet has a little protection. In Panguana, we always wore rubber boots when we went into the forest, because of the snakes. Nor is my thin minidress, printed with a colorful patchwork pattern, sleeveless and with a fashionable double-frilled seam, the ideal clothing for an expedition. On top of that, the long zipper in the back has partially burst. When I feel around, I find another wound on my upper arm, all the way in the back, where it's hard to see. It's the size of a dime, and it's about an inch deep. This cut isn't bleeding either, no more than the one on my calf. I take notice of my open wounds, but they don't alarm me.

Much later doctors will determine that I jarred my neck during the crash and from the resulting spinal injury I still suffer regularly recurring headaches to this day. This also explains why I felt for so long as if I were packed in cotton, for it would take days before the dazed feeling would completely subside.

Suddenly I'm seized by intense thirst. Thick drops of water sparkle on the leaves around me, and I lick them up. I walk in small circles around the seat. I'm well aware of how quickly you can lose your orientation in the jungle. Everything looks the same everywhere, and I wouldn't be the first to get helplessly lost after a few steps. At home in Panguana, I never went into the forest without a machete, and whenever I left the observation trails we had made, I cut signs at regular intervals in the bark of the trees, as my parents had taught me. Once it happened, anyway, that I had lost my orientation for a while and had gone in circles. That's why I'm on alert; lacking a bushwhacker, I memorize a particularly striking tree and don't take my eyes off it.

At first, to my boundless astonishment, I find not a trace of the crash, nothing. No wreckage, no people. Then I discover a bag of sweets and a typical Peruvian Christmas stollen, a panettone, originally brought to the country by Italian immigrants. I'm very hungry and eat a piece of it, but it tastes awful. The hours of rain have softened it completely, and it's soaked with mud. I leave it where I found it. The sweets, however, I take with me.

All morning and into the afternoon, I stay at my crash site, explore the immediate surroundings and gain strength. I search for other survivors—above all for my mother. I shout as loudly as I can: "Hello! Is anyone there?" In response, there's nothing but various frog calls, for it's the rainy season.

And then suddenly I hear the hum of engines. It's airplanes circling over me. I know immediately what they're looking for. I look up into the sky, but the jungle trees are too dense. There's no way I can make myself noticeable here. A feeling of powerlessness overcomes me. And the thought: *I have to get out of the thick forest.* And then the airplanes depart, and only the voices of the jungle remain.

Later I find out that I was only about thirty miles from Panguana. I have no awareness of that, but it's clear to me that I know this forest. And suddenly I notice a very particular sound, which has been there all along, from the beginning, but only now penetrates my consciousness. The sound of dripping, tinkling water, a soft burble.

Immediately, I try to locate where these water sounds are coming from, and indeed: nearby I find a spring, feeding a tiny rivulet.

This discovery fills me with great hope. Not only have I found water to drink, but I'm also convinced that this little stream will show me the way to my rescue. I suddenly remember clearly an incident that occurred when I was living with my parents at Panguana.

At that time a group of scientists from Berkeley visited us. They were on their way to the nearby Sira Mountain Range at the upper reaches of the Yuyapichis to study that as yet unexplored area. When they arrived, there was an accident: The leader of the expedition inadvertently shot himself in the leg and urgently needed medical attention. Since the man was over six feet tall and much too heavy to be carried straight down, a student was sent to get help. The young man promptly lost his way in the jungle, but he was resourceful. He looked for flowing water and followed it until he came to a stream. This brought him to a larger channel and ultimately to a river, which, fortunately, was the Yuyapichis. After two days and two nights, he reached Panguana. This episode really made an impression on me, and I never forgot it.

And now, after quenching my thirst and washing myself a little, I make a decision. By now, I've become convinced that there are no survivors of the plane crash nearby. I still have no inkling that I am the sole survivor and believe that there must be others somewhere, but after crawling around on the forest floor near the spot where I landed, calling out constantly, I am certain that there is no one else in the vicinity. There's no sense in waiting any longer. The search planes will never find me here. I hear the voice of my father, who said to me time and again: "If you get lost in the jungle and you find flowing water, then stay near it, follow its course. It will bring you to other people."

Later I was accused in the press of simply leaving selfishly, without worrying about the injured. In other newspapers it was even written that the survivors were wandering around in the forest, screaming and crying, and I ran off on my own. The truth is, I found no survivors. I don't know what I would have done if I had actually found injured fellow passengers and possibly my mother. Probably I would have stayed with them and we would have perished together. Today we know that the wreckage never would have been found without my information.

So I follow the rivulet, and at first that's not so simple, because there are often tree trunks that are lying across it this way and that, or dense undergrowth blocks my way. Little by little, the rivulet grows wider and ultimately turns into a stream in an actual bed, which is partly dry, so that I can walk relatively easily along what is meanwhile about a twenty-inch-wide channel. How far do I come on that first afternoon? I can't say. Around six o'clock, it gets dark, and I look in the streambed for a suitable spot, protected at the back, where I can spend the night. I eat another fruit candy. I have no way to light a fire; even though my father taught me how to do so by rubbing sticks or smashing stones, it is the rainy season, so everything is soaked. Once the darkness sets in, it is pitch-black. Exhausted and alone, I fall asleep.

Later on, my nights will be plagued by insects, rain, wind, sleeplessness and despair. But, probably due to my concussion, my sleep that first night is more like a state of oblivion.

Meanwhile, the news of the LANSA crash has reached the Módena family at the mouth of the Río Yuyapichis. Don Elvio, Moro's uncle, goes to my father. But my father only shakes his head: "My wife and daughter can't possibly have been on board that plane," he says full of conviction. "I specifically told them not to fly with LANSA. My wife never would have set foot on that airplane!"

Don Elvio doesn't know what to say. He hopes my father is right.

The next day my father turns on the radio. In a special announcement the passenger list of the crashed plane is read. What a shock it must have been for my father as he heard the names of his wife and daughter among the victims. To this day I can barely imagine what hell he must have gone through, all alone in Panguana.

I wake up on December 26 and realize I slept deeply. Still, I feel apathetic. That's probably from the concussion. I'm not afraid and feel no pain. I only know one thing: I have to get out of here.

So I continue to follow the stream. I slowly make headway. Time and again I have to climb over tree trunks. On top of that, the stream meanders a great deal. That costs me time and strength. But since I can't see well into the distance without my glasses, I don't dare to take any shortcuts. The risk of getting lost is simply too great. Besides, the terrain is extremely hilly. Occasionally I pass slopes that rise up a hundred feet or even more. Only here, where I'm walking, the water has found itself the simplest, slightly sloping path, and I follow it, making progress slowly but steadily on its course.

At one point I encounter an imposing bird-eating spider, which could pounce on me and bite me. But it's on the other side of the stream; we eye each other cautiously and then we each continue on our way.

The streambed is rocky and shallow. The stream increasingly widens, until ultimately it fills its whole bed. I begin to wade in the water, always stepping first with the foot in the sandal. I frequently hear the search planes circling over me. I shout, even though I know how futile that is. The forest I'm in is still too dense. I'm invisible to the rescuers and there's no way to change that. My only chance is to go on and at some point reach a wider river, where the closed canopy of jungle tree crowns will open and I can make myself noticeable to the airplanes. Maybe they'll find the others, I think, maybe my mother is among the rescued. I cling to this thought. As mild as my injuries are, it seems impossible to me that others haven't survived the crash too.

What I don't know is that the airplanes are searching in vain. Two days after the crash, there are numerous leads from the population, but most of them turn out to be false. A hunter supposedly saw a bright light and then heard an explosion. A forest worker reports having sighted the airplane on December 24 flying at a low altitude along the Sira Mountain Range. Pilots among the American linguists located on the shore of the Yarinacocha Lagoon, those missionaries studying the language of the Indians in order to translate the Bible for them, join the Peruvian Air Force, the Fuerza Aérea del Perú (FAP). They focus on a trapezoidal area between Tournavista, a town named Aguas Calientes and Puerto Inca, for there are three possible accounts, which all point to the correct area. I hear search planes almost all day. And yet the operation is unsuccessful. The jungle seems to have simply swallowed the airplane with its passengers.

Due to the many false reports, a news blackout is imposed. Only official announcements are permitted. The commander of the FAP, who is leading the search, reacts drastically: It is said that people who raise an alarm will be arrested and interrogated. That unsettles the population. Still, more rumors circulate. Anonymous letters appear, in which there's talk of divine punishment. The victims were punished for their many sins.

For many family members of the missing, the uncertainty grows too great and the waiting unbearable. They feel like they have to do something, and ultimately band together into a civil patrol to finally get answers to their many questions. From Puerto Inca, they make their way into the rain forest, but the search is hampered by torrential rainfall. The despair and helplessness grows when a man named Adolfo Saldaña, whose son was on the plane, has a car accident on the Carretera Central, a bad road, muddy and riddled with holes, while attempting to bring food to the rescue teams. He dies at the scene of the accident.

Unaware of all this, I set one foot in front of the other in the jungle, always stepping first with the shod foot. I fight my way through dead wood that blocks my path in the streambed, climbing unswervingly over every obstacle. On the third day after the crash, I find in the streambed the first piece of wreckage since I set off—a turbine. On one side it's completely black. *Aha, I think, this must be where I saw the lightning strike.* The sight merely fills me with amazement, because I'm still in severe shock and suffering from the effects of the concussion. It will take years before I will grasp the whole significance of this find. For the improbable occurs, and twenty-seven years later I will return to this place, with the filmmaker Werner Herzog. What I can't imagine in the days after the crash will then become reality: I will retrace parts of this path, I will see even more pieces of wreckage, and I will still ask myself how all this was possible. And still I will find only some answers to my questions.

In the first days of my trek, I don't ask myself any questions. I'm still in a daze. On December 28, my gold confirmation watch, a gift from my grandmother, stops for good. The watch is actually not even waterproof and has just undergone an extreme endurance test. I briefly think of my confirmation, which took place the previous spring in Lima. My father was even there and picked out my confirmation motto: "Blessed is the one who finds wisdom, and the one who gets understanding, for the gain from her is better than gain from silver and her profit better than gold." It doesn't occur to me how aptly this proverb fits my situation. Only much later will that make me self-reflective. For without knowledge and understanding of the laws of the jungle, I would probably not be alive today.

And then, on the fourth day of my trek, I hear a sound that makes my blood freeze in my veins. It's the flapping of large wings, unmistakable, louder and lasting longer than that of other birds. Of course, I can only know this because my mother is an ornithologist and she explained it to me, and I hope and pray that she's not the reason for the presence of the king vulture. For the *cóndor de la selva* always goes into action when there's a great deal of carrion in the forest. *The king vultures there, they're feeding on the dead.* It's not even a thought, more an intuition or still more a certainty.

And for the first time since I set off on my own in the jungle, I'm horrified. I come around the next river bend, and there I see it. A three-seat bench, just like mine, only this one here is rammed headfirst about three feet into the earth. The heads of the passengers—two men and a woman—are also stuck there in the rain forest floor, only their legs jutting grotesquely upward.

I've seen a corpse only once before in my life. That time I was six years old and visiting Pucallpa. My mother went to observe birds and left me in the care of friends who owned a sawmill. They took me along to their neighbors' home, where a child had died that night. We arrived for the *velorio*, the day that a dead body lies in state and friends and acquaintances come to pay their last respects. There the child lay with a bloated belly. At the time I viewed all that with interest, as only children can naively confront death. When my mother came home in the evening, I told her: "Guess what I saw! A dead child!" But my mother was really angry, I was even scolded for going along at all, for the child might have died of yellow fever or typhus, and I could have been infected.

As a child I had been more inclined to gaze in wonder at the whole thing as if it was an interesting novelty. But today the sight of the dead pierces me to the core. A nameless horror seizes me. Still, I force myself to stay and take a closer look at the corpses. They're still intact, but in the trees sit the king vultures. They're waiting. It's not a good feeling. A terrible thought crosses my mind. *What if it's my mother?* Very slowly, carefully, I approach the corpses. I look at the woman's feet as if I could recognize by them who it is. I even grab a small stick and with it I turn the foot carefully so I can see the toenails. They're polished. I heave a sigh. My mother never polishes her nails.

At the same moment it dawns on me how stupid of me this is. This woman can't possibly be my mother, because she was sitting right next to me on the same bench. *Why didn't I realize that right away?* I think. And I'm relieved. Later I will feel ashamed.

I look around to see whether there might be more dead or even injured people here. A few pieces of metal lie scattered around, nothing else. And so I turn away and go on. Again I hear the search planes. I know I have to hurry.

8 Pucallpa Today

Noisy modern times in Pucallpa, caused by the thousands of motocars, 2008.
(Photo courtesy of Juliane (Koepcke) Diller)

Today we land safely on the small airfield, which back then was the setting for so many scenes of anguish. Moro is waiting for us, and as always we fall into each other's arms. Neither of us has gotten any younger. His full beard, once so black, is now interspersed with silver threads. We've experienced so much together! And yet, in accordance with the custom, Moro rarely calls me by my first name. In front of other people, he addresses me stubbornly and with a touch of pride as *"la doctora."* If we're alone with his family, I'm *"la vecina,"* the neighbor. His wife, Nery, turns that into an affectionate *"vecinita,"* which is what I call her too.

At the point where the airport road enters the *carretera* is a cemetery. Over the wall you can make out the taller grave monuments, among them an especially large one. It's a memorial to the victims of the LANSA crash, and here fifty-four of them are interred in the traditional *nichos*, burial niches. Two angels stand atop a gigantic block, which holds the coffins. One is weeping and the other is consoling a mourner. Between them is a round slab. On it is a stylized map with the relief of a crashed plane, and a dashed line marks the path I took back then. On the edge is written: *Ruta que siguió Juliana para llegar a Tournavista,* which means "the route Juliane followed to reach Tournavista." And inscribed in large letters, at the base of the group of sculptures, is *Alas de Esperanza,* which means "wings of hope."

Werner Herzog named the documentary film we made together after this. I often ruminated on that strange name for a monument built for people for whom there was no more hope. At best my survival could be viewed as a temporary sign of hope, but in light of the numerous victims, I always found that somewhat presumptuous. Only recently did I learn that there was a missionary aid organization at the time with bush airplanes called Alas de Esperanza, which, of course, makes much more sense. This organization was among those that participated in the search for the crashed plane, and one of its pilots, Robert Wenninger, is said to be the one who finally sighted the first piece of wreckage from the fuselage of the plane.

It's strange, but for many years I knew nothing of the existence of this memorial. No one told me about it, until Werner Herzog brought me here in 1998. At that time I was already shocked by how young most of the victims had been. One family lost two daughters, one fifteen years old, the other eighteen. Another had three dead daughters to mourn, all of them still children. Mary Elaine López was going to get married on January 22, 1972. She died together with her sister. The Sales family lost three members, among them a mother with her five-year-old child. Later I learned from a special edition of the Pucallpa newspaper *Impetu*, dated January 24, 1972, more details about the victims, such as the fact that one girl was not even on the passenger list, because she had taken her ticket from a friend who was ill. A young man had booked a flight for December 26, 1971, but he really wanted to fly earlier. After a passenger canceled, he got a seat. Another man couldn't fly for professional reasons and gave his girlfriend the ticket. And Rodolfo Villacorta had won the LANSA flight in a prize competition.

Whenever I'm in Pucallpa, I visit the monument. I always look at the little photos that, according to local custom, are attached to the front of the niches in oval lockets. Here are the two sisters. There's the girl who took her friend's place. Some of the *nichos* have apparently been emptied since my last visit. Here and there, the names of the victims have been painted on by hand in black, stubborn attempts to retain memory and hold off the decay that accompanies gradual forgetting. As I'm leaving the cemetery, an elderly man who is cleaning the paths speaks to me. It's very nice of me, he says, that I still come here. He knows who I am. Even here in Pucallpa, he adds sadly, people are gradually forgetting.

From the cemetery we head to the home of Tío Bepo, an uncle of Moro's. His shaded farm, no more than three hundred feet from the bank of the Río Ucayali, will be our base station today between our many errands. For here, too, we have things to do. Anxiously wrinkling his forehead, Moro spreads out several documents in front of me on Tío Bepo's garden table. They're the papers for the acquisition of one of the plots of land that is to expand the area of Panguana. Apparently, one of the previous owners wasn't telling us the whole truth, Moro determined after an inspection of the property.

Because these parcels are in the middle of the jungle, it is not always easy to determine properly the exact lay of the land and the boundaries between neighboring plots. Some of the older documents that are supposed to prove ownership are of historic value, handwritten on crumbling, soft paper and frequently authorized with a thumbprint. In the case of some properties, the sale was confirmed by nothing but a handshake between the previous and present owners. Most of the eight property owners avoided the elaborate and costly entry in the registry of deeds, and, of course, I now have to ensure that all that gets rectified. For if I want to have Panguana, in expanded form, declared a nature reserve by the ministry of the environment in Lima, I can't show up with papers like these.

"Here," Moro says glumly, "look at this."

One of the property owners sold us a parcel as primary rain forest. And that's true for the majority of the area. But a remainder, fortunately small, is pasture, which has been used by a neighbor for years.

That is aggravating. But now it comes down to how exactly the boundary runs, and whether the owner of the adjacent property is willing to have his cattle graze somewhere else. This matter shows how urgently necessary it is to protect the remaining rain forest from deforestation. Here fences will probably have to be erected. Moro frowns, less than thrilled about this, for he will be stuck with this job. Since 2000, he has been the official administrator of Panguana.

Today our journey takes us to a lawyer who will now deal with the entries in the land title register. At least that's my hope. For my visit last year with a notary in Puerto Inca, the provincial capital with jurisdiction over Panguana, did not have the successful outcome I'd hoped for. Aside from a bill that the notary issued relatively quickly, nothing happened. For that reason I'm a little skeptical regarding how the new lawyer will handle things. But after the sweat-inducing visit in his tiny office directly next to a sun-drenched roof terrace, I'm in good spirits. Finally I seem to have found a lawyer who knows what he's doing. So I don't mind learning that I have to go from Panguana to Puerto Inca to pay a long-overdue fee for all eight plots of land at the city hall there. I might already be able to deal with one of the registrations there. Here in Pucallpa, no one can tell me whether that will be possible. We'll find out once we're there. On top of that, the cattle-ranching neighbor lives in Puerto Inca, and I hope to be able to resolve then and there with him the question as to the use of the pastures.

Cheerfully, Moro, his wife, Nery, my husband and I take two of the countless, colorful *motocars* zooming around like mad; they are funny rickshaws propelled by motorcycles. For several years they have defined the streetscape of Pucallpa, filling the city with their pandemonium and stinking exhaust gases and making it easy for people to move from one corner of the city to another. I find it fun to go for a bumpy ride in these covered two-seaters, into which three can squeeze if necessary, chatting with the mostly young drivers and hearing the latest stories from the city.

Our destination is the market, where there's always something we need to buy, whether it's a new pair of rubber boots or a sheet or bath towels for Panguana, or some airtight sealable plastic containers for the insects my husband (a zoologist, like me, who studies parasitic ichneumon wasps) is hoping to capture, or the rain forest honey, which is liquid and not very sweet at all, but rather tastes sour and bitter. The wild stingless bees nest in hollow trees, and to harvest their honey one has to saw open the tree carefully from behind and swiftly remove the pot-shaped honeycomb. After the closing of the nest, the bees then produce new honey again. Since we're already there, we also go by the stands that sell medicinal herbs and remedies of all sorts. We buy a cream from the plant, *uña de gato*, "cat's claw," which is supposed to help treat all sorts of things, and a root to alleviate toothaches. A few days before my departure, of all times, the dentist determined that one of my teeth needed a root canal treatment!

I love this market, the colorful supply of fruits, vegetables and tubers, the hodgepodge of things you simply need for everyday life in a jungle city. I often came here with my mother, passing through on our journey between Lima and Panguana, and we always had a long shopping list.

We have one today too. For we have to buy our provisions for Panguana here—everything, from drinking water down to the last piece of toilet paper—and take them with us. We do that in one of the large grocery stores, where the goods are cheaper by the dozen. They already know us here, because this is where we stock up on supplies before every excursion to the Yuyapichis.

Once all the packages are loaded onto various *motocars* and are zooming off toward Tío Bepo, we heave a sigh. It's already late afternoon, and since breakfast we've eaten only a snack.

"What do you say," I ask my companions, "shall we head out to Yarinacocha and have something to eat in one of the floating restaurants?"

I hear no objections, and a taxi has already stopped. The lagoon, an oxbow lake of the Río Ucayali, is quite far for a *motocar.*

We get a seat all the way out on the water. Of course, we order fish, which is fresher here than anywhere else. I look out on the lagoon, where fishermen in their boats spread gill nets. It was a boat just like that, I think, that brought me back to life back then. And as the others chat, the memories come back, of following the stream in the hope . . .

9 The Large River

Birds of hope: Hoatzins, a symbol for my rescue. The calls of these large birds showed me the way out to the large river, Shebonya, which eventually led to my rescue, 2010. (Photo courtesy of Juliane (Koepcke) Diller)

. . . of finding human settlements. The water flows around my feet. Doggedly I set one foot in front of the other. The stream turns into a larger stream, finally almost into a small river. The days are all alike. I try to count along, so I don't lose my sense of time. The intensity of the daylight indicates to me the approximate time of day. In the tropics it gets light at six o'clock in the morning; at six o'clock in the evening, on the dot, it gets dark. The sun itself, however, I see rarely, for the canopy of the jungle giants is too dense.

Eventually I've sucked the last candy. I don't dare to eat anything else. Since it's the rainy season, there's barely any fruit. I don't have a knife with me and cannot hack palm hearts out of the stems. Nor can I catch fish or cook roots. I know that much of what grows in the jungle is poisonous, so I keep my hands off what I don't recognize. But I do drink a great deal of water from the stream, which is brown with floating soil. That might be the reason I don't feel hungry. I do not feel any particular aversion to drinking this water. From living in the jungle, I know that the water of the forest creeks is clean. There is not much danger of dysentery in uninhabited areas where people do not contaminate the water. Still, in Panguana, we had always boiled the river water before drinking it. That crosses my mind as I take in the muddy water from the stream, but I am aware that I have no choice. Because I haven't had any food, I must drink a lot to survive.

Despite my counting, the days get mixed up for me. On December 29 or 30, the fifth or sixth day of my trek, I hear a birdcall, and my apathetic mood immediately turns into euphoria. It's the distinct, unmistakable call of hoatzins, a mixture of buzzing and groaning. At home in Panguana, I heard this call often. These birds nest exclusively near open stretches of water, near larger rivers, and that is my hope exactly, for that's also where people settle!

With new impetus I try to make more rapid progress and follow the birdcalls. And indeed I soon find myself at the outlet of "my" stream into a river. But if I was hoping to reach it quickly now, I was deceiving myself. The mouth is blocked by a great deal of driftwood and overgrown with thick underbrush. Soon I accept that I will never get through here with nothing but my bare hands. So I decide to leave the streambed and go around the barriers. It costs me hours to fight my way through the jungle here. The mouth is densely covered with about fifteen-foot tall reeds, the *caña brava*, and the sharp stalks cut my arms and legs when I'm not careful. But the calls of the hoatzins and the roar of the search planes embolden me.

My mother had studied the hoatzins extensively, observing and describing important details of their breeding behavior. These interesting animals not only look gorgeous, but they also belong to a very primitive family and are faintly reminiscent of the archaeopteryx. Like that first-known bird, their young also have claws on their wings. Since their parents build their nests not only extremely sloppily but also over the water, they can really use the claws. Frequently a hoatzin chick falls out of the nest, catches itself on the branches with the help of its wing claws and climbs back up. The chicks can also swim outstandingly.

Finally I'm standing on the bank of the large river. I estimate its width at thirty feet, a beautiful stretch of water, but there's not a human soul in sight. Immediately I notice that it cannot be navigable, for numerous logs and other driftwood make that impossible. I look up at the sky. After so many days in the half-light of the jungle, I can finally see it open above me again. Where are the search planes? I hear them only in the distance. At one point one more makes a halfhearted sweep over me, and I wave and shout, but it's in vain. It turns away and disappears, just like the others. Silence. *They'll come back*, I tell myself, *for sure*. But time passes, and the engine noise I heard almost constantly over the past few days doesn't return. Finally I grasp it: They've apparently given up the search. Probably all the others have been rescued, except me. *Except me.*

A boundless anger overcomes me. I had no idea that I still had the strength for such intense feelings. How can they simply turn around, now that I've finally reached an open stretch of water after all these days! Now that I can make myself noticeable! But as quickly as the anger flares up, it dies out and gives way to a terrible despair. Here I am on the bank of a really large river, feeling utterly alone. Only now that I have a little bit of distance from it do I become distinctly aware of the vastness of the jungle around me. I fear that it's uninhabited for thousands of square miles. I know that there's an extremely slim chance of meeting a person here. I suspect that my odds are virtually zero. But I don't give up.

This is still a real river. And where there's a river, people cannot be far. My father repeated that all the time. *Sooner or later,* I now encourage myself, *I will reach them. There's no reason to despair right now. On the contrary, my rescue lies just ahead.*

I pull myself together. Think about how best to proceed. The riverbank is much too densely overgrown for me to go on hiking along it. I'm also afraid that I might step on a poisonous snake or spider with my bare foot. I begin to wade downriver in the shallower water near the bank. But beforehand, I look for a stick, not only to avoid slipping but also to check the ground in front of me. I know there are dangerous stingrays resting in the mud of the riverbanks or lying in rapids, and they can't be seen. If you step on them, they plunge a poisonous stinger into your foot. The leg swells intensely, and you get a high fever. Though the stingray's poison isn't deadly, mud often gets into the wound with the stinger, which can lead to blood poisoning. In my situation such an injury could end fatally. I learned all this in Panguana from my parents and our neighbors. I know the dangers in the water, and so I walk carefully and warily.

My progress is very arduous. There are branches and many logs in the water, the ground consists either of slippery rocks or deep mire into which I sink. So I soon decide to swim in the middle of the river. In the deep water I'm at least safe from stingrays. Instead, there are piranhas, but I've learned that they only become dangerous in standing water. Certainly caimans are to be expected, but they, too, generally don't attack people. So I yield to the current. I still have no fear. Plus, the confidence that I'll somehow make it has returned.

It's good that I don't know but only suspect that they will soon stop searching for survivors. It's also better that I can't imagine that so far no one has been rescued—and that the searchers haven't even been able to find the slightest trace of the plane wreck. But most important of all is that I don't know that besides me some people actually did survive the crash, without being lucky enough to be able to leave the spot where they hit the earth. As I later found out, my mother was among those people. And I think of my mother during each of my nights, in which I barely sleep. For, ever since my concussion has abated, I no longer fall into that sleeplike state that is more akin to a stupor. My nights are long, pitch-black and without peace.

When the sun descends and I estimate the time at around five o'clock, I search for a reasonably safe spot on the bank where I can spend the night. I always try to find a place where I have protection at my back, either from a slight slope or a large tree. Still, sleep is almost unthinkable. Either mosquitoes or tiny tormenting midges, which are also among the gnats, keep me awake. They seem to want to devour me alive. There's buzzing around my head, and the bothersome pests try to crawl into my ears and nose. Those night hours are unbearable. Dead tired, I fall into a half sleep and wake up again and again from the burning and biting of new stings. Or, even worse, it rains. Then the mosquitoes leave me alone, but the ice-cold rain pelts mercilessly down on me. I freeze in my thin summer dress, constantly soaked to my skin. As hot as it may be in the daytime, during the rainy season it cools down drastically at night, and each of the hard drops torments me like an icy pinprick. And then the wind comes and makes me shiver to my core. I search for spots under dense trees or in bushes, collect large leaves and try to protect myself with them. Nothing helps. On those black nights, which seem never-ending, as I cower somewhere soaked to the bones, I cannot protect myself, a boundless feeling of abandonment arises in me. It is as if I were all alone, somewhere out in the universe. Those are the moments when I despair.

I think about my mother a lot. How might she be doing? Was she already rescued? I don't dare to think of the possibility that she could have suffered the same fate as the three people who had been rammed into the ground, along with their seat bench. I wonder what my father might be doing right now. How is he? Where is he? Has he heard about the crash yet?

I ruminate a great deal on how it could have happened that I awoke alone in the jungle. I wonder where all the other passengers are, why I couldn't find a swath cut anywhere in the forest, where in the world the airplane itself has gone. I think about my life up to now, which was so completely unspectacular. At least in my eyes, nothing really exciting happened before. I'm a young girl, like all the rest. I love animals, read avidly, go to the movies with my friends, get good grades, adapt to whatever place I'm dragged to—whether it be the jungle or Lima. I've never worried much about the meaning of my life. Though I was baptized as a Protestant and was just recently confirmed, my parents adhere more to a sort of philosophical nature religion and view the sun as the basis of all life. They have not raised me to be particularly religious. They believe that I should form my own opinion; they certainly provided the fundamentals for a Christian upbringing, but more was not necessary, in their view.

On those nights I pray. The prayers are mainly about my mother. I've always had a very close relationship with her. She is my mother and a sort of friend. We're more intimately bound to each other than I am to my father, who scarcely lets anyone get close to him besides my mother. I'm aware that it's a miracle that I'm still alive, and I wonder why me of all people. I have survived the crash and believe that I now have to get through this too. I pray that I will find people. I pray for my rescue. I want to live. With every fiber of my gradually weakening body, I want to live. And then I wonder what I will do with that life when this is finally over.

I think about that for a long time.

Of course, like all my friends, I've thought about what I will do after school. From an early age I wanted to study biology, like my parents. But I never asked myself why and for what purpose. I was fond of animals, interested in plants, and I liked what my parents did. Up to now, that was reason enough for me. On those rainy nights I now think that it would be great to devote my life to something big, something important, something that would benefit humanity and nature. What that might be, I have no idea. I just feel that my life from now on should have a meaning in the fabric of the world. For it has to mean something that I fell out of the airplane and walked away from that with only a few scrapes.

Those "few scrapes," though, do begin to worry me somewhat in the days that follow. The cut on my calf swells with rampant whitish flesh. Still, I feel no pain. The hidden wound on the back of my right upper arm is a different story. I have to twist my head far to see what's going on there. To my horror I discover white maggots, whose bodies peek out of the wound like tiny asparagus heads! Apparently, flies have laid their egg packets in my wound, and the brood is now already half an inch long. That is something else I know all about, and this time my knowledge worries me.

For Lobo, my German shepherd mix, was once infested with fly larvae. Unbeknownst to us, he had a small cut in his shoulder, and the flies laid their eggs in it. Hidden under the skin, the maggots hatched and burrowed ever deeper into the flesh. They do that very skillfully, avoiding blood vessels so that the wound doesn't bleed. Back then, they ate a deep canal for themselves under Lobo's fur, down his leg to his paw. At night Lobo whimpered, and we wondered what was wrong with him. The maggots were still completely invisible. Then the leg eventually swelled and began to smell. By then, it was already so bad that the dog would no longer let anyone touch him. Finally we discovered what had happened. Normally, you can get maggots out of the body with alcohol, but my father said we couldn't do that, because the dog would go crazy with pain. So we poured kerosene into the wound, which doesn't burn, until the maggots came crawling out, one after another, and we could patch up poor Lobo. Fortunately, his wound healed without any problems after that.

So I know what I have to do: The maggots have to come out. But I have neither alcohol nor kerosene. Only a silver spiral-shaped ring, and I now bend it open and try to fish out the maggots with it. But as soon as my self-made tweezers approach, the maggots disappear into my flesh. I try it with the buckle on my watchband, but that, too, gets me nowhere. Then a rather queasy feeling creeps up on me. It's not a pleasant thought, to be devoured alive from within. Though I know that the maggots themselves would not do anything dangerous to me, for like all good parasites they initially avoid harming the host, the wound can, of course, get infected. After all, I swim all day long in brown, dirty river water. And if that should occur, then it's not out of the question that my arm would ultimately have to be amputated. I've heard of cases like that. I wouldn't be the first person to whom this happened.

Since there's nothing I can do about it at the moment, I go on swimming. I noticed a long time ago that the wild animals on the riverbank are extremely trusting. I see martens and brocket deer, which aren't frightened of me at all. I hear howler monkeys, very close, and that makes me think, because usually those animals are extremely shy. I know what that means, but I try to keep the thought at bay: This river and the surrounding forest have not yet come into contact with people, and that it will be many miles before that might change.

Meanwhile, I'm getting weaker all the time. Though I don't feel hungry at all, I notice how everything is getting harder. I drink a lot of the river water, which fills my stomach, and I know that I should eat something. How many days have I already been on the move? Seven? Or eight? I count on my fingers, and I realize that the new year of 1972 has possibly already begun. My mother really wanted to celebrate the turn of the year with my father. That was the reason she didn't want to wait any longer for a flight. And now I wonder where my father might be.

Only recently did I find among my aunt's posthumous papers letters that my father wrote during those days. On December 31, 1971, he wrote:

> Now a week has already passed, and still the plane
> has not been found. The weather is mostly good, so that
> search operations could be launched in all directions. I'm
> on Herr Wyrwich's hacienda, which has an airfield and
> is therefore equipped with transmitters and receivers. We
> can inquire in Pucallpa and are then informed on the
> status of the search operation.

This paragraph is followed by an enumeration of the various theories and statements of witnesses, all of whom claim to have heard the airplane itself or a detonation. But it turns out that in the nearby Sira Mountain Range, due to the constant rainfall, a landslide had occurred, which might have caused this sound. As I read this letter for the first time in my father's typical neat handwriting, I tried to imagine what might have been going on inside him. Only the second part of the letter, written after an interruption, bears witness to his emotions. For in the meantime an American missionary named Clyde Peters had landed his plane on Herr Wyrwich's airfield and had given him encouraging news. There was some support for the theory that the LANSA plane must have made an emergency landing somewhere. I could tell even by my father's handwriting how hope was rekindled in him.

Of course, I don't have the slightest inkling of all this during my odyssey. I have only one thing in mind: I have to find people. During the day I swim or let myself drift, and at night I now have a few encounters with larger animals. At one point, while I'm trying to sleep in the middle of some bushes, I hear a hissing and pawing right next to me. I know it's most likely not a jaguar or an ocelot. Probably what's making noise next to me is a *majás*, known as a paca in English, a rodent as large as a medium-sized dog, with brown fur and white spots arranged in rows. I clear my throat, which gives the animal a terrible scare. It runs away in wild bounds, loudly grunting.

The next morning I feel a sharp pain in my upper back. When I touch it with my hand, it's bloody. While I've been swimming in the water, the sun has burned my skin, which is already peeling off. They are second-degree burns, I will later learn. I can't do anything about that either and continue to let myself drift in the water. Luckily, the current is getting stronger. As weak as I am, I only have to be careful not to collide with a log floating in the river or injure myself on another obstacle.

My bad eyes repeatedly fool me. Often I'm convinced that I see the roof of a house on the riverbank. My ears deceive me too, and I'm completely sure that I hear chickens clucking. But, of course, it's not chickens; it's the call of a very particular bird. Even though I know this call well, I'm taken in by these sounds, again and again. Then I'm annoyed and scold myself: *How can you be so stupid, you know that those aren't chickens.* And yet it happens to me, again and again. The hope of finally, finally finding people is stronger. And ultimately I fall into an apathy unlike anything I've ever experienced before.

I'm tired. So horribly tired. During the nights I fantasize about food. About elaborate feasts and completely simple meals. Each morning it gets harder for me to stand up from my uncomfortable spot and get into the cold water. Is there any sense in going on? *Yes,* I tell myself, mustering all my strength, *I have to keep going. Keep going. Here I will perish.*

At one point I sink in the middle of the day onto a sandbank in the river under the glaring sun. It seems to me an ideal place to rest a bit. I've almost dozed off, hardly noticing anymore the ubiquitous blackflies on the riverbank that are constantly pestering me. Suddenly I hear a squawk near me that I know; young crocodiles make those noises. When I open my eyes, I see baby caimans, only eight inches large, very close to me. I jump up. I know that I'm in danger. As soon as the mother of these babies notices my presence, she will attack me. And there she is already, very close. She rises on her legs and comes toward me threateningly.

And me? I slide myself back into the water and drift on. I've already had encounters with spectacled caimans, which were dozing on the riverbank. When they had noticed me, they were frightened and jumped into the water toward me. If I didn't know this jungle so well, I undoubtedly would have gone ashore full of panic and run into the forest, where I would probably have died. But instead I trust that what I've learned in Panguana is true: that caimans always flee into the water, no matter what direction they suspect danger is coming from, and that they will swim past me or under me but definitely won't attack me. But the very presence of so many caimans is a sign for me that there are no people living on this river. Later I will learn that at that time the entire river was uninhabited. If I had simply lain down somewhere and stayed there, I would never have been found.

So I keep going.

I'm getting weaker, can scarcely struggle to my feet anymore. I know that I have to eat something if I don't want to die. But what?

It's the rainy season, and frogs are jumping around everywhere. And I'm seized by the idea that I have to catch one of these animals and eat it, even though I know they are poison arrow frogs and will not agree with me. The Indians use certain species to poison their arrows, but the effect of these frogs here is too weak to kill an adult. Still, I'm not sure how well I will stomach them in my weakened state. Nonetheless, I try again and again to catch one of the frogs. But I don't manage to do it. At one point one of them is sitting less than six inches from my mouth. The moment I grab it, it's gone again. And that depresses me more than anything else.

And again I hear the false chickens clucking, and again I am fooled by them. At one point I'm close to tears when I realize I've been deceived again.

I spend the tenth day drifting in the water. I'm constantly bumping into logs, and it costs me a great deal of strength to climb over them and to be careful not to break any bones in these collisions. In the evening I find a gravel bank that looks like a good place to sleep. I settle down on it, doze a little, blink; then I see something that doesn't belong here. I think that

I'm dreaming, but I open my eyes wide, and it's really true. There on the riverbank is a boat. A quite large one, actually, of the sort the natives use. I tell myself that it's not possible, that I'm hallucinating. I rub my eyes, look three times, and still it's there. A boat.

I swim over to it and touch it. Only then can I really believe it. It's new and in full working order. Now I notice a beaten trail leading from the river fifteen to twenty feet up the slope of the bank. There are even visibly trodden steps. Why didn't I see that before? I have to get up there. Here I will definitely find people! But I'm so weak. It takes me hours to cover those few yards.

And then I'm finally there. I see a *tambo*, a simple shelter, poles with a palm leaf roof, a floor made out of the bark of the pona palm, about ten by fifteen feet. The boat's outboard motor is stored here—forty horsepower, I observe, as if that were important right now—and a barrel of gasoline. No people can be seen far and wide, but a path leads into the forest, and I'm certain that the owner of the boat will step out of it at any moment. As I look at the gasoline, I remember my maggots, which sometimes hurt horribly and have already gotten a bit bigger. I will trickle some of the gasoline into my wound, and then they will come out as they did with Lobo. It takes an endlessly long time for me to get the barrel's screw cap open. With a little piece of hose I find next to it, I suck up the gasoline and let it drip into my wound. At first that hurts excruciatingly, for the maggots inside my arm try to escape downward and bite their way still deeper into my flesh. But finally they come to the surface. I take thirty of them out of the wound with the bent-open ring, and then I'm exhausted. Later it will turn out that that was far from all of them, but for the time being I'm pretty proud of my achievement.

Still, no one has come. It gets dark, and I decide to spend the night here. At first I try the floor of the hut, but the pona bark is so hard that I'd rather find a spot on the sandy riverbank. I borrow a tarp that is also lying in the hut, cover myself up with it and, thus protected from the gnats, sleep divinely that night, better than in any five-star hotel.

The next morning I wake up, and still no one has shown up. I wonder what I should do. Perhaps no one will come here for the next few weeks. I know that there are shelters like this in the jungle that trappers or woodcutters use only sporadically. Perhaps I really should keep going?

Only briefly do I consider taking the boat and heading downriver, but it doesn't seem right to me. Who knows? Perhaps the owner is somewhere in the forest here, I think, and when he comes back, he'll need his boat. I cannot possibly save my own life and jeopardize another's. Besides, I'm not sure whether in my weakened state I'm even capable of maneuvering the boat down this river. While I'm thinking about this and unable to decide whether to get back in the river, midday comes. And then it begins pouring rain. I crawl into the *tambo*, wrap the tarp around my shoulders and feel nothing. Now and then I try to catch a frog, in vain.

In the afternoon the rain stops, and my mind tells me that I have to keep going. Against all common sense I simply remain sitting. I don't have the strength anymore to struggle to my feet. I will rest for one more day, I think, and tomorrow I'll go on. Despair alternates with hope; powerlessness with new resolve.

I think that all the others must have been found a long time ago, and I'm the only one still out here. The thought occurs to me how strange it is that a person can disappear just like that, and no one knows about it. It's a peculiar feeling, which fills my chest and goes to my depths. I worry that I might die here, and no one will ever know what became of me. No one will ever find out what an arduous journey I undertook, how far I have come. I'm aware that I am slowly but surely starving. I have gone too long without eating anything. I always thought that when you starve, it hurts terribly. But I have no pain. I don't even feel hungry. I am only so horribly exhausted and weak. Again I try to catch one of the frogs. Again and again. Thus the day passes.

It's already twilight when I suddenly hear voices. I can't believe it! After all this time in solitude, it's inconceivable to me. *I'm imagining it,* I think, *as I have so many other things already.* But they really are human voices. They're approaching. And then three men come out of the forest and stop in shock. They even recoil involuntarily. I begin to speak to them in Spanish.

"I'm a girl who was in the LANSA crash," I say. "My name is Juliane."

Then they come closer and stare at me in astonishment.

10 The Return

A witness to the devastation: a temperature gauge from the cockpit of the LANSA plane, 1998. (Photo courtesy of Juliane (Koepcke) Diller)

It's January 3, 1972. Some of the LANSA passengers' family members have lost hope. Ten days after the disaster, the prospect of finding survivors fades. The search for the missing airplane is officially abandoned. Only the patrol made up of civilians and family members does not yet give up. The numerous journalists who came to Pucallpa on Christmas, and have continuously besieged the city since then, depart—the story seems to be over. My father is staying on the farm belonging to his acquaintance Peter Wyrwich. Has he, too, accepted the fact that he has lost his wife and daughter?

Meanwhile, Beltrán Paredes, Carlos Vásquez and Nestor Amasifuén, for those are the names of the three forest workers who find me in their camp, kindly take care of me. They give me *fariña* to eat, a mixture of roasted and grated manioc, water and sugar, the typical fare of the forest workers, hunters and gold panners. But I can get almost nothing down. As well as they can, they attend to my wounds and take still more maggots out of my arm.

"By all that's sacred," Don Beltrán confesses to me as he picks one after another out of my wound, "at the first moment I thought you were the water goddess, Yacumama."

"Why?" I ask with surprise. I know whom he means. Yacumama is the name the Indians give to a nature goddess who lives in the water. Pregnant women have to avoid looking at her at all costs, or else she will come later and take the child. But why did they think I was she?

"Well, because you're so blond. And because of your eyes. And because there's no one living here far and wide. Especially not any whites. Good thing you spoke to us right away."

That's how I learn that this river really is completely uninhabited.

"What about the other passengers?" I ask the men. "Were they rescued?"

Speechless, the men look at me with wide eyes. Finally one of them pulls himself together. It's Don Nestor, and his voice sounds hoarse.

"No, *señorita*," he says, "not even the airplane has been found. It has simply disappeared in the jungle, as if it closed its fist around it. As far as I know, you are the only survivor."

The only survivor? Me? That seems inconceivable to me. *If I'm the only one . . . that means . . .* I try not to finish this thought, but can't help it: My mother wasn't found either?

"No one," confirms Don Carlos, who has been silent until now. Only now do I realize that I spoke my thought aloud. "It's a miracle that you've turned up here, that you're alive, able to talk to us. And that we came here. For we actually weren't going to. When the rain came today, we considered whether to go to the shelter or not. To be honest, we check on the boat pretty rarely. We might well not have come at all. But Nestor said, 'Oh, come on, the weather is deceptive. Let's go to the *tambo*. There we'll at least have a roof over our heads.' I can still hardly believe it. How long were you on the move?"

The men give me pants and a shirt to put on. I eat one or two spoonfuls of the sour-smelling *fariña*. Then I'm already full. Apparently, my stomach has shrunk.

Suddenly another two men come out of the darkness. The bad weather—or fate?—leads them all to this shelter, today of all days. It's Amado Pereira and Marcio Rivera, and they, too, are thunderstruck when they see me.

"Whom do we have here?" Don Marcio asks with surprise.

And again I have to tell what happened. Again the response is pure astonishment. We exchange information, and I learn details about the large-scale but unsuccessful search operation. That evening we speak for a long time.

"We'll get you out of here," says Don Marcio, and he confers with the other men. Actually, they want to get me as quickly as possible to a doctor, as if they were afraid I might have more serious injuries, after all, and could die on them. But then they agree that it's safer to spend the night here. The three men who first found me will remain in the forest, as they originally intended. Don Marcio and Don Amado volunteer to take me to Tournavista early the next morning in the boat.

That night I don't dare to say how uncomfortable I find the palm-bark floor in the shelter and that I'd rather sleep in the sand. So all six of us spend the night in the *tambo*. The men give me their only mosquito net, but I sleep poorly, anyway. My wounds, out of which we have meanwhile taken about fifty maggots, hurt unbearably. Early in the morning, when it's still dark, we set off. I try to walk, but they carry me over the last stretch, lay me in the boat and cover me with a tarp.

And then I simply let go. I'm so boundlessly tired. I doze off, again and again. During my waking hours I look at the riverbank gliding past me and talk to the men. I learn the name of the river. It's the Río Shebonya, and it really is still completely uninhabited.

It's not long before the story of my rescue fills newspapers all over the world in the most unbelievable variations. The wildest version is the myth that I built a raft for myself, out of branches and leaves, and floated down the Río Shebonya on it. Indians saw me drifting by, unconscious, and pulled the raft ashore. When I came to, I said only: "There are dead people," and then I passed out again. Once it's out there, hundreds of journalists copy this account. Even today you can still read it in newspapers or on the Internet. I've received letters mainly from rational-minded children like those first graders from Warner Robins in the United States who were justifiably eager to know how I managed to build a raft without any tools. And why didn't my raft made of branches and leaves sink? Other reports describe my journey on the boat with Don Marcio and Don Amado like this: *Then she fell into a deep oblivion.* That was not the case. On the contrary—though I repeatedly nodded off, I took in much of the monotonous journey.

The trip goes on forever, and it's a long time before we finally reach the mouth of the Río Shebonya where it flows into the Río Pachitea. On the bank of the Pachitea lies the village of Tournavista. It becomes clear to me: I could never have managed this alone.

Around noon the men stop to eat something. We go ashore to a house in the middle of a pasture. As I approach, some children run away, screaming; and a woman turns away with horror, her hand pressed to her mouth: "Those eyes! I can't look at them! Oh God, those terrible eyes!"

I ask my companions: "What's wrong with her? What's going on with my eyes?"

And then they explain to me that my eyes are completely red. Apparently, all the blood vessels have burst, and there's no white left, everything is bloodred. Even the iris has turned red. I'm surprised, for I can see quite well.

Later I will look in a mirror and understand well the woman's terror. It really does look as if I no longer have eyes, but only bloody sockets. No wonder these people here think I'm a jungle spirit. Nonetheless, they give me a bowl of soup, but again I get almost nothing down.

Around four o'clock in the afternoon, we dock in Tournavista. Our arrival provokes great excitement. Immediately a stretcher is brought over, and I find that embarrassing, for I can walk on my own!

The nurse who comes to meet me I know from the past. Her name is Amanda del Pino, and she once gave me a tetanus shot, back before I came to Panguana. Now she wants to give me penicillin, but I refuse. My father is highly allergic to this antibiotic, and I don't know whether I might have inherited this intolerance from him. Sister Amanda lets herself be persuaded, and she injects me with a different medication.

Everyone is very careful with me. They handle me with kid gloves. Someone takes a photo that will soon appear in *Life* magazine. In it, I'm standing on a porch. Someone has put a bathrobe over my shoulders. The nurse is holding me by the arm and looks very concerned. She barely asks me any questions. Still, the next day there's an interview in the newspaper that I definitely didn't give.

After my wounds have been cleaned and disinfected, and I've received an injection, an American female pilot named Jerrie Cobb appears and offers to take me on her plane to the Instituto Lingüístico de Verano in Yarinacocha, where the missionaries are studying the languages of the Indians and translating the Bible. There are some doctors there, she says, and I could get better treatment and recover comfortably. Though the prospect of getting on a plane again frightens me, I'm too weak to protest energetically. And she's probably right, I think.

So a short time later, I'm aboard a twin-engine Islander, and as Jerrie Cobb tries to reassure me with the information that she's the first woman in the world to be trained as an astronaut, and with her I will fly as safely as in the arms of an angel, I don't find the strength to insist on being allowed to fly sitting up. Jerrie finds it safer for me to lie down, and so the twenty-minute flight becomes a torment for me. Above all, it happens when Jerrie, who apparently doesn't notice my fear, really leans the airplane into the turns.

The "linguists," as the missionaries of the Wycliffe Bible Translators in Yarinacocha are generally called, give me a warm welcome. The family of Dr. Frank Lindholm takes me in, and immediately I receive medical attention again. The doctor removes more maggots from my arm, as well as from the cut in my leg, in which the beasts had also nested. The hole in my arm is deep. How deep no one knows exactly, and therefore I now receive the first of countless treatments during which I have to clench my teeth to keep from screaming loudly: Dr. Lindholm soaks a twenty-inch strip of gauze in iodoform and stuffs it deep into the wound. It has to remain there until the next day, when it will be pulled out and replaced with a new one. That's the only way, he explains to me, to make sure that the tubular wound heals cleanly from the inside to the outside. Then he pulls a pretty long wooden splinter out of the sole of my foot, which I hadn't even perceived. All over my body I have insect bites, which are inflamed and swollen. These are now treated too.

When this is over, I'm asked what I'd like to eat. On impulse I say: "A chicken sandwich." To my great joy they immediately make me one, and I eat it very enthusiastically.

I'm safe. And with this certainty I fall into a deep sleep.

In the restaurant our food is served. It's a gorgeous late afternoon. The light glistens gold on the water, gently rippled by the wind. Over there, a bit farther up the lagoon, is where I rested back then in Dr. Lindholm's house. Today there are only a few linguists left there. When I came with Werner Herzog, they already had to reduce the size of their camp. Just a few months ago, after an interview with me was broadcast on CNN, the widow of another doctor, whom I had moved in with after several days, Mrs. Fran Holston, sent me a photo showing me with her two daughters in the garden. You can scarcely tell by looking at me in this picture that I had just gone through that eleven-day odyssey. In a skirt and blouse, borrowed clothes, I'm smiling at the camera. I was surprised how little I felt at the sight of this photograph, as if the girl in it were someone else entirely. I had a similar experience during the shooting of the documentary *Wings of Hope* with Werner Herzog.

To this day it seems to me a stroke of good fortune that in 1998 our telephone rang at home in Munich and a man introduced himself with the words: "My name is Werner Herzog. I'm a film director. I would like to make a documentary about your fate."

By that time the crash was twenty-seven years in the past. I hadn't had many good experiences with journalists and filmmakers, and so had shied away from all that, years ago. Those days I rejected interview requests categorically, and was all the more averse, of course, to appearances on talk shows. I was tired of being asked the same questions over and over again, all my life, and being perceived exclusively as the rare survivor of an unbelievable story. Since then, I had a life of my own, had been married for nine years, and there was in my opinion a host of topics more exciting than rehashing, again and again, the details of the crash. Especially since it had been my experience that, whatever I said, the journalists seemed not to listen and in the end would write what they had already imagined, anyhow, or what they thought the readers wanted to hear. But suddenly I had Werner Herzog on the telephone, and he wanted to shoot a film with me!

He apparently sensed my hesitation, for he said: "If you want more information about me, then you can read about me on the Internet. I would also be happy to send you a few of my films."

"That's not necessary," I said after I had overcome my initial surprise. "Of course, I know who you are, Mr. Herzog." I had always admired this extraordinary director. I had seen many of his films. I could hardly believe I was talking to him on the telephone. And his proposal also seemed unbelievable to me at first.

For Werner Herzog did not just want to conduct interviews with me, as so many others had done. He was planning something unheard of: twenty-seven years after the crash, he wanted to return with me to the place where everything had happened. He also wanted to retrace my path back to other people. Should I actually do it? On the other hand: How can anyone really turn down an offer like that?

Herzog suggested that I think about everything. He sent me books and some of his films I hadn't yet seen, and gave me time. I consulted with my husband, for his opinion was always really important to me. He has incredible insight into people, and I know that I can rely on his advice. He said: "Maybe it will be good for you. You will probably never have an opportunity like this again."

And so I contacted Werner Herzog and informed him that I was interested in his project. We met at an excellent Munich restaurant. On this occasion I became acquainted with the cameraman Erik Söllner. Later, too, during the filming, Werner Herzog set great store by his opinion.

That evening Herzog explained his plan to us: He wanted to send an expedition to find and make accessible the spot where the wreckage of the Lockheed L-188A Electra still lay scattered in the jungle, for the crash site was still roughly known among the locals. I put Werner Herzog in contact with Moro, who had looked after Panguana over all the years during which I couldn't come to the research station. Despite his help and that of several natives, three expeditions Herzog sent to locate the wreckage of the Lockheed Electra returned empty-handed. Only the fourth was successful. Together with his then-eight-year-old son, the director proceeded to the location to view the pieces of wreckage, which were strewn over a stretch of about ten miles in the jungle.

On his return to Munich, he told me that I'd be amazed how well some of the wreckage was still preserved. But he also had to face the fact that the terrain was so rough that on some days it took experienced native *macheteros* hours to advance even only a hundred yards. The film crew, along with all the equipment, couldn't possibly make it to the crash site on foot. Several times it looked as if the project might fail, but not with Werner Herzog. He balked at no means or exertion to put his plan into action. If you couldn't get there on foot, then it would have to be by air. And so he decided to have a small swath cut in the jungle near the largest pieces of wreckage, just large enough so a helicopter could land.

Everyone thought that all this would upset me terribly, but to my astonishment I realized that I was confronting everything oddly emotionlessly. More than the prospect of seeing the place again, what made me nervous was the fact that I'd have to speak on camera, and I wondered whether I would manage that well enough. My husband always says that I'm a perfectionist, and he is undoubtedly right. But when you're standing in front of the camera for someone like Werner Herzog, then you ultimately want to do a good job. And then, in early August 1998, things got under way.

With American Airlines, we flew via Dallas to Peru, which was not the shortest route and made the trip still longer and more arduous than a direct flight from Europe already is, anyhow. But that airline permitted substantially more baggage than any other, and, of course, a film crew has a great deal of luggage and equipment. Some of it had been sent ahead already, and once again it was Alwin Rahmel who saw to it that everything got through customs smoothly.

With the crew we got along excellently from the beginning. Everything was perfectly organized, and I enjoyed not having to worry about anything, for once. In Lima, we visited the archives of the two large newspapers, La Prensa and El Comercio. Here I saw photos of another LANSA crash, the one near Cuzco, pictures of corpses on a field that were so horrible that they could not be published at the time. The bodies were battered, twisted and contorted from the impact, and the sight shocked me profoundly, for I, of course, could not help thinking constantly of my own accident and in what condition the people must have been who had not been as lucky as I was.

It really was a strange journey the director took me on. To persuade me to get on an airplane again, twenty-seven years after my accident, that flew the exact same route as the one on which I crashed was still relatively simple. After all, I had already had to take that flight several times since then to save time getting to the jungle. But he even put me in the same seat as on the LANSA plane out of which I fell from the sky back then: row 19, seat F. Actually, I would have preferred to have traveled by bus, for here, too, a great deal had changed since the days of my youth, and now it took "only" twenty hours from Lima to Pucallpa. But Werner Herzog is a man with great powers of persuasion, and so I changed my mind and agreed to fly with him. Today I'm glad I did so. For if the filmmaker had not brought me face-to-face with that part of my past and drawn me closer to the public again, who knows whether I would now be capable of advocating this way for Panguana to a larger audience?

So I overcame my fear. And on camera we flew over the spot where it had happened. Werner Herzog used that moment, of course, and interviewed me: At that exact point I recounted how I had experienced the crash. And fortunately it went so well on the first try, we didn't have to repeat it. My husband was at my side the whole time, and that was enormously important for me. I believe that you can tell in this film how much we support each other, how much we're there for each other when the other needs it.

On the way from Pucallpa to the jungle, I experienced many a surprise. Along the new Carretera Marginal de la Selva, the forest was being cleared everywhere. With saw and fire civilization was boring its way into the wilderness. My heart bled, for I knew quite well how much life perished in the flames. Meanwhile, an iron bridge had been built across the Río Shebonya, the river I followed; and a couple miles from it, a woman from the Andes had opened a kiosk, where we stopped to get something to drink. I did not believe my eyes when I saw what she had leaned against the outside of the house: It was actually a fully intact door from the LANSA plane, which someone must have brought here. On it the Indian woman had written in flawed Spanish: *Juliana's door*. This enterprising woman had apparently realized immediately what a magical appeal this relic of my past would have. Indeed, everyone I talk to about it calls this kiosk, which has meanwhile grown into a small grocery store that sells drinks, "The Door." Of course, Werner Herzog filmed me there. Whenever I've passed by since then, the people accompanying me say, "Juliane, stand there for a moment, please," and they take a photo. That still feels strange to me. I find it unpleasant, because for me it's not a tourist attraction, but a door through which ninety-one people went to their deaths, including my mother. I was the only survivor. And that has preoccupied me a great deal ever since.

That door changes constantly: each time I come by, it looks different. Something new is written on it, or something is painted over. For example, written on it recently was: *This is the door through which Jhuliana escaped.* Which is, of course, not true. Once the owner of the kiosk heard that she had misspelled my name and the date was incorrect, she took me aside and said: "Now you have to write down your name correctly for me, so that I can do it right." And those are the moments when everything comes up in me. Have things already come so far that someone can do business so directly with the horror of that time? And then they are back again, the feelings of those days, even if only for brief moments.

Of course, I quickly push all that back down. For people can't help it, and, of course, they don't mean any harm. And I realize how deadened I've become since then, out of sheer consideration and understanding. Was there ever actually a time in which there was space for my original, unbridled feelings, uncensored by rationality? I was preoccupied with these questions as I traveled on toward Panguana with Werner Herzog's film crew.

I had not been back to Panguana for fourteen years. Until recently the presence of the terrorist organization Movimiento Revolucionario Túpac Amaru in the area had made any trip into a life-threatening risk. Meanwhile, the original houses in which I had lived with my parents had decayed. My father had hired Moro to build a new guesthouse: a wooden hut on stilts, like all the houses here in the rain forest, with three small rooms and a covered terrace. Now I could take a close look at it for the first time. My husband and I stayed with Moro's family, who had relocated their farm to the edge of Panguana's grounds, so that they could better look after everything. And the not-exactly-small film crew managed to pile into the rooms of the guesthouse and onto the deck.

How many memories came back up! The river was still the same, and fortunately the forest too had scarcely changed. The calls of the birds that my mother had studied so extensively, the wonderful lupuna tree towering at its 150-foot height far over all the others, the butterflies and other insects—everything reminded me of those years when my world was still intact. I wandered as in a dream through the places of my childhood, grateful and amazed that I could still move in the rain forest in the exact same way I had learned to do as a child. "It's like riding a bike," my husband observed, laughing. "You never forget how to do it."

We went to Puerto Inca, and there we met Don Marcio, who had brought me to Tournavista back then. It was a really moving encounter for me, after all those years. Along with many others, Don Marcio had helped search for the wreckage for the documentary. Once, he had even set off on his own. Unfortunately, he was injured by a stingray. It stuck its poisonous stinger through Don Marcio's rubber boot and into his heel, causing his foot to swell intensely and become inflamed. Due to this incident he might almost have died in the jungle, if a boat hadn't passed by. But since Don Marcio had almost no money with him, these people didn't want to take him along. So out of necessity he offered them his rifle, a valuable item in the jungle, and so they let themselves be persuaded to take the injured man onto their boat.

I'd heard of his bad luck, and bought back the rifle with Werner Herzog's help. Now we brought it back to him, a small favor in return for what he had once done for me. At that meeting I said: "Don Marcio, you saved me back then." But he shook his head and said earnestly: "Not I, but God saved you, Juliana. I only got to be his vessel."

When we were about to depart in the helicopter that was already waiting for us in Puerto Inca, there was a delay. For the pilot had discovered on an earlier flight that the trees in the clearing where we were supposed to land had not been cut down low enough. The stumps were still a few feet high, and that was life threatening. So they had to be cleared again, and only then could we set off.

I'd never flown in a helicopter before, and I found that really interesting. How you can simply rise vertically and hover in one spot in the air—that was extremely exciting for me, as someone who as a little girl had already been more interested in technical things than dolls.

And then we landed there, in the middle of the jungle, on top of a hill. We were a large crew with a cook and macheteros, who helped us cut the path. Some had flown ahead and had already set up a temporary camp with mosquito nets under large plastic tarps. My husband and I got a two-person tent somewhat away from the others, which was a luxury in this jungle camp. All provisions, including drinking water, had to be brought with us, for it was the dry season. And with German thoroughness a toilet was immediately dug as well, a simple pit with an outhouse over it.

To my surprise there was a tremendous number of sweat bees there on the hill. Even though they don't sting, hundreds of them stick to you, which is very bothersome. All of us suffered from it. The crew was impressed with how stoically I endured this, but that was simply due to the fact that I was intently focused on speaking my lines as well as possible and not having to repeat them all the time. In the film there is a shot of my arm, where these creatures are just romping about. At the time of my journey through the jungle, I did not have to endure this, for down by the stream there were no sweat bees.

It was a peculiar place, our camp in the jungle. All around us in the forest, the parts of the airplane were scattered. At first they couldn't be seen at all. Over all those years the jungle had absorbed them. But then, all of a sudden, they revealed themselves, and that was always an extremely astonishing sight—above all, because they were still in such good condition.

We found wreckage that looked as if it had just fallen into the jungle. Since most of the pieces were made of stainless steel or aluminum, all the years in the humidity of the jungle had apparently passed them by without a trace. The rain forest had appropriated them, grown over and around them, pulled them into its ground as if they belonged to it. Often you couldn't recognize anything until one of the *macheteros*, who had helped find the crash site, set upright a pretty large piece of the airplane's sidewall and brushed off leaves, moss and lichens: The paint and writing on it were like new. It was as if I were in a dream.

I saw all the pieces of the airplane in which I had once sat, in which I had crossed the Andes, surface from the green of the rain forest. And yet it scarcely affected me. I found it extremely interesting, even the smaller finds like a piece of one of the trays from which I, too, had eaten my last breakfast before the crash, or the remains of a plastic spoon, a wallet containing coins that had since become invalid, fragments of the carpet on which even the color could still be made out, the heel of a woman's shoe, the metal frame of a suitcase whose clasps were incongruously still locked while the material that had originally covered it had disappeared. All that fascinated me profoundly, but it didn't strike any chord inside me. It was as if I were an outsider viewing a distant spectacle.

What astounded me was: The airplane parts seemed so untouched. We also found a propeller and the turbine I had already encountered on my trek back then. And a three-person seat that was better preserved than all the others we found. We assumed that it could be the one with which I fell from the sky. It also fascinated me that airplanes were flying over us. We were exactly below the flight path between Lima and Pucallpa. So the pilot back then had not even tried to avoid the storm.

To see the stream again that had led me out of the forest and thus saved my life was also strangely unreal to me. The courses of streams can certainly be altered over the years in the rain forest, just as the vegetation is constantly changing, and yet I had the distinct feeling that I had been in that spot before. When we arrived at the Río Shebonya, we came upon a lot of butterflies at one point on the bank, and Werner Herzog had the idea of shooting a scene in which I walk through their colorful cloud. But how to explain to them that they should gather at Werner Herzog's direction? Our knowledge as zoologists helped there, for my husband said: "That's very simple! All of us have to pee there now, and then the butterflies will come in droves."

No sooner said than done. The whole film crew peed on that spot, and that's how the beautiful scene was made in which I walk through a fluttering swarm of butterflies—a fitting metaphor for my flight, the crash and my journey back to life.

And finally we found among all the wreckage something that did affect me deeply. Again it was initially hard to recognize, even though it was gigantic in size. It was part of the landing gear still lying in the forest with the wheels pointing upward. Lying there like that, it reminded me terribly of the remains of a dead bird, a real living thing stranded helplessly with its feet pointing upward.

I don't know what people were expecting—whether they thought that I would burst into tears or undergo a powerful emotional eruption. I've never been the type for that. On top of that, some survival instinct must have formed a protective shield around me over the years, allowing me to lead a so-called normal life. Today I also think: The shock I undoubtedly suffered during my plunge from a height of ten thousand feet lasted until during the filming. To this day it has not yet completely dissipated. And probably that's all right. It's a mechanism that allows us to live with a monstrous experience, to deal with it as if it were a birthmark that belongs to us, a scar, an affliction. Or sometimes even a blessing. Who can decide?

But today, as I look out over the Yarinacocha Lagoon, I sense that the time when I have to keep those memories at a distance is now over. Now the time has come to speak about it. All those years it wasn't possible. The work with Werner Herzog, which I really enjoyed and for which I am still extraordinarily grateful to him, helped me a great stretch of the way to working through my past. For me, someone who has never gone to a therapist, Herzog's film work, his empathetic questions and his ability to truly listen, as well as the chance to return with him to the site of terror, were the best therapy. Since then, I have found peace and inner stability. And yet another thirteen years had to pass before it would become possible for me to tell my story more fully than I had done ever before. Werner Herzog's careful documentation had set the course for that, making it possible for me to write this book today. I've put it off for a long time. Today I am ready for it.

Surveying the LANSA wreckage site with the famous film director/producer Werner Herzog, 1998. (Copyright ©1998, Werner Herzog Film)

An examination of the wreckage: the frame of a suitcase and a part of the side panel.
(Copyright ©1998, Werner Herzog Film)

11 One Survived!

After the crash, I recovered in the doctor's home at the mission station in Peru's Yarinacocha district, 1972. (Copyright ©1972 Stern magazine)

While I'm lying in a deep sleep in Dr. Lindholm's house the night after my rescue, all hell breaks loose in Pucallpa. And not just Pucallpa—the unbelievable news of my miraculous rescue spreads all over the world! No sooner had we arrived in Tournavista than an amateur radio operator already broadcast the news over the ether at four o'clock in the afternoon. The other passengers' families, having just reconciled themselves to the inescapable and trying to come to terms with the death of their loved ones, now revert to a mad euphoria. The hope that others might also have survived is rekindled. In the evening everything that has legs goes out into the streets and streams to the Plaza de Armas. At first people cannot even believe the good news.

That same night the *comandante* of the Fuerza Aérea del Perú, Manuel del Carpio, who is in charge of the search operation, calls a press conference. He confirms my rescue, but prohibits any contact with me with the argument that I'm in shock and have to recover. He mentions that I'm only mildly injured, which only increases the hope among the passengers' families. If Juliane isn't seriously injured, then shouldn't others be able to be saved too? And another valuable piece of information spreads like wildfire. For during our trip on the Río Shebonya, I described to Don Marcio and Don Amado how the spot looked where the stream I was following flowed into the Río Shebonya. I mentioned the *caña brava*, and since they were familiar with the area, they knew that those gigantic reeds grow in great abundance by only one outlet: that of the Quebrada Raya, the "Stingray Stream."

So it happens that early the next morning, the pilot Robert Wenninger, from the missionary aid organization Alas de Esperanza, boards his airplane and is directed by the two forest workers Marcio Rivera and Amado Pereira. They fly over the mouth of the river and follow the Quebrada Raya. At around ten o'clock in the morning, they already sight

117

the first large piece of wreckage from the LANSA plane's fuselage.

When I wake up that morning, I have no idea about all this, of course. Everything appears so unreal to me. I'm lying in a pretty large, divinely comfortable bed. Then I remember: I am at home; I have returned to the world of the living. Still, I'm hovering in a state that I can't describe. To this day, after so many years, I find it hard. It's the way you might feel after handling a very urgent matter for which you have to be in top form, and afterward you fall into a void. You're neither upset nor happy about what you've achieved. You simply feel nothing.

I'm in this sort of limbo when my father walks through the door. He simply comes in and asks, "How are you doing?"

I say: "Good."

And then we take each other in our arms. Neither of us cries. I'm so happy to see him. But it's more something I *know* than something I *feel*. There's no space in me for big emotions. I am simply relieved. At that moment there are no words for what I experienced. Nor are there any for what is still to come. And there are definitely no words for what I'm feeling. For at the moment it's as if I'm cut off from my own feelings.

My father sits down next to me on the bed, and we just look at each other silently. He was never a man of many words. And I prefer it that way.

Later I will worry about this emotional void, will wonder whether something might be wrong with me, whether I might be coldhearted. This inner apathy will occasionally cause me anxiety. But today, forty years later, I know that this was a protective mechanism I developed at that time. During my trek through the jungle, it was necessary for survival; and when I was rescued, I could not just shut it off. My psyche was on autopilot. Inwardly I was still making my way through the rain forest. My mind had not yet made it back to civilization. Perhaps it's still not completely back today.

But my body grasps very well that it's safe, and all of a sudden it lets go. From one hour to the next, I get a very high fever that lasts a few days and then just as suddenly disappears. The doctors are at a loss.

On top of that, my left knee swells up a great deal. No one knows why. A few months later I will find out that I tore my cruciate ligament during the crash. "And you're telling me you walked on that for eleven days through the jungle?" the orthopedist will ask me with consternation.

"Medically, that's actually completely impossible."

Isn't it incredible how my body was able to suppress the natural reaction to this injury until I was rescued? During my eleven-day journey, I had neither pain nor swelling. If I had not been able to move away from the crash site, I certainly would not have survived.

There are constantly people around me, and there's always something going on. The linguists' small airplanes, which are participating in the search operation, come and go over the settlement. When my father finally breaks the silence, he asks about my mother. How disappointed he is when I'm able to tell him so little! In a telegram to his sister, he writes: *Unfortunately, we cannot say anything about Maria. Juliane did not see her again after the accident.* And for me, too, it's incomprehensible how she, who had just been sitting next to me, could disappear from one moment to the next *so completely* from my life.

On that first day after my arrival in Yarinacocha, the *comandante* of the FAP, Manuel del Carpio, visits me too. He asks me politely for information. I tell him what I know. Afterward, he asks me to report nothing in detail about the events of the crash to press people until everything has been cleared up. I comply with his request. But an official statement on the cause of the crash would never be made.

On that day, to quote the local newspaper *Impetu*, a "deluge" of journalists inundates Pucallpa. They plunge the small city into chaos, and they're all searching for me. Luckily, the *comandante* issues a report that I am in the famous Hospital Amazónico Albert Schweitzer, with Dr. Theodor Binder, who is as well known in Peru as elsewhere. Not only the journalists, but also many locals besiege the hospital. Everyone wants to see me.

Despite the red herring, Comandante del Carpio orders police to guard the house where I'm staying. The crash area is closed off too and is only accessible to police and military personnel. Nonetheless, once again a group of ten civilians and family members sets off, extremely motivated by my fortunate rescue and the locating of the crash site. Among them is Marcio Rivera, who serves as a guide with his good knowledge of the area.

On that same day, the pilot Clyde Peters, the missionary who gave my father so much hope on New Year's Eve, 1971, parachutes to the crash site. His plan is to cut a clearing in the jungle so that helicopters can land there safely. That would facilitate the rescue work immensely. At the same time an official delegation of three members of the Guardia Civil and six military personnel, among them a radio operator and two medics, set off on foot from Río Súngaro, near Puerto Inca, more than twelve miles away from the wreckage. Meanwhile, Clyde Peters's heroic attempt fails. Not only does he lose his equipment—most important, the power saw bound to his leg—but he also injures himself landing. Cut off from the helicopter crew without radio contact, he follows the flight noise, because he thinks it will lead him to the crash site. But this is not the case, and instead of a rescuer, he becomes a missing person himself. It will be three days before Clyde Peters resurfaces.

The military delegation doesn't have much luck either. It takes them two days to cover the twelve miles. It turns out to be intensely arduous to cut one's way through this part of the rain forest, for the terrain is extremely hilly and the constant rain has made it completely muddy. When the leader falls and injures himself as well, progress becomes still more difficult.

The next afternoon, January 6, some civilians follow Clyde Peters's example. But instead of parachuting, they are lowered down from helicopters on ropes, equipped with power saws, over the crash site. The military delegation and the civil patrol arrive there on the same evening and decide to work together. Thus it is now a total of twenty men, among them two newspaper editors, who approach the crash site.

Meanwhile, my usually composed father loses his temper: He starts a huge quarrel with the comandante and accuses him of not doing enough for the rescue of possible survivors. In my father's opinion, the rescue teams' progress is too slow. A lot of energy and precious time are being lost by infighting over jurisdiction. In a letter to his sister and his mother, which I found only recently in my aunt's posthumous papers, he writes two days later:

> Unfortunately, not everything that can be done is being done by the Peruvian side here. If Juliane had not come and said where to look for the airplane, they probably would have abandoned everything already. The day before yesterday I had a very intense confrontation with the highest authority in the search operation,

Comandante del Carpio. The special North American airplane has been requested much too late: the linguists and Adventists (none of them Peruvians), who are experienced in the jungle, have not been sufficiently brought into the effort or permitted to help. They could have long since requested about 30–50 jungle Indians from among the linguists, etc. The "señor comandante" declared that he was canceling the police protection for my daughter. The police guarding us are no longer standing outside the house.

My father is not the only one to criticize del Carpio. The *comandante* is also attacked sharply by the press and other family members, but I don't hear about any of this. I notice only that there's now much more going on around the house and that our hosts, since the police protection was canceled, have their hands full trying to shield me. From that point on, a whole horde of journalists besieges the linguists' settlement.

My father tells me that he has decided to make an exclusive deal with *Stern* magazine. "They're serious," he says, "and then we'll have our peace from the others."

Two men will come and interview me. Do I feel strong enough for that yet?

I nod. I agree with everything my father decides. He must know what he's doing, and I just accept all this.

And so the next day, January 7, 1972, becomes visiting day: Not only Gerd Heidemann and Hero Buss, of *Stern*, arrive and introduce themselves to me, but also the British journalist Nicholas Asheshov, who accompanied my father on an expedition years ago and found favor with him. He is a reporter for the *Peruvian Times* and also the Peruvian newspaper *La Prensa*. From that point on I will have daily conversations with the *Stern* journalists.

In his letter to his sister, my father writes on January 8: *All the rest* (he means journalists) *I "chased away". . . . I made an appointment with the two from* Stern *for this morning: Juliane will describe in detail to them everything she knows.*

My father is always there during the conversations with Gerd Heidemann and Hero Buss, and I'm glad about that. Every day they knock on my door and stay one or at most two hours. At first a brief preliminary report appears, then four detailed accounts with large photo spreads. No wonder I don't really get a chance to rest. Especially since I receive other visitors from Lima.

My godfather's daughter arrives, as well as my former English teacher, who immediately wants to pray with me. But that's too much for me. Though religious, I prefer to pray alone, and I tell her that. In addition, old friends of my parents come. They are Hannelore and Heinrich Maulhardt, who own the lovely bungalow hotel La Cabaña, on the Yarinacocha Lagoon, and put up my father. The director of the natural history museum in Lima visits too, as well as a doctor friend, a nurse and many others. Many of my friends write to me and send me sweets.

Meanwhile, the various, now relatively smoothly cooperating search parties made up of civilians and military personnel continue to fight their way through the jungle. On the morning of January 7, they already reach the first airplane wreckage. It takes six hours before—mainly due to the tireless effort of the family members—a landing site has been cleared. The first FAP helicopter lands around five o'clock in the evening. Within a distance of just a few hundred yards, they find the LANSA's galley, the intact tail of the plane and the completely destroyed luggage compartment, the contents of which have been scattered far over the ground.

That day a seaplane also lands in Puerto Inca to the great jubilation of the local children. Here the base is established for the whole operation, and the small jungle settlement experiences a boom such as it has seen only once before. That time, too, a plane had crashed, though not over the lowland rain forest but in the Sira Mountains, where it was never found. Now there's a flurry of activity in the small city. The few hotels, which raise their prices on the spot, are immediately booked up. The restaurants are simply overrun, and soon it becomes apparent that there's not enough food—the people of Puerto Inca are not prepared for the feeding of such masses. There are no more hotel rooms available in Pucallpa either. And the flights out of Lima are booked up for days.

The next day, January 8, more pieces of wreckage are found at the crash site, as well as the first twenty corpses. There are reports of gruesome finds and awful images that can never be forgotten. Most of the corpses are dismembered or horribly disfigured. In the press there are comparisons to Dante's *Inferno*. According to press reports, the coroner flown in at the behest of the authorities becomes "ill" when he sees the scene of the accident and the remains of the corpses and finishes his work as quickly as possible. Apparently, over a diameter of around two and a half miles, there are gifts, pieces of luggage or their contents, clothes, shoes, Christmas stollens in their packaging, but also parts of corpses hanging in the jungle trees all around. Over everything hovers a terrible smell of decomposition. In the branches sit vultures, which have clearly been disturbed by the search team.

The new hastily flown-in coroner inspects the crash site for fifteen minutes; then he orders the recovery of the corpses and departs again. No wonder the true cause of the crash was never determined.

The first dead to be identified are the pilot and a fourteen-year-old girl. The pilot, Carlos Forno, has to be sawed out of his cockpit, and is recognizable only by his seat in the plane, his uniform and papers. In the young girl's case, it is the sad remains of Elisabeth Ribeiro, who is able to be identified by her own father on the basis of her jewelry, which he himself gave to her as a gift. He insists on carrying by himself what is left of his daughter in one of the black plastic bags that have been provided. He brings her remains into the helicopter that will take the corpses to Puerto Inca. From there they are flown to Pucallpa to the morgue that is specifically established for them on the Carretera Central. There the dead are laid out in an empty factory building for identification. Here, too, the smell of decomposition soon attracts the vultures.

Again and again there's pouring rain. The civilians, mustering all their strength for the recovery work, complain that the authorities are not providing them with the right resources. The distributed gloves and black plastic bags could not be less suitable for the task and make more difficult the often-arduous recovery of corpses that have fallen into ravines or are lying on steep slopes. And so the already extremely problematic work becomes agonizing.

And me? I'm shielded from all this. I want most of all to have my peace. But there are the conversations with the journalists from *Stern*, who come daily, and my visitors, who think they have to cheer me up. My father goes to Pucallpa daily. As I learn later, he is waiting day after day at the temporary morgue. He is waiting for my mother. But none of the found corpses are identifiable as hers.

When he's not in Pucallpa, he sits silently most of the time in a corner of my room. Once, after the children from the mission station, who unfailingly visit me every day, have left, I look at him sitting there, completely absorbed in himself.

"What's the matter?" I ask him.

Then he looks up as if returning from another world.

"Oh, nothing," he answers, forcing himself to smile, which doesn't really succeed. "I was just grieving a little bit for your mother."

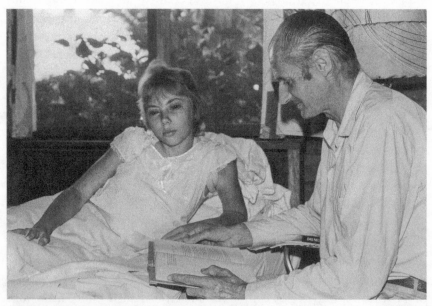

Our post-crash meeting: my father visiting my sickbed.
(Copyright © 1972 Stern magazine)

Reflection: looking behind the mirror, I think back on my youth.
(Copyright © 1972 Stern magazine)

12 Greetings From This World and the Next

Letters congratulating me on my survival arrived from all over the world.
(Photos courtesy of Juliane (Koepcke) Diller)

Over the days, weeks and even months that follow, mail is brought to me, mountains of letters. Each day there are more. They come from all over the world, and I'm overwhelmed and moved, as well as occasionally put off, by the lines that complete strangers feel compelled to write to me. Most are from the United States, Canada, Australia, Germany, France, England, Poland, Italy, Sweden, Argentina and, of course, Peru. But also people from Burundi, New Zealand, French Guiana, Uruguay, Cuba and Costa Rica have something to say to me. The addresses on the envelopes are often curious. Sometimes they consist of only the words "Juliane Koepcke–Peru," but they always arrive. The ages of the letter writers range from nine to eighty years old. Among them are many children, young people and mothers, who usually feel sympathy with my fate and apparently simply have the need to write and tell me that I'm not alone. For instance, there is a nice woman from Australia who writes: *I'm no one special, just a mother of a family.* . . . All over the world many people think of me during those days and wish me the best.

Many want to let me know how much they admire how I found my way through the jungle and think I'm enormously "brave," "coolheaded" and "fearless." I'm happy about that; but actually, I think, I simply had no choice.

Then there are people who were acquainted with my parents either closely or more distantly, had studied with the same professor in Kiel or had toured the Peruvian jungle in earlier years. Some German exiles in Latin American countries write how proud they are that "a girl from the old country" could achieve such a feat. An American airplane pilot believes that "his" stewardesses could learn a lot from me—I'm not entirely sure what he means by that. Bob from Colorado used to study aviation technology and would like to know whether I fell to earth together with a piece of wreckage or on my own. He even writes a funny sentence in flawed German.

Doctors or others who possess special expertise comment on my injuries and give good advice, as in the case of a Belgian who warns of lung damage—caused by the collarbone fracture—or a Munich entomologist who writes to me that it could not have been the case that there were worms (*Würmer*) in my wounds. He's right: It's the fault of German newspaper articles with incorrect translations of the English "worms" and Spanish *"gusanos"* as *Würmer*, "worms" in the strict sense, instead of *Fliegenmaden*, "maggots" in the sense of fly larvae. Some boys my age and younger ask for zoological details. A few, like Peter from Australia, who would like to learn more about the stingrays, are interested specifically in fish; others, like Brian from Canada or Herbert from southern Germany, who want to know whether it's true that the jaguar in Peru has gone extinct, have general questions about the wildlife of the Amazon Rain Forest.

But occasionally letters also offer me a glimpse into a stranger's fate: A woman from San Antonio, Texas, had lost her then-seventeen-year-old daughter three years earlier, who—so she claimed—not only had a strong resemblance to me, but also loved animals and wanted to become a veterinarian. She died in a diving accident. Now the woman is inviting me to live with her and her other daughter and study at a Texan university. Perhaps she thinks she can replace my mother and I her lost daughter?

I also can't rule out the possibility that one or another young man has fallen in love with me from afar. Usually, they write me charming letters assuring me that they will always be there for me if I should need them. One of them even composes a religiously themed poem. Another sends me his message in minute handwriting on a postcard in Italian, French and even Latin. Unfortunately, there are also some who become pushy. When I don't reply to one of them, he ultimately appeals indignantly to my father!

An American artist expresses the desire to make a bronze sculpture of me—if we could meet someday. And a sixteen-year-old girl from Munich would like to write a short story about my accident and asks me for details.

A zealous supporter of the international artificial language Esperanto writes me a bilingual letter in English and Esperanto, which begins as follows:

Now that you have become a world famous person, probably you will find [it] useful to learn the international language, Esperanto. The world famous "Football King," Pelé of Brazil, wrote an autobiography "I am Pelé" and published it in Esperanto, and it makes history because Esperantist footballers over the whole world can read it, whatever their national languages are. Please learn Esperanto and write a book about your life and adventures so that Esperantists male and female around the whole world can read it. . . .

Conveniently he has also enclosed a small handbook with the grammar rules and a vocabulary book for learning Esperanto.

I also find funny a postcard from Hildesheim, Germany, on which the following poem is written:

An angel came from heaven,
ate a piece of cake,
then went wandering,
and all was well again.

Oh, if only things were that simple!

I also find pleasure in the letters from school classes that have many questions, and now and then they enclose pictures they've drawn of me in the middle of the jungle next to the airplane wreckage.

Then there are letters that make a strange impression on me, which I occasionally even find abhorrent. For there are people who have supposedly managed to do what has remained denied to us—that is, to make contact with my mother in the afterlife. Even before her death was officially confirmed, such people sent along her "warm greetings." A psychic from Freiburg, Germany, is firmly convinced that her soul was with me at the moment of the crash and I was able to survive only because—unbeknownst to me—she showed me the way. Meanwhile, she describes the circumstances as they are portrayed in the error-ridden newspaper reports: I climbed out of the wreckage; there were many corpses around me; at her advice I picked up a cake and took it with me, would almost have fallen into the hands of cannibals if her invisible soul had not lured me onto a safer path. In her last vision she saw me sitting in a clearing, encircled with light, eating the last cake crust. I can still take all that with a sense of humor. However, when she then passes on messages from my dead mother as well, it becomes too much for me.

It's neither the only nor the last odd letter I will receive. Some even try to hitch their wagons to me. Several months later a biorhythmist from Switzerland is convinced that *during this almost superhuman exertion, I was in an optimal biorhythmic state.* She goes on: *For even if such perseverance is largely a matter of character, it would not help much if one were in a weak rhythmic state.* That's why she writes that she is *convinced that your jungle odyssey constitutes a perfect test case for the doctrine of biorhythmics.*

To verify this, she asks me to indicate my birth date, if possible also the time of day. This is very important to the woman: *For if my suspicion regarding your experience is correct, then this would be such a persuasive test case that even the most malicious doubter and opponent of biorhythmics would have to admit defeat.*

An extremely excited woman from New Jersey will write me a discomfiting letter two years later. It begins like this: *Juliane: I have found new patterns in air crashes—planetary positions.* Starting with my case, she calculated the horoscopes for those days on which airplane accidents took place and stumbled on a shocking theory. Apparently, quite particular configurations of planets made the metal birds fell from the sky. *Most of my friends think I'm going mad,* she writes, *but I've become obsessed with research.* In her view, a plane crash is caused by a square between the sun and Pluto. But on Christmas in 1971, Venus, Pluto and Saturn formed a triangle to spare me. Apparently, something similar repeated itself a year later, and again a plane crashed, this time a French one over the Caribbean. What am I to make of this? I understand nothing about astrology and can unfortunately contribute nothing to this discussion.

Still odder is a letter that also reaches me two years after my accident. This one reads: *I have found the right circle relation number . . . and with it would like to start a worldwide intellectual revolution in the field of mathematics with the help of your high-school graduate* (this refers to me). The complicated, supposedly groundbreaking new formulas for a "Pitel year" I cannot understand even after my Abitur–on which I scored rather well–and the intellectual revolution will apparently have to wait.

But I'm getting ahead of myself.

I'm still lying in my bed in the mission station of Yarinacocha as a guest of the hospitable "linguists." Each day I receive a new basket full of letters, read them all and ask myself the anxious question: How in the world am I going to answer all these people? There are so many that it's simply impossible. I choose the letters that especially appeal to me. Some even turn into friendly correspondences, as happens with a student from Sweden and a woman from Poland.

But some letters do not require any postage stamps and do not have to traverse any great distance to reach me, for they come from next door. The community of missionaries, who so kindly took me in and cared for me, has lost members too. I am all the more grateful to be able to recover with them. Deep in my heart I feel guilty for having survived, while all the others had to die. "Why," my father asks me at an especially hard moment, "did the two of you have to take that LANSA flight?"

. . . *Even though I'd explicitly warned you not to.* Though he doesn't say the second part out loud, I know that he's thinking it. I also know that it's my fault that we didn't take the flight with the safe airline Faucett, as my mother would have liked to, just because I was so childish and insisted on participating in the school graduation celebration. I feel guilty and full of boundless regret. I'm sorry that I didn't skip the school event. I'm sorry that I survived and she didn't. I'm sorry that so many families are in mourning, and only I am sitting here in my bed and already doing so well again.

I don't find words for all this, am not even aware of it. The fact that every survivor of a disaster goes through this, I learn only much later.

13 Terrible Certainty, Agonizing Uncertainty

en el Aeropuerto de Pucallpa, en donde familiares de las víctimas, así como periodistas y curiosos, indagan sob
n LANSA caído. Las maniobras e intentos de rescate fueron seguidos minuto a minuto por toda la opinión públi
la región.

NADA DE SOLES HABRIA EN
S DEL TRAGICO AVION LANZ

istas De
El Mundo

or   do la estricta vigilan-
ez   cia policial se vieron
de   obligados a marchar a
i-   campo traviesa, pero
n-   fueron devueltos a la
e-   ciudad por patrullas mi-
os   litares y policiales.
de
u-   Los intentos para in-
ternarse nuevamente
os   en la Selva se repiten
r-   aprovechando lanchas
es   que se desplazan río
de   abajo, ya que la carre-
el   tera que conduce a
or   Tournavista está cel-
sente vigilada.
l-
de   El número de perio-
de   distas sigue engrosán-
i-   dose, decenas de ellos
an   llegan por vía Faucett
en los aviones de itine-
rario.
n-
u-   Ayer cuando faltaban
l-   pocos minutos para llegar a esta ciudad,

PUCALLPA, 6 (Por Car-
los Cómena Alvarez, Enviado Especial de ULTIMA HO-
RA).— Treinta millones de
soles se hallarían entre los
restos del avión LANSA que
se estrellara el 24 de di-
ciembre en las faldas del
Sheboya.

Esta fuerte suma de di-
nero en billetes circulares
se envió desde Lima con
destino a Intuto, vía Iquitos, para pagar a los tra-
bajadores que se hallaban o-
perando en esa zona donde
hace algunas semanas se
encontrara petróleo.

También trascendió que
el dinero habría sido en-
viado para el pago de los
militares que cumplen ser-
vicio de guarnición de fron-
teras en alejados puntos de
nuestra Amazonía.

Esto justifica las extremas
medidas de seguridad que
han sido adoptadas por los
militares y la Guardia Civil.

Hay un verdadero cerco
de vigilancia, tanto en esta ciudad como en Tourna-
vista y Puerto Inca. Así
mismo, todas las vías que

ayer a Pucallpa, al igual
que colegas capitalinos y
extranjeros, hemos tratado
de desplazarnos hacia la
zona de desastre, pero la
vigilancia es estricta.

Se controlan todos los
puntos de donde parten a-
viones, al igual que las
troncales carreteras y los
terminales fluviales. In-
cluso los radioaficionados
parece que han quedado ba-
jo control policial.

Pucallpa y todas estas lo-
calidades y puntos de sali-
da dan la impresión de que
hubieran sido convertidos
en zona de seguridad mili-
tar.

Recién esta madrugada yo
y mi reporter gráfico he-
mos podido conseguir una
avioneta y en cuanto acla-
re nos desplazaremos al
lugar para poder informar
a los lectores de ULTIMA
HORA.

Esta ciudad se ha con-
vertido en una población cos
mopolita, por sus calles y
oficinas de transporte aé-
reo, terrestre y fluvial se
ven personas de toda na-
cionalidad, se escuchan di-
versos idiomas y lo que es

Militares entrevistac
este Enviado Especial
nifestaron que han re
órdenes estrictas de :
periores para no dej:
sar a ningún periodis
zona del desastre.

Sin embargo, sin (
mar se sabe, que vari
riodistas alemanes y :
americanos burlaron .
gilancia y se han inte
selva adentro acompa
de expertos guías con
pósito de llegar lo
pronto posible al luga
ir al encuentro de p
sobrevivientes que de
lan por la jungla.

En vista de la grav
manda de guías, dece
ellos han llegado a es
dad de los alrededore
valor de sus servicios
elevado tremendamer

El aeropuerto de Pı
es un inmenso col
donde entran y salen
nes, avionetas, autos,
bombas, motocicletas,
bulancias, militares, (
peruanos y extranjerc

El ambiente de esti
dad ha cambiado poi
pleto la tristeza que l

A town in uproar: thousands waited at the Pucallpa airport for news about the vanished
LANSA aircraft. (Photo courtesy of Juliane (Koepcke) Diller)

As the fever with shivers weakens me and the twenty-inch strip of gauze is stuffed, day after day, into my arm wound, I, wrapped in my cocoon, can still scarcely grasp what has happened. I experience my first nightmares in my sleep and am not yet able to make sense of them. My father sits in my room, and now and then leaves quietly and comes back; and during all those days, more and more corpses are recovered. Every day I talk to the journalists from *Stern*; and their Peruvian colleagues are terribly upset when the first pictures of me appear in the foreign magazines *Life*, *Paris Match* and *Stern*. Meanwhile, Comandante del Carpio, apparently to protect me, forbids the local press any contact with me. On January 9, a delegation from the company Lockheed arrives. The participants visit the crash site, but they will provide no new details about the reasons for the accident.

On January 11, I move from the Lindholm family's to the Holstons' house. The next day a funeral service is held for the thirteen-year-old Nathan Lyon and eighteen-year-old Dave Ericson. What I don't know, and will find out only years later: They are the two boys who were waiting in line in front of us on that morning of December 24, 1971, when none of us suspected what would happen a few hours later. That day the recovery of corpses is officially ended.

That same day, January 12, my father goes to Pucallpa. When he returns in the afternoon, he is serious and very pale, but composed.

He says he has identified my mother. He tells me very calmly that he had a scuffle with a journalist who tried to hold his camera into the zinc coffin and photograph my mother's remains. He even knocked the camera out of this fellow's hand. I'm horrified. Ordinarily, my father would never do something like that.

He goes on to say that he's not 100 percent sure that the female corpse is my mother. Apart from the lower jaw, the head was missing.

However, he took a closer look at the corpse's foot. My mother had very distinctive feet. Her second toes on both feet were much longer than the big toes, and the little toes were very bent—my father often used to tease my mother about that. And that was the case with this corpse too. My father asks me whether I can remember what shoes my mother was wearing on the day of the accident. When I describe her flat leather shoes with the saddle-stitch seam, which she had brought back a few years ago from a Europe trip, my father nods imperceptibly and looks down at the floor. There was a shoe like that with the corpse.

So my mother is really dead. At that moment, when it becomes a certainty, I feel nothing at all. And I'm surprised at myself. But hadn't I actually known it for a long time? Had there really still been reason to hope nineteen days after the crash? My emotional void disconcerts me. Shouldn't I break down crying now? Neither my father nor I do that. He, too, is completely unemotional, and today I know that was our way of protecting ourselves at that time: Everything drips off me as if I were made of glass. And he speaks about it as if it were one of his scientific cases. Which doesn't mean that all this doesn't matter to him. It actually matters to him immensely, occupies all his thoughts and feelings.

My father can best show his feelings through angry outbursts, and that's what he does now too, toward the journalists who bother him during what are, with certainty, the worst moments of his life, as he stands before the remains of the person he loved most in the world. Or he directs his rage toward the authorities who work with appalling sloppiness and trample on his feelings. He will expend a great deal of energy to achieve complete certainty about whether that corpse shown to him in the zinc coffin no. 22 was really Maria Koepcke, born von Mikulicz-Radecki.

During those days he tells me that he's not entirely sure, that he's plagued by doubts. He also tells me that the state of the corpse raises big questions. Why was the upper part of the head missing, if the corpse otherwise appeared fully intact? And most disturbing of all: Why was the corpse in such a fresh state? I, too, know very well that a corpse in the jungle can remain intact at most for a few days. I remember all too well the presence of the king vultures, which I found near the three corpses four days after the crash. Ants, bugs, flies, turtles and vultures, specialized in feeding on carrion, promptly find any cadaver, however well concealed it may be.

So why was my mother's body still so well preserved? There's only one answer, and it's horrible: She must have still been alive for a long time. In fact, she cannot have died more than a few days ago. If that's really true, what must she have suffered in the two weeks before? My mind takes in this information, but my protective mechanism doesn't let it get close to me. Perhaps I appear completely coldhearted to my father? Her mother lies for two weeks helpless in the jungle and for some reason cannot move—perhaps her pelvis is broken or her spine—and this girl, her daughter, doesn't say a word. She leans back in bed and simply falls asleep again. Wakes up and asks when the men from *Stern* are coming today. Eats dinner as if nothing happened.

But maybe he understands what's going on with me. Or he's too preoccupied with himself to worry about me at all. Maybe he's going through the exact same thing, for he's speaking as if someone else was in the morgue and had a fight with journalists there. What he's really thinking and feeling at that time—to this day, I don't know. Later on, we never again spoke about those days.

A brief letter to his sister, which he wrote a day after the identification, perhaps best conveys my father's distraught state:

> *Yesterday I looked at Maria's corpse. The coffin was already soldered up; everything was difficult. I had to have an actual scuffle with the journalists. I was shown Maria's wedding ring. Whether it was found on the hand no one knew. The definite identification is supposed to have been made through the dental bridge, but the upper part of the skull was missing. Incidentally, the corpse was astonishingly fresh, that is, only destroyed a little bit by vultures and insects. According to our experiences with mammalian corpses laid out in the forest, after about five or six days only bones and pieces of skin should be left. One foot was still relatively recognizable. It could be Maria's foot (which does have a very distinctive toe shape), but I'm not entirely sure. I would like to ask you to have the corpses examined and assessed there. It's not impossible that Maria was still alive for days*

and that the missing parts of the skull were removed later. It would probably be best for you to get in touch with Johann-Georg (my mother's brother, who was himself a doctor). The rest of the family doesn't need to know any of this for the time being. Before January 7, no corpse was found. Many of the corpses are unidentifiable. Skulls might be needed to reach the quantity of 91.

Thoughts like these are tormenting him as I, too, write to my aunt and grandmother at the same time. The contrast between our letters couldn't be greater:

Since Daddy is writing you a letter right now, I wanted to send you a few lines too. Please excuse the poor and uneven handwriting! It's because I'm writing in bed. I've also broken my right collarbone, so I have to be careful.

I'm already doing much better. My wounds are healing well, and I can move really well. All the people here are friendly to me and bring me books and chocolate (unfortunately much too much). The food is always very good. At the moment, I'm living in the house of my doctor, an American. I like it here.

Now I would like to end my letter, because I have another to write.

Considering that I'm seventeen years old and rather eloquent, my dazed state in light of the terrible events all around me, in which I feel like I'm cut off from myself, can be read from these lines. Clearly, I am extremely eager to assure everyone how well I'm doing. In German, the little word "gut," meaning "good" or "well," appears four times in this short letter! And this is a day after my mother's corpse was found.

Today it seems to me as if I had to tell myself again and again: *You're doing well, Juliane, you did it! You're doing so well.* As if at least I didn't want to worry the people around me, who were consumed by grief and sorrow.

Only since my aunt's death in the summer of 2010 do I know that my father didn't give up his inquiries into the corpse's identity and cause of death. He wanted to have certainty. But it was as if the chaotic and corrupt circumstances in Pucallpa and the confusing results in Germany, where the corpse was transferred, wanted to confound him more than ever. Due to the difficult circumstances of the recovery, no one had taken photos of the place where the corpse was found or the original position of the body. The surrounding area was not investigated. No one even knew with certainty where the shoe was found.

What is taken for granted for any accident in Germany was completely neglected in those days in the Peruvian jungle—perhaps because of the extreme conditions during the recovery. Eventually the corpses were apparently just packed in bags and taken away.

The day my father stood before the corpse that he thought was his wife, and yet wasn't certain, a wedding ring was shown to him. He could identify that definitively, for the date of his engagement with Maria and his first name were engraved on its inside. It was clearly my mother's wedding ring. When my father asked whether it was found on the corpse's hand, no one could confirm that for him. When he wanted to keep it, they refused him the ring with the argument that the judge had to see it first. My father never saw the ring again. When he inquired with the judge, the military and the responsible hospital, no one would admit to hearing anything about the ring.

The coffin was closed and soldered up again, while my father was still there. On that same day, January 12, it went on to Lima. Here Dr. Luis Felipe Roveredo embalms the corpse on January 13, so that it will make it through the flight to Germany. From my godfather's garden, a small bouquet is attached to the coffin. It comes from the same bush from which a wreath was woven for my mother on the day of her wedding. On January 14, at six o'clock in the evening, in a hangar at the Jorge Chávez International Airport in Lima/Callao, a funeral service is held. Friends tell us later that the ceremony was really moving and was given an especially dramatic effect by the taking off and landing of airplanes. Many friends and colleagues pay their last respects to my mother. The next morning her coffin is transported on a Lufthansa plane to Frankfurt, and on another to Munich. On January 21, what are thought to be my mother's remains are buried in Aufkirchen on Lake Starnberg, where her father was buried too. My father and I did not attend either ceremony due to my condition—though I suspect that his reason for staying with me was not only that he did not want to leave me alone but also that he could not have endured the grief.

Why was the burial in Germany? Why not in Peru? I can only surmise the answer, for my father didn't speak to me about his reasons. I knew that my parents were planning to return to Germany in a few years. How much my father was preoccupied in those days and weeks with his own death is evident to me from another letter to my aunt Cordula, in which he explains in detail how he would like the grave to be designed, which also already provides a place for himself. My aunt clearly found it advisable to write in her reply: *Please also consider in all your decisions that you have to be there for Juliane. Having already lost her mother, she needs her father twice as much.*

A lot is going through my father's head those days, and they're not pretty thoughts. At one point he says to me that he doesn't consider it out of the question that my mother might still have been alive even when she was found. "But then why is she dead?" I ask with consternation.

For a while he doesn't speak. Then he says: "Perhaps she was killed?"

The answer is terrible and inconceivable to me. Why would someone have done that?

As a matter of fact, my father cannot get the thought out of his head. He wants to know whether the corpse is his wife or not. He also wants to know when and how my mother died. He asks his sister Cordula to arrange an autopsy in Munich, which she does. But the results are long in coming.

In February, four weeks after the burial, Gerd Heidemann, of *Stern*, will attend to this at my father's request. Heidemann even engages the district attorney's office. The outcome will be more than shattering for my father: the postmortem examination not only neglected to resolve clearly whether the remains are identifiable as Maria Koepcke, but to his horror he finds out that instead of an embalmed and still well-preserved body, only several bones arrived in Munich.

How can that be? A satisfying answer was never found. Was the coffin inadvertently switched? But then why was Maria Koepcke's lower jaw, the only part of the corpse that could be clearly identified based on her dentist's casts of the jaw, in the coffin? Both doctors—the one in Lima who performed the embalming, and the one in Munich who conducted the autopsy, or was supposed to conduct it—indicate that it's impossible for the corpse to have decomposed so completely within those few days. Did someone want to cover something up? My father is inclined to suspect that. But then, what would there be to cover up? It's a mystery that will never be solved.

In the weeks that follow, my father does everything he can to arrange an exhumation. He sends a sworn statement to Hamburg, in which he describes meticulously what he saw on January 12, 1972, in Pucallpa and compares his observations with his experiences with vertebrates laid out in the jungle. He also encloses a notarized statement from the doctor in Lima, who was the last to see the corpse before its transfer. My aunt translates it into German. But aside from a notice in *Stern* on February 23, 1972, the matter comes to nothing. The report reads:

WRONG CORPSE

The plane crash in Peru, which only the seventeen-year-old Juliane Koepcke survived after an eleven-day march through the jungle, has found a mysterious epilogue. Fifteen days after the crash Juliane's father saw his wife's corpse "astonishingly intact," had preservatives poured into the coffin and the corpse sent to Munich for examination. But only parts of the skeleton arrived there, from which it cannot even be ascertained whether they belong to a man or woman. Among them, however, was the lower jaw of Frau Dr. Koepcke. Now it can no longer be determined whether the ornithologist had survived the plane crash and died only later.

My father spared me all these nasty details in the time after my recovery in Yarinacocha and in the weeks that followed. But how hard it must have been for him not only to accept the loss of the only person to whom he had ever opened up, but also to be cheated of her corpse, never to know how his beloved wife had died and where her mortal remains might have been in the end.

Even though I knew of my father's grim suspicions, I myself did not doubt until recently that my mother lies buried in Aufkirchen on Lake Starnberg. It was simpler for me that way. I knew instinctively how important it was to recover my inner balance. Since there was nothing more my father could do, he let the matter rest. Or so I thought—until, after my aunt's death, I found all these shocking documents.

I also heard nothing back then about the fact that on January 24, 1972, a funeral service was held in Pucallpa for the fifty-four dead who came from the city, and the corpses were interred in the mausoleum inscribed as *Alas de Esperanza*. Only recently did I find the special supplement that appeared in the newspaper *Impetu* in Pucallpa that day. According to it, the authorities had originally planned to bury the unidentifiable body parts in a mass grave. The families of the victims, however, found that "impious, godless and inhumane," and successfully fought this measure. And so these human remains, too, were laid to rest in the mausoleum that I visited for the first time twenty-seven years later with Werner Herzog.

During the recovery work, a twenty-six-year-old voluntary helper named Mario Zarbe displayed an incredible intuition and found almost half of the corpses on his own. According to the information in the special supplement, which contained personal statements along with numerous obituaries, at least six people survived the crash; according to other accounts, it was twelve. After the official end of the recovery, a group of civilians, who didn't want to give up, found six more corpses, among them that of the one American boy, the eighteen-year-old David Ericson, for whom a funeral service had already been held.

Personally, I've never believed there was a crime against my mother and regard my father's suspicions at that time as the grim thoughts of a distraught person. The horrible suspicion he was harboring shows me what a devastating condition he must have been in.

As for her final resting place, I think that her mortal remains are probably mainly in the *Alas de Esperanza* monument. What's the difference if her name isn't written there? Perhaps it's as good a place for her as Aufkirchen on Lake Starnberg. And what's much more important: I'm certain that she has found her peace.

A breathtaking sunset, such as occur only in the tropics, turns the sky bloodred. In a few minutes it will be night.

"Shall we get going soon?" my husband, who knows me as no one else does, asks cautiously. It's a suspicious sign when I say nothing for longer than ten minutes. Then he knows that I'm back in the past again with my thoughts.

He's right: Tomorrow we have a long day of travel ahead of us. When I think of it, my heart leaps for joy. Soon I will be in Panguana.

An hour later we're packing again. And suddenly I can't help thinking of the suitcase that was so unexpectedly brought to us back then. It was one of the suitcases that my mother and I had packed in Lima for the Christmas celebration in the jungle in 1971. It was completely intact. Only the outside of it was soaked. Among other things, there was a Christmas stollen in it, very similar to the one so often described in the newspaper reports. My father and I actually ate this one.

Tapes with birdcalls were also delivered to us, and then something else that made me especially happy: my fountain pen, on which I had written my name with waterproof ink to avoid any mix-ups. After all, almost all my friends wrote with an identical fountain pen. For a long time it was among my greatest treasures—until it was stolen from me years later, along with my purse, during a trip to San Ramón. This loss pained me deeply. Since the crash it had been my faithful companion and a constant reminder of the fact that the two of us found our way against all odds out of the depths of the jungle, not unlike a lost needle in a haystack, back to life.

The next day the time has come once again: We set off for Panguana. . . .

141

14 Nothing is the Same as It Was

Recovery after the crash: embracing a giant tree at Panguana and regaining strength, March 1972. (Photo courtesy of Juliane (Koepcke) Diller)

A Toyota pickup with four-wheel drive picks us up early in the morning. For a few years we have always booked the same drivers. They know the difficult route like the back of their hands, and so far their vehicles have always been reliable.

"The road is open," he says, after greeting us, and I heave a sigh of relief. For a few days the route was impassable due to the heavy rainfall. "The conditions aren't great, but we'll get through. Yesterday it took one of our drivers seven hours."

Seven hours—that sounds good. The most important thing is that we arrive in Yuyapichis at daytime, for at night the crossing of the Río Pachitea and the hike to the research station are still more arduous than usual.

"It will be fine," Nery reassures me. "If need be, you could always spend the night in my house in Yuyapichis."

As always it takes a while before all the baggage, including all the provisions that we brought, is stowed in the open truck bed. Then a board is put over the gasoline canister for refueling as a seat bench for Moro and the second driver. They will spend the drive up there—as I know from my own experience, not always a pleasure under the scorching sun and on dusty or muddy bumpy roads. But Moro laughs: he's used to it and will sleep—he's sure of that.

When we turn onto the *carretera* that leads into the jungle toward the Andes, and will ultimately end in Lima, I'm happy. This evening I will be in Panguana! Even after all these years in Germany, it's still a homecoming for me.

It's just like back then, when after a four-week stay in the Instituto Lingüístico de Verano, my attentive doctors finally allow me to leave my bed. For a few days I live with my father with the Maulhardt family, who hospitably

143

put me up in their bungalow hotel La Cabaña. Here I also have my last interviews with a new reporter from *Stern*, Rolf Winter. I have to confess, all the questions are starting to get on my nerves. The meetings with Gerd Heidemann and Hero Buss had gone pleasantly. Even though errors crept into their accounts, which would be copied a thousand times.

In the preliminary report, which appeared before the two of them had even spoken to me, so much of the groundwork was laid for rumors, which would never again be eradicated. This piece was clearly based on the article that had first appeared in *Life* magazine, for which the reporter had interviewed various people, such as the nurse in Tournavista, the pilot Jerrie Cobb and probably also the woodcutters who had rescued me. So *Stern* wrote that I took a cake with me from the crash site. This cake, which unfortunately did not exist, for I couldn't eat the completely mud-soaked panettone, will spread worldwide through all the coverage and take many strange forms. For the one cake soon turned into several! Finally–in *Paris Match*–it had transformed into so many that I can't even carry all of them with me, for want of a bag, and I have to leave them behind. Later the cake will turn into a Christmas stollen I baked for my father; in another newspaper I hold on to it in my lap the whole time during the Electra flight, so that after I wake up on the forest floor, I conveniently have it right at my fingertips.

The *Stern* reporters are also surprised that I left the crash site and even write of a "mistake" that saved my life. But I knew very well what I was doing. I had realized that no one would ever find me in the place where I woke up. I certainly did not run panic-stricken through the jungle, but followed with good reason the course of the water.

In the preliminary report the absurd myth of the self-built raft is also taken from the *Life* article:

> The fact that Juliane knew which branches and lianas are suited for the building of a raft was the second stroke of luck that saved her life: If she had chosen the wrong material for her raft, she would have been in the middle of the river without a chance, for in the rainy season even the small rivers, which are all tributaries of the Amazon, have a raging current.

Nothing is the Same as It Was

The detail that I had "many worms" (*viele Würmer*) in my arm, which provoked the expert from Munich to write a reader's letter, is also in this very first article.

In the second part of the report, there's a sentence that many later held against me: *After the crash Juliane resolved: "Now Father has lost his wife, but he's not going to lose his daughter too."* This suggests that I had seen my dead mother and possibly other corpses or injured people as well, which was, of course, not the case. This then led to the false reports that injured people were wandering through the forest, crying and screaming, but I ran off on my own. But these are basically all the typical inaccuracies from which journalists all over the world are clearly not immune. What affected me much more was the tone and content of the last part of the report, written by Rolf Winter. Here, in issue no. 9, February 17–23, 1972, I am portrayed on page 54 as an unfeeling, arrogant, precocious child. (In the article the phrase "little Juliane" appears a total of seven times!) I am depicted as someone who remains completely unmoved by her experiences and also incomprehensibly would like to go back to the jungle. He apparently doesn't notice that I'm still suffering from the aftereffects of an intense shock. To my knowledge, people had heard of this phenomenon even in 1972. Fundamentally, I'm anything but a vindictive person, but to this day I have not forgiven Rolf Winter his last paragraphs:

> It need not be feared that she will have to suffer on her continued life's journey from an excess of feminine emotions. Nor will she lose sleep over the tragic circumstance that her now dead mother and she actually didn't even want to take the crashed plane, but rather already had tickets for another airline. Someone told them mistakenly that the flight was canceled, so they flew with LANSA–the mother to her death, the daughter to tragedy-enveloped luck.
>
> Little Juliane, who looks so fragile and in need of help, much more child than woman, will cope with these sorts of things. Still, she is only human. Someone tells her that at the station in Panguana her bird "Pinxi" has died. She found him once after he had fallen out of the

nest, she loves him, and now he's dead.
Now little Juliane cries.

I will get used to reading my story in variations that are constantly surprising to me and to the fact that complete strangers know how it was at that time much better than I myself do. But there are certain things I will never get used to. I find it uncanny how my trek through the jungle stirs people's imaginations, right up to the lurid novel *A Jungle Goddess Must Not Cry*. It's quite possible that my fate "inspired" Konsalik to write this shoddy work, an unspeakable story about a blond, likewise seventeen-year-old, girl who survives a plane crash in Amazonia—conveniently, along with a brave young man—and is found by dangerous headhunters and abducted as a sun goddess . . . and so on and so forth. Of course, many reports also mention that my dress was completely in tatters and I was half naked. I saved the minidress, and aside from the defective zipper and a small hole in the side seam, it's in astonishingly flawless condition. But apparently the truth is eventually no longer so important. It has to take a backseat to what people imagine in their wildest fantasies.

So it's no wonder that I'm relieved at the end of January 1972 when I've finally recovered enough so that I can travel. With my father I go to Panguana. Our relationship has changed radically due to what has happened. Overnight, it seems to me, I've turned from a carefree child into an adult, and nothing has prepared me for it—neither the school in Lima nor the school of the jungle. I might be able to keep myself alive for days in the rain forest, but I'm unarmed against what pelts down on me after my rescue.

Up to that point I had a much closer relationship with my mother. She was my confidante, as much as my father's. Perhaps, I realize only now, she was always a sort of intermediary between my father and the world. The void she left behind brings us closer to each other. And yet my father, who will never get over losing her, will always remain to some extent a stranger to me.

I don't have many concrete memories of the five or six weeks in Panguana between the crash and my departure to Lima. My mother isn't there, but she might just as well have been on one of her trips abroad. I get a young coati as a gift, and I name him Ursi. He really keeps me on my toes.

He gets up to a lot of nonsense and, of course, cannot be housebroken. At one point he devours our entire supply of aspirin pills. Another time he snatches our valuable thermometer and disappears with it onto the roof of the hut. I have a lot of fun with him, even though he ravages our kitchen repeatedly in search of something delicious.

Unfortunately, as Rolf Winter reported, Pinxi, one of my blackbirds, died during my stay in Yarinacocha. My father had put the birds in the care of friends, and there they had probably eaten something that Pinxi couldn't tolerate. Now I begin to gradually return the other blackbird, Punki, to the wild. I release him, and he immediately joins a group of blackbirds building their hanging nests in a nearby tree. Still, he keeps coming back to me when he sees me. He really loves to come swooping into the kitchen hut and plunge without warning into one of the bowls of bread dough or whatever else happens to be standing around at the moment. Eventually he gets on my nerves so much with this that I offer him a spoonful of mustard, and greedy as Punki is, he immediately sinks his beak into it. From that point on, he's more careful and no longer comes smashing immediately into any bowl.

The familiar surroundings, spending time with my beloved tame animals and those in the forest outside our door—all this does me good. When my father and I speak about the future, then I know exactly what I want: to return to Lima, to go to school for two more years and then to take my Abitur. This was just what I was planning before the crash.

I want to pick up my life again where the thread broke on December 24. I want to go on living my completely normal life, just like before. At one point my father speaks of sending me to Germany. I argue with him, which I rarely do. I don't want to go there now. Germany is a foreign country to me. Anything but still more change. I want everything to go on the way it was. Or at least *almost*.

No one can bring back my mother. And even here in the jungle, where everything is actually the same as it used to be, nothing is the same as it was. This paradox will stay with me for many years. For my desire for normality is so strong that it sometimes almost hurts. Here, in February 1972 in Panguana, I really think I've moved on from "it." I will soon find out how much I'm deceiving myself.

The grief for my mother—it still has not reached me. Not until about three years later, on a Christmas Day, will I grasp with full force the irretrievability of this loss. Only then will I cry, all day long, almost without cease. But until that point her death remains for me like a distant theory. As if my mother might step out of the forest at any moment, shout to me with a laugh about whatever exciting thing she has discovered this time. For many years I dream again and again that I suddenly spot her by chance on the other side of the street. I run to her, call to her, we fall into each other's arms, and all is well. I'm boundlessly relieved and *sooo* happy—until I wake up.

I know that this will never happen. But thinking and feeling are separate from each other. In those days and weeks between the crash and what will follow, I learn that *understanding something* and *grasping it* are two different things. At least here I have a little peace and quiet, even though some especially tenacious journalists even follow me all the way to our very difficult-to-reach refuge.

At one point, for example, to our great surprise a nurse arrives, claiming to have to examine my wounds. Her face looks familiar to me. "Don't I know you?" I say. "Didn't I see you in Yarinacocha?" It's a journalist, who that time already tried in a different role to force her way to me. Now she has disguised herself as a nurse. My father drives her away. The rest of the day, his expression is gloomy. I'd like to know what's going on inside his head. Or rather: I don't want to know.

The weeks pass, and life goes on. I'm looking forward to seeing my classmates who, like me, will be preparing for the Abitur. And I'm looking forward to life in Lima with movies and milk shakes and excursions to the beach. After the Abitur, I'll study biology. For that, I will go to Germany, as I already had discussed a long time ago with my mother. The universities are better in Germany, she had said. I would like to study in Kiel and become a zoologist, just like her and my father. But that will still take two years. Two years are a long time in the life of a seventeen-year-old. And then the time has come, and the new school year is just around the corner.

If only I were already there! But before I can go to school again in Lima, I have to cross the Andes.

"I'll fly with you," says my father. I have a lump in my throat. Of course, we don't book with LANSA. Even if we wanted to, that wouldn't be possible, for with the Electra the airline lost not only its last plane, but also its license. My father, who tries to sue the company in Lima, will learn that it was long since liquidated. But the fact that we're flying with a different airline doesn't dispel my fear of this flight.

"Do we have to fly?" I ask my father.

He casts a brief glance at me. Then he says: "It will be better than winding across the Andres for three days, don't you think?"

I'm not sure whether it will be better. But I don't say anything else. I learned a long time ago to be brave.

If I thought that the world had forgotten me in the meantime, I'm already disabused of that notion in Pucallpa. I have no idea how the journalists know that I will fly at this particular time to Lima. In any case they hold microphones in front of my face from all sides. Cameras hum; flashes blind me; flowers are handed to me; questions bombard me. Am I doing well? How are my wounds healing? What am I going to do with my life? Would I like to greet the girls of Pucallpa? Am I afraid to get on an airplane again?

I don't know what to say. Of course, I'm afraid. But being mobbed so suddenly by this pack scares me even more. I'm almost relieved once I'm sitting in the airplane. But that is only until it takes off. Then I notice how every muscle in my body tenses.

I close my eyes and try to take a deep breath. Strain to listen to every sound, however slight. Today no storm can be seen far and wide. Fortunately, the flight takes under an hour. But fifty minutes can be so terribly long.

I've almost made it through the flight when I hear a noise that makes me panic. It's a rattling and banging—my heart skips a beat; sweat breaks out from all my pores. I cling to the seat in front of me.

"Relax," says my father. "It's only the landing gear. It's being lowered now. In a few moments we'll already be landing."

I heave a sigh of relief. Shortly thereafter, I climb, my knees still wobbling, out of the plane.

But what are all these people doing at the bottom of the steps? A whole crowd besieges the airfield, surrounds the airplane. Are they allowed to do that? Are they waiting for me? Once again I'm photographed. Here, too, people hold microphones toward me. I'd like best to turn back around and hide myself away in the airplane. But the other passengers are pushing from behind.

It's like running the gauntlet: "Juliana," I hear, "smile for us!" "Juliana, have you recovered well from the green hell?" "Juliana, what will you do now?" I don't want to say anything. I want to disappear into thin air. I'm generally a shy person, and this attention is getting to be too much for me. "Juliana, do you already have a boyfriend?" "Juliana, is it true that you pray to San Martín de Porres, the black saint?"

Finally we've gotten through. I can hardly believe it. Why are all these people still interested in me? During the weeks in Panguana, I saw barely a handful of people. And here I'm being overrun.

As he often does, my father lives during this stay in Lima in the guest room of the natural history museum. He withdraws from everything. He doesn't want to see or hear anything, but prefers to be alone with his grief. And I move back into my room in my schoolmate Edith's grandmother's apartment. But if I thought everything would be the same as it was before the crash, now I realize that nothing is the same as it used to be. Complete strangers approach me on the street, want my autograph or just want to touch me. I find this incredibly trying. I haven't yet learned to deal with this sudden "fame." And the journalists don't give me any peace either. When I step out of the house, they're already there. When I take a walk with my friends in the city, they follow us. When we go to the beach, they're already waiting for me. They even try to photograph me in my room with a telephoto lens. Ultimately I feel as if I'm under siege. It's no fun at all to do anything anymore. This isn't how I imagined my return to Lima.

In this mood my friend Edith persuades me to go swimming with her in the German Club. I've been there only rarely, for my parents didn't visit that place, but Edith doesn't relent.

"Oh," I say, "I don't know. I'm sure to be ambushed by journalists there. I'd rather not."

"But you can't sit in your room with the curtains drawn forever," she replies. "It would be best if you just got used to the press. And you'll see, it's not as bad as you think."

Edith knows what she's talking about. She has already won numerous medals as a track athlete for Peru, and she is famous herself. She has experience with press people, and she promises to stand by me.

"Besides, you're imagining things," she says. "They don't let journalists into the German Club. Come on, the weather is so beautiful."

Finally I give in. Edith is right, I think, soon school will be starting again, and we don't have much time left for things like that.

At first, everything seems to be quiet in the German Club. But no sooner have we stepped out of the changing room than they are already there: I have no idea how they got in, but suddenly the press has surrounded me once again. This time there's even a television camera pointed at me.

"Come on," Edith says softly to me, "it would be best if you very agreeably answered a few questions now. Then they'll quickly leave you alone again."

And at her advice I sit down obediently on a swing, smile pleasantly and answer the journalists' harmless questions. And indeed, after a brief time, the television crew departs. Still, the incident leaves me with a bad feeling. The way that the press follows me in a pack, almost like wild carnivores, is awful; though no jaguars or other animals attacked me in the jungle, these supposedly civilized people never stopped hunting me.

My life would have taken a different course if my godfather hadn't invited my father to his home that particular evening. They turn on the television for the main news. And there he sees, to his boundless dismay, his daughter. She's sitting in a bikini on a swing, smiling into the camera and telling the world that she's doing well. It's quite a coincidence, because my father doesn't usually watch television. But during those two minutes, of all times, he is watching. First he is thunderstruck. Then he sees red.

"So that's how you mourn your mother!" He hurls the words angrily at me when he finds me that same evening. And then he announces to me his irrevocable decision. I will leave this country immediately. I won't take my Abitur in Lima, but in Germany. As soon as possible he will put me in an airplane and send me to my aunt Cordula.

I'm horrified. Cry. Beg to be allowed to stay. I don't want to go to Germany. *Don't take away my home too,* I want to scream, *not that too. I've already lost so much.* But the severe reprimand of his "So that's how you mourn your mother" seems to deprive me of all my rights. I'm doing well, after all, you could hear that on television. Only he is consumed with grief for his beloved wife. Over the next few days, I hope and pray that he will come to his senses. Once he's calmed down, I think, he'll reconsider. But my begging is in vain. His decision has been made.

"Here in Peru," he says a few days later, "you'll never get any peace. These journalist vultures will keep you from being able to lead a normal life. Believe me, this is for your own good. In Germany, you'll be able to start a new life."

A *new life*. But I don't want a new life. I just want to be able to go on leading my old life like every other girl in my class, to go to school and take my Abitur. After that, I'll go to Germany. But not now, not after everything that has happened. . . .

It's no use. My passport photos have to be taken. In them I have tears in my eyes. Everything happens so quickly, as in a bad dream from which I just can't wake up.

When my schoolmates hear of my imminent departure, they organize a farewell party for me. On this occasion they give me a beautiful ring, red gold with a pink tourmaline, so that I should never forget them. They chipped in to be able to buy it for me. I'm touched and have to cry once again.

I remember an afternoon walking through the streets of Miraflores with my father. He's trying to explain something to me, talking about the philosophy to which he and my mother adhered, the ancient Egyptians' belief in the significance of the sun as a life-giving power. I notice that he's searching for words. He makes a strange movement with his hand, as if he had to wave something away, but there's nothing there.

"What are you doing?" I ask with alarm. "What's that about?"

"Oh, nothing," he says, and stops walking.

"Juliane," he then says in a completely different tone, "your mother and I, we had a few rules we always adhered to. One of them is never to say good-bye to each other in a fight or even to go to sleep at night without making up first."

I look at him and wait for him to go on. He runs his hand over his face. "That's important," he says.

Nothing more. I look into his face, observing his deep wrinkles, the hint of despair around his mouth, his alert, almost burning eyes, which seem to have sunk even farther back into their sockets. And suddenly I realize: My father is completely at the end of his nerves.

152

Was he trying with those words to make up with me, awkward as he was in emotional matters? At the time I was too young, too distraught and confused to recognize that. To my friends' grandparents, with whom I was living, I said in farewell: "I'll be back soon!"

But they only looked at each other and then said: "We don't really think so, Juliane. It won't be that soon."

But I didn't want to hear that. I replied: "Yes, it will. I'm sure of it."

There are photos from the airport in Lima. Of course, the Peruvian journalists followed me up to the very last moment, and in Germany their colleagues were already waiting for me. In these photos I'm waving sadly at the camera, while my father keeps an eye on me with a rather pinched face. He looks nervous in these pictures. Perhaps he's having doubts about his decision? Or he's afraid I'll thwart his plans at the last instant, after all? The fact that I was sent to Germany against my will—for many years I successfully suppressed that, at least on the surface, like so many things. For a long time I said: ". . . and then we decided I'd be better off going to Germany." But, in actuality, my father decided that, and I was really unhappy about it. Today I have, of course, come to realize that his decision was right in the end.

But at the time there was so much that filled me with anxiety. First and foremost I had to face, alone, my first overseas flight ever.

15 Homecoming to a Foreign Country

My new life in a foreign land, residing at the home of my aunt and my grandmother in Germany, 1974. (Photo courtesy of Juliane (Koepcke) Diller)

I had to conquer the stress of sitting in an airplane again, and this time it would not be only fifty minutes, but a whole eighteen hours. Fortunately, I got to spend some of these hours in the cockpit, which made the time pass much more quickly for me and to some extent allayed my fear. I found especially fascinating the evening stopover in New York, which I got to witness from the cockpit. I was immediately seized again by my enthusiasm for all things technical, and the friendly pilots patiently answered my questions.

And yet on this flight over the Atlantic, I was in a sort of psychological no-man's-land. My previous life had come to an abrupt end. I had not yet begun a new one. And I was gradually grasping that the crash was more than an unpleasant incident to be experienced, worked through and then forgotten. Even though I had miraculously landed relatively softly on the rain forest floor—I still felt as if I had no ground under my feet, no basis, no foundation.

I had lost my mother. My home had just been taken from me. And I had no idea what would await me in my new life. I had set off with the firm conviction that I would return as soon as possible to Panguana. In reality many years would go by before I would see my beloved jungle again.

Perhaps that's why it is always really special for me to return to this spot in the middle of the Peruvian rain forest. Today it turns once again into a test of patience. No sooner have we left the *carretera* and turned onto the dirt road toward Yuyapichis than there's one mud hole after another. After rainfall the red laterite ground causes cars to slide all over the place, and after the past few weeks of heavy showers, it requires a lot of experience to steer the fully laden truck safely through these perils. Several times even I, who have by now already traveled here in the jungle so often and with all sorts of road conditions, think: *We're not going to make it over this obstacle*

155

here! Especially when the road heads steeply downward for a few yards as on a slide into a water hole of indeterminable depth, and then, after ten or twenty yards, back up an equally steep slide. But our driver is not so easily impressed, and he unswervingly maneuvers us through this mess. On the way we meet small and larger trucks and pickups, fully laden with goods and people. Like bunches of grapes they cling to the load on top and hold on as tight as possible. You can't be timid when the vehicle really pitches; but for a lift for a few *soles*, people here in these remote areas will put up with a lot.

"Once we've reached The Door," says the driver, "things won't be so bad."

And he's right. We only have to change a tire once, and the two drivers take care of that as routinely as if they did it every day. And that's actually the case. "A tire?" laughs the second driver, who is clearly happy to have something to do instead of just being tossed about on the truck bed. "That's nothing!" The "new" tire has almost no tread left at all, but that doesn't bother anyone.

And then the journey continues.

At The Door we make only a brief stop today. The *señora* is not at home, and I give her daughter a few photos I took of her mother on the last trip through. We have a beer and move on. It's not long before we cross the Río Shebonya. Here I have the truck stop briefly, for this river remains special to me. I walk to the bridge, cross it halfway and look between the iron trusses into the water. How often have I asked myself whether I passed by here too, swimming or drifting in the water, wading along the riverbank, always on the alert for stingrays? Everyone I asked about where the plane wreckage was from here gave me a different answer. It's back in the clutches of the jungle, disturbed only once by the tenacity of Werner Herzog.

And on we go across the wide, earthy white-water Súngaro River and through the settlement of the same name, continuously heading south. It's not far, and yet the journey drags on. My impatience grows with my anticipation. After crossing the beautiful black-water Yanayacu River, we reach the dead-end road to Yuyapichis. When we finally arrive in the village, it's still three hours before twilight. I urge Moro to hurry, for now it's time to arrange boats for us and for our cargo. But things don't go that quickly here. I should actually know that.

And eventually the hectic pace of the city simply falls away from me. The jungle has its own tempo, and people adapt to it. And so I don't get worked up when Moro is standing in front of me an hour later, sweating and gasping for breath, with the news that he was able to find a boat for us and our suitcases, but not for our food. So we store it for the time being in Nery's house and head to the river. Mañana, mañana–tomorrow is another day.

The journey across the river has always been like the crossing of a mysterious border for me. On one side lies real life; on the other is Panguana. Of course, Panguana is just as real as life in Lima or Munich. But it belongs to another world. In the city nature is a tolerated guest: you plant a few trees, put plants in front of the window and keep a pet. Here in Panguana, nature is the host, and we are the visitors. Even if this spot belongs to me on paper, I view it more as borrowed, or better still: entrusted. We biologists come, marvel, learn, describe and try to make our newly attained knowledge accessible to humanity.

"What's the point of knowing how many beetles, ants, bugs, mites and other creatures are crawling and flying around there?" I'm often asked. "What good does that do us?"

"You can only protect what you've first studied and gotten to know," I usually answer, "and at some point people will realize here, too, that it's more beneficial and valuable to preserve the forests and their biodiversity in the long run instead of destroying them for a short-term profit." But as long as we regard the rain forest as nothing but a wilderness, a "green hell," we're behaving like children setting fire to a heap of money just because they don't know what the paper is worth.

I prefer not to talk about my love for this green universe, whose secrets we have still barely penetrated. Many people view feelings as an unsound argument. And there are, of course, really enough good arguments: If the tropical forests are destroyed, then the CO_2 previously stored in the biomass will escape into the atmosphere, and that's several billion tons. And other harmful gases will be released as well. If the forest cover is decimated, it will get increasingly dry, the groundwater level will sink and the temperatures will rise. The consequences are vast, and they have alarming effects on the entire global climate.

When my parents came here over forty years ago, the Amazonian forests were still as good as unexplored. It was their idea to investigate in a particular, well-defined area what cohabits here in a small space. They chose Panguana, in order to direct their focus on this exemplary area, less than a square mile, in the immensity of the rain forest. To begin with, they simply wanted to observe and compile what lives and grows here. The bulk of their work, therefore, consisted in making lists of species. At the same time they wanted to study the ecosystem of the lowland rain forest, in which these many species interact with one another, especially the "ecological niches" of animals and plants, for every species finds itself a niche in which it can exist alongside the others. This is usually a very complex and exciting web of relationships. While my mother as an ornithologist focused mainly on bird life, my father always set his sights on the "big picture," and he was actually working ecologically from the beginning, even though in his day that wasn't the term for it.

Originally my parents wanted to stay here for five years and then go back to Lima to analyze their results. At that time they probably couldn't imagine living longer than five years in this isolation. But soon they realized that the diversity in the lowland rain forest near the Andes is so tremendous that you would need more than a whole lifetime to come even close to completing the lists of species. At that time the lists existed only for the large or common animals and plants. There were some superficial compilations for wider regions or the whole country, which disregarded biological contexts and did not particularly take into account the rain forest. What my parents achieved here by striving for exhaustiveness in a small area and illuminating the depths of this ecosystem was thus truly pioneering work.

The news of the enormous diversity of life-forms in Panguana lured scientists here from all over the world. My parents, especially my mother, had an excellent worldwide network of colleagues—and this at a time when e-mail and the Internet did not yet exist and a letter usually required several months to reach us. In her letters my mother often mentions the difficulties with the mail. Nor did she shy away from tracking down those responsible and asking them why a piece of mail sometimes even took a whole five months to make it from Pucallpa to Panguana.

My mother repeatedly traveled to the United States or Europe to participate in conferences. I remember particularly well one of her longer absences in early 1970, shortly before my return to Lima. At that time we had numerous scientists visiting, and I had to cook daily for everyone, which I found rather grueling.

My parents were the first to investigate how any life-form they found integrates itself here in its environment, how it escapes enemy pressure, what strategies it develops to challenge food competitors, and much more. Since they intended to take everything into account, to exclude nothing and set no priorities, it swiftly became clear to them that this work was as good as endless and would take a very long time, unless they had help. For that reason they were happy to be able to interest many of their colleagues in Panguana as a new field of study. Even today, far from all the life has been catalogued, and yet Panguana is the best-explored jungle station in the Peruvian rain forest, east of the Andes. It is also the oldest, though not the largest, and most of the others are equipped with significantly more resources. When my father left Panguana in 1974 and taught as a professor in Hamburg, he assigned thesis projects and dissertations to his students on ecological problems that were not yet so well investigated in Panguana. In this way a lot of knowledge was gathered in the course of time. But still no one has done more extensive systematic work on Panguana's fish. Once, my parents spread a gill net in the river and soon found thirty-five different species in it. Here, too, there would still be so much to do.

If my mother could see what has become of Panguana since then, I think, as I climb down the bank to the Río Pachitea, where the boat is waiting for us, she would definitely be happy. And perhaps she would say with a wink: "What? In all these years you still haven't managed to complete the species list of fish?"

With two or three steps, I climb spiritedly aboard our boat, *Panguana I*, a *canoa*, a traditional dugout canoe, reinforced and enlarged on the sides with boards. It's best to step exactly in the middle, or else you might fall in the water faster than you can say "oops." During my two years in Panguana, I even used to be able to pole a simple *canoa* without side reinforcements by myself. I haven't tried it in a long time. Nowadays they use the typical seven-horsepower outboard motors, known as *"peque-peques"* because of their loud chugging noises. They have a long steering rod, with the help of which you can lift the screw out of the water in no time, which is really handy if you inadvertently run into a shoal. And to my ears even the *peque-peques* sound like home.

In the evening it's especially beautiful on the rivers of Amazonia. The water, usually the brown color of coffee with milk, receives a golden shimmer, the sky takes on an unreal tinge, and the background noise of the riverbank birds, frogs and insects changes its pitch. No one speaks. The river is like a magical ribbon on which we're gliding along, downstream and across the stately breadth of the Pachitea, past the huts of gold seekers, past houses in front of which children are playing, and above all past the green wall of the forest. I keep an eye out for hoatzins, which once saved my life and which my mother studied so intensively. To do so, she would climb down to the river on countless evenings and observe with her unique saintly patience the behavior of these strange birds. But today the hoatzins don't show up anywhere.

We reach the mouth of the Yuyapichis River. Our boatman changes his course and heads for a sandy pier. On top of the hill I spot the old Módena farm, which Moro's grandparents once cultivated.

The last leg of the journey, our hike, begins.

In the past we used to have to fight from here on—of course, only after a revitalizing stop at Doña Josefa's—through dense secondary and primary rain forest. Today the forest between the Módena farm and Panguana has been largely cleared. Even though that makes our hike easier, I regret it, of course. Over the past thirty years, more and more landowners have switched to cattle ranching and cleared the forest for that. But they have not had much success. For the pastures attained in this way by no means meet the requirements for profitable cattle ranching. After a brief fertile phase, due to the slight amounts of nutrients in the wood ash remaining from the slash and burn, the already nutrient-poor grounds become barren. Since they don't have the forest's network of roots, they can no longer become saturated by the rain, and they dry out. The water drains much too quickly. The already scarcely present topsoil is washed into the rivers, and there's increased erosion. The grass grows sparsely and is not particularly nutritious, so that the cattle rancher is forced to supplement it with expensive concentrate feed. The infrastructure in the jungle also makes it hard for him to make a profit on his cattle. On the long journeys, often crammed together on boats, the animals lose weight and are usually lean by the time they arrive in Pucallpa, where they don't sell for a good price. Nonetheless, every year many acres of rain forest are destroyed. For want of knowledge and genuine alternatives, the myth of possible affluence through cattle ranching persists.

In the evening of this long journey, we now march cross-country over the pastures of the Módena farm and are glad that the sun is no longer so high in the sky. We wade through a deep mud hole and the Río Yuyapichis at an old ford, where the water reaches just up to the upper edge of our rubber boots. Moro's wife, Nery, and their two daughters, who joined us in the village of Yuyapichis, are already far ahead of us. Now we continue a couple more miles along an oxbow lake of the river, where caimans have recently started living again, which pleases me immensely. For too long they were gone, eradicated by the Indians and farmers, who were afraid for their small animals, and for whom the really tasty meat of the caimans, which they hunted and ate as a delicacy, was nothing to sneeze at either.

And then, finally, I can see the lupuna tree. It rises proudly from the multitude of other trees and spreads its mighty crown—the emblem of Panguana, 150 feet tall and many hundreds of years old. Moro's house comes into view next, then the two guesthouses. They're unremarkable wooden huts, nothing more—for me they mean heaven on earth. For two years we have even had a shower cabin; and even though there is only cold water, it's an enormous luxury for us. Previously we washed down in the river, where there are many blackflies and midges, whose stings often get unpleasantly inflamed and itch terribly. River water is regularly pumped into a large container on the roof of the cabin. The earth that washes in with it settles to the bottom, and out of the pipe comes clear, gloriously refreshing water. Drinking water, however, we have to bring with us from Pucallpa, like most other food.

Moro's dogs bark. We're home. Smoke is rising from the chimney of Moro's house: Nery has already lit a fire in the stove and begun preparing dinner. I'm sure that she will conjure up a customary delicacy for us even without the provisions that were left behind in Yuyapichis.

On this first evening in Panguana, despite our fatigue after the arduous journey, we remain sitting for a long time by candlelight on the terrace, so that the generator can remain shut off. We share a few beers, which Moro wonderfully took along in his backpack, and listen to the noises of the tropical night. The sounds of the jungle envelop me. Above us circle bats. There are over fifty species of these alone here in Panguana. I studied them for several years and recorded the results in my dissertation. For even though it would take years after my departure in 1972, eventually I returned to Panguana.

Back then, when I flew from Lima via New York to Germany, and finally landed completely exhausted in Frankfurt, I just accepted the fact that here, too, journalists were waiting for me and trying eagerly to shoot a photo of me. I hadn't slept a wink during the flight, and I still had to get used to the phenomenon of the time difference.

In Frankfurt, friends of my parents were waiting for me, who had arranged a plan for my stopover. I still had to continue on to Kiel.

So it happened that among the first people I met in Germany was Bernhard Grzimek, who was not only a popular animal expert, well known through the media, but also director of the Frankfurt Zoo. I've always liked visiting zoological gardens, and now I had the opportunity to see that famous one. But I was so tired by that point that I was indifferent even to the visit to the zoo, and I just accepted stoically everything that was proposed to me. Only later, when I learned that Grzimek's son Michael had been the victim of a plane crash in the Serengeti thirteen years before, did I realize that our encounter must have been moving for him too. Michael had been exploring the Serengeti in a small plane, had collided with a vulture, lost control of the aircraft and died in the crash.

From Frankfurt, a smaller airplane was to bring me to Kiel, where my aunt and grandmother lived, and I had a terrible fear of getting on this plane. Perhaps the kind married couple looking after me in Kiel could sense my fear, for they asked me several times whether I wouldn't prefer for them to drive me to Kiel. I would have so liked to say "yes!" But I didn't have the courage. And so I clenched my teeth, sat down in the turboprop airplane—like the LANSA plane, but smaller—and made it through this flight as well. Everything went well. But when I arrived in Kiel, I was completely beat, and the first thing I did was sleep thirteen hours straight.

My aunt Cordula and my grandmother gave me the warmest welcome imaginable. In the three-room apartment, I got my own little realm—for that, my aunt gave up her room and slept and worked from that point on in the living room. She never made me feel that this might have been a sacrifice. For her, it simply went without saying. From the beginning I got along well with both women. My aunt, in particular, took care of me devotedly, and I will never forget that as long as I live. Still, the adjustment was anything but easy for me. The first thing that struck me about Germany was that I was freezing all the time. It was early April, and I had previously experienced coldness like that only in the Andes.

Here in Kiel my aunt also told me how they had found out the terrible news in Germany. For at that time there wasn't any e-mail, and even making a phone call to a distant continent was not so simple. My father couldn't be reached in Panguana, anyhow, and so my aunt's contacts as a journalist came in useful for her.

At first they thought that my mother and I had already flown on December 23, so they were not yet that worried when they heard about the crash. But then they heard that we were on the plane, after all, and the uncertainty began. During those days the Bonn, Germany, office of the Agence France-Presse proved extremely helpful. On December 26, the editors obtained the passenger list of the LANSA plane within three hours with the help of their office in Lima. Aunt Cordula's colleagues also kept her updated on the rescue operation. In a thank-you letter, she wrote: *The news that my niece was found late in the evening of January 4, 1972 was of extraordinary importance for the family members living in Germany, for whom I'm speaking.*

To this day I find it fascinating how difficult it was in those days to get reliable information and how resourceful and well connected my aunt, nonetheless, was.

Yes, I spent those first weeks in Kiel in a daze. I didn't feel good, I was constantly nauseous, and so I just let everything wash over me. First of all, because I had come so hastily, a school had to be found for me, where I could take my Abitur. I was lucky, for the husband of one of my mother's relatives was the principal of the Wellingdorf Gymnasium in Kiel, which had been the first school far and wide to introduce a reformed Oberstufe, which is the higher secondary-school level in which students obtain their university entrance qualification. He offered me the opportunity to go directly into the eleventh grade. Then we would see how I did. Indeed, that level was simpler for me. I could choose the subjects that suited me best. In Lima, however, the school year began in April and here in the autumn, so I was barging into the middle of the ongoing classes, which I found really awful.

The first day of school confirmed this: I didn't find the right classroom immediately and so arrived late. The teacher scolded me: "First you're new and then you also come late!" On top of that, I first of all had to adapt to the German customs; for example, in Lima, you stood up when it was your turn to say something. I quickly broke that habit, though, after I had provided general amusement with it in the class.

I was immediately accepted by the other students and soon had a really nice circle of friends. Of course, here, too, people knew who I was and what I had experienced, and curious questions were inevitable. I found it hard to talk about the whole thing, especially ever since I had also been "exiled" from my homeland of Peru. But all the people in my new surroundings strove to make the adjustment as easy as possible for me. And yet—what had been rushing in on me over the past weeks was simply too much, and my body made it clear to me once more that I had far from gotten over everything.

Ever since my knee swelled up back in Yarinacocha, I had intense pain when walking. My aunt brought me to an orthopedist to have it looked at. He not only looked at my knee, but also into my face and said: "Your eyes are really yellow! I'm sending you immediately to a hospital for examination!" They admitted me then and there and put me in the isolation ward, for I not only had a cruciate ligament rupture, but also a full-blown case of hepatitis. This was most likely caused by the water I drank from the stream in the jungle, which I had needed in order to survive without food. My liver was swollen—that was the cause of my constant nausea.

So there I lay, and it was basically all right with me. All I wanted was to have my peace, and now I had it. I had to maintain a strict diet, but that didn't bother me either. Yes, I liked it in the hospital.

The doctors and nurses were friendly, I had a lively roommate, and I felt more secure than I had in a long time. As far as I'm concerned, I thought, I could stay here forever. Isn't it strange that I had to be admitted to the hospital before I finally got some peace? But everything I'd gone through had overwhelmed me.

In Yarinacocha, despite the restful environment, too much had still been rushing in on me: There were the journalists, the daily accounts of the recovery of corpses, the gruesome news and the realization that I was the sole survivor. And ultimately there was the fact of my mother's death. On top of that, there was the imperceptible tension between me and my father, and his grief, which he couldn't show, but also couldn't hide. There was so much that had remained unsaid between us, and ultimately my hasty departure from Peru, which I had yet to get over. Now I had time; now I had the peace I so urgently needed. That's why I didn't want to leave this isolation ward.

After four weeks, when I was already doing much better, the doctor found out that I did not have health insurance in Germany and had to bear the costs myself. Bed rest and diet, he said, I could also maintain at home, and he released me then and there. And I thought: *Oh no, now I have to go somewhere else yet again!* But my aunt took such loving care of me that I gradually began to feel at home. I remained bedridden for a few weeks. My new classmates came to visit me now and then, and summer break, by then, had already arrived.

In September, I began the new school year at the normal time, and lo and behold: With my aunt's support I got into the twelfth grade and did not have to repeat the eleventh. I chose a concentration in biology—of course!—and German, the latter at the advice of my aunt, who was a writer and supported my enthusiasm for literature in any way she could. I was always good in that subject, but she helped me improve my style. Only in mathematics was I downgraded, because we hadn't done set theory in Peru and the curriculum was somewhat different there. In the end I aced my German Abitur, and I was very proud of that.

Aunt Cordula was an extremely interesting woman, and each day I came to appreciate more the opportunity to live with her. She was, as mentioned, a journalist and a writer. Because she was unmarried, she lived with her mother. She was always in the know about everything that was going on in politics and in art. My aunt sharpened my awareness of such things, which had not particularly interested me before. Among other things, she wrote quite successful biographies of the intellectual Lou Andreas-Salomé and the philosopher and nun Edith Stein.

When she could help me with my essays, especially interpretations, she was really in her element. I'll never forget how she taught me to interpret poetry. She wanted me to figure out for myself everything that was in a poem. She encouraged me until I succeeded. Those were hours that brought us very close to each other, and I remain grateful to her to this day for opening my mind to all things cultural.

In those first two years in Kiel, I drew and painted a lot. I liked to use chalk and charcoal. Certainly, I inherited the abilities for this from my mother, who was an excellent animal illustrator. She had learned under Professor Hans Krieg in Munich how to draw birds in flight and other animals in swift motion, and perfected her rapid sketching technique. She also illustrated my father's books and made hundreds of drawings for them. In Peru, a set of postage stamps with five of her bird drawings came out after her death. My mother had been commissioned to design these stamps half a year before the crash and completed the task shortly before her sudden demise; for my father and me, the issuing of the stamps became a sort of posthumous testament to my mother's life's work.

Now I, too, took great pleasure in drawing, so that I even seriously considered studying art instead of biology. A teacher at the Wellingdorf Gymnasium, with whom I had a special connection, encouraged my interest too. She took me with her on trips to view this or that exhibition. She also invited me to her home, and on those occasions I met some artists of the Kiel cultural scene. All this was really enriching for me, for in Peru I experienced nothing of the sort.

Even though I would have liked to forget the past, it was necessary time and again to remember what had happened. *Stern* had sold the rights to my story to a film production company, and an Italian director named Giuseppe Scotese (not to be confused with the famous American directer Scorsese) visited me to get firsthand information. So I had to tell him everything again from the beginning and answer his numerous questions. I did so patiently, but was not involved further in the film work. That was all right with me. The less I had to do with it, the better, I thought.

My first year in Kiel was approaching its end. My aunt might have been wondering anxiously how I would feel during Christmas, the anniversary of that terrible experience. But it was strange: Maybe because Christmas in Germany was so completely different than it was in the jungle, maybe because I still could not really acknowledge my grief—another relapse did not occur. Instead, I made plans for the coming summer. That might have been my way of coping with my homesickness. And so my aunt wrote to my father that I would like to visit Panguana over the next summer break in 1973.

Actually, the most normal thing in the world, you would think: A daughter wants to return home over summer break. Wasn't I doing everything my father expected of me? Hadn't I, despite my serious illness, mastered the foreign school curriculum with flying colors and even skipped a grade? In my aunt's letters, which she wrote to my father during my first year in Germany, I repeatedly find the same refrain: *These weeks Juliane has to work very hard for school.* Curiously, I don't remember at all having so much to do. Undoubtedly, that was the best way for me to put all I'd gone through behind me and keep homesickness at bay.

So I had slowly arrived in Kiel, not only outwardly, but also in my heart. I had recovered to the point where I was healthy, and was looking forward to seeing Panguana and my father again. Until I calculated how little of my five-week summer break would remain once I subtracted the long and arduous journey. My aunt advised me gently against it, and stressed what a strain it would be: so much time in airplanes for a mere two weeks in Panguana. At the idea of having to fly again, I got goose bumps. And when my maternal grandmother urged me to come and finally visit her on Lake Starnberg, I gradually abandoned my plan to go to Peru.

What I didn't know was that my father had forbidden me to come, anyway. In my aunt's posthumous papers, I found a letter that made my blood freeze in my veins. While my father accepted various visits from zoologists, he wrote:

> I am dismayed that Juliane wants to come back here already. I don't find that advisable at all. Please talk her out of it: there are too many things that make her coming here appear ill advised. If Maria's brother wants to come, he should do it. . . . He should take into consideration that I have no staff here and that this is no summer resort. If Juliane shows up here against my will, then she will experience something she wasn't expecting.

My aunt replied:

Juliane has already abandoned her Peru travel plans on her own, when she realized that she could have had at most seventeen days in Panguana, for the break is only five weeks long. You certainly don't need to threaten with angry words, as in your letter of December 30. That will only jeopardize her difficultly attained and easily shaken mental and physical equilibrium. That's why I didn't tell her about it at all.

Only now, forty years later, do I learn about this, and wonder: *Why didn't my father want to see me? What "things" made my visit "appear ill advised"? Was he unable to bear my presence? Did he resent that I was alive instead of my mother?*

Even after so many years, his roughly phrased letter forbidding me to come home still hurts me. But what is still odder: Until I found this letter a few weeks ago, I had completely suppressed the fact that I had at that time considered going to Panguana at all. If someone had asked me, I would have denied it with utter conviction. And yet here it is in writing. Why did I forget that so completely?

And why did I abandon the plan of my own accord? Seventeen days—that's not such a short time if you're actually really homesick. Did I sense without words even across the great distance that I wouldn't be welcome with my father? I don't know and will never find out. My father died in the year 2000. Why do we so often neglect to ask the important questions before it's too late?

And yet I cannot really be angry with my father. His Christmas letter to me, which he had already written at the end of November 1972 so that it would arrive in time, begins with the following sentences:

Dear Juliane!
I wish you all the best this Christmas and also much, much happiness for the new year of 1973. Since last Christmas, this time of year has taken on a particular face for us. For you it will always be the holiday on which your life was given to you anew. For me it is from now

168

on a sad holiday, which is followed by a still sadder time, that is, the period up to the real date of Mommy's death, which is to be estimated around the sixth or seventh of January.

The harsh letter in which he forbids me to come to Panguana he wrote to my aunt on December 30, 1972, just after the anniversary of the crash. He had just had the first Christmas without my mother, and I don't dare to imagine what might have been going on inside him.

"Well, *vecina*," Moro says, breaking the silence and jolting me out of my thoughts, "aren't you tired at all?"

"I am," I say, "it's been a long day. I'm just so happy to be here again."

"And we're even happier! Welcome back to Panguana!"

With flashlights we find our way to the shower cabin to brush our teeth and then head to our beds. They're hard, but that doesn't bother us. I already know that I'm going to sleep deeply.

Following in my parents' footsteps: at fourteen years old, I'm catching a butterfly by the Yuyapichis River, 1969. (Photo courtesy of Juliane (Koepcke) Diller)

16 Miracles Still Happen

A comic-strip version of my ordeal was published in a Peruvian newspaper.
(Photo courtesy of Juliane (Koepcke) Diller)

A few days later the time has come to go to Puerto Inca and settle the matter of the deed registrations in the city hall there. Early in the morning Moro and his helper Chano bring us in the *canoa* to the ford to spare us a stretch of the way.

To my joy, large birds flutter up from the riverbank. It's hoatzins, a whole colony.

At the Módena farm we meet Don Elvio, Moro's uncle, who gives us a warm welcome and is happy to ferry us across to the village of Yuyapichis in his boat. There we soon find a car that takes us to the village of Súngaro, on the river of the same name. And then we will see what comes next.

Once I've adjusted to this jungle life, its rules and customs, I enjoy it to the fullest. One way or another you always reach your destination, even though there's no public transportation system with an exact departure schedule. There are always drivers shuttling between the different far-flung jungle villages. Usually, you can find a lift in this way, and if you're unlucky, you have to wait a few hours. That's just how it is, no reason to get worked up. Still, for a European, it takes getting used to. But the sooner you resign yourself to this rhythm, the better. For there's no use grumbling and complaining—all that accomplishes is to spoil your mood.

The road to Súngaro isn't clayey, but instead it's littered with fist-sized pebbles. There are potholes too, of course, and our driver apparently makes a point of racing as fast as possible over this rumbling road, which is more reminiscent of a marble run for gigantic children than a street. This is a challenge for the vehicle's suspension, but also for our backs and bottoms. When we arrive in the small village, we're all a little bit dazed and rather jolted. From here it's only another half hour to Puerto Inca. A station wagon, which by European standards is already fully occupied, lets us get in as well. Everyone just pushes together. My husband and I squeeze into the passenger seat, and so the driver manages to pack into a normal passenger car with a four-person capacity twice that number of passengers. A particularly intrepid traveler even sits in the open trunk, true to the motto: "Better a bad ride than a good walk."

Whenever we arrive at the bank of the Río Pachitea and I see Puerto Inca on the other side of the river, I remember the many times I stopped here with my mother. But my main connection with this small city, just over ten miles from the crash site, is the story of my accident. For even though I'm known all over Peru as "Juliana, the survivor of the LANSA crash," here I'm a local celebrity. Even the ferrymen who are standing around on the riverbank waiting for customers recognize me immediately. The old man who "gets to" ferry us across beams across his whole toothless face.

It's noon now, and when we climb the concrete steps on the opposite bank to the riverside road, the sun burns down mercilessly on our heads. Though it isn't time for lunch break yet at the real estate department, the responsible official "isn't here at the moment." Will he be back later? The secretary isn't really sure. We can give it another shot after two o'clock. So we try our luck at the city hall.

And here—I'm convinced that there's no such thing as coincidences—we actually meet an old acquaintance. Don Marcio, who brought me from the jungle to Tournavista back then, is suddenly standing in front of me, aged as we all are. His features are more striking than before. He beams when he sees me. And for me, as always, it's a very touching encounter. He's doing well, the old woodsman. He has become more sedentary; after all, he turned seventy-three this year.

"Those days—those were some times," he says. "How much we experienced." And then he asks me whether I still have a copy of "my" movie. He would like to show it to his grandchildren.

Yes, the LANSA crash and the ensuing search operation were definitely a highlight in the history of the small city. Another followed when the Italian director Giuseppe Scotese made a movie of the story, partially shot on location.

There were scenes in the Pucallpa airport, Yarinacocha, La Cabaña and Puerto Inca. My part was played by the young English starlet Susan

172

Penhaligon. Some say she looks exactly like me—so much so that many people thought I was playing myself. Others assert that she doesn't have the slightest resemblance to me. That goes to show how opinions can differ. The roles of my parents were also cast with actors. Otherwise, the director worked a lot with nonprofessionals. So it happened that many people played themselves. Don Marcio participated too and took on the role of my rescuer in the movie. To this day funny stories of the filming circulate in the small jungle city. People still find especially comical a brief appearance by Pampa Hualo, a genuine local original nicknamed after a rainy-season frog.

The director Scotese also visited my father in Panguana and apparently considered shooting the relevant scenes in the original location. But then he decided against it, and our huts were re-created on the grounds of the hotel La Cabaña in Yarinacocha—in my father's view, quite poorly.

Like everyone else, I first got to see the film in 1974, when it was showing in Germany. The owner of a movie theater in Kiel invited me and my aunt to the premiere and asked me whether he could introduce me to the audience afterward. I happily accepted the invitation, but preferred to come incognito and was very nervous. In our lovely box seat, I found myself trembling and freezing during the screening. Above all, the depiction of the crash really upset me, and this is also one of the best scenes in the movie.

I can still remember well a young couple talking behind me. She said to him: "How far-fetched! That's impossible!" I almost wanted to turn around and say: "Actually, it is possible! It really happened to me!" But, of course, I remained silent.

But unfortunately, there were also a number of scenes that were rather corny. At one point the girl who's supposed to be me is cowering on a slope, utterly exhausted. It's nighttime. And suddenly a mother monkey comes along with her child, pursued by a jaguar. The mother quickly throws her little one into the girl's arms. Then she is dragged away by the feline predator. And now, of course, the girl and the little monkey cling to each other and give each other comfort. When the little monkey goes on his way in the morning, she cries desperately after him: "Don't go away! Don't leave me alone!"

What can I say? The film wasn't a masterpiece. Even though the actress who played my part was really dedicated and spared no effort, flung herself into the mud and showed intense engagement in many scenes—for long stretches, the movie is simply boring. The director sought to remain authentic, the many nonprofessional actors did their best, but on the whole the movie wasn't really convincing.

Still, here in Germany, under the sensationalistic title *A Young Girl Fights Her Way Through the Green Hell*, the movie was in theaters for twelve weeks, and in Peru and other South American countries, as *Perdida en el Infierno Verde*, still longer. In the United States, too, it came out, but under the title *Miracles Still Happen*; in contrast to the German and South American titles, which stressed the comparison of the jungle to hell, this suggested a triumphant survival tale. Nonetheless, I was ultimately informed that the film only incurred losses, and so I didn't get a penny from the worldwide earnings. The movie was also shown on television under the strangest titles. Unfortunately, I never received an official copy of the movie. Meanwhile, the director has died, and the production company was dissolved a long time ago.

What really angered my father was the fact that Susan Penhaligon also made films in which she had nude scenes. In many newspapers pictures of me in jeans and a T-shirt then appeared next to a nude picture of her. That didn't bother me personally. But many people asked me whether that was me, and whether I was really making nude films now.

According to a false newspaper item, incidentally, Susan Penhaligon supposedly died in the 1990s in an accident in the United States. That's another nice illustration of how inaccurate media reports often take on a life of their own. For even though it's not true, and the actress enjoys good health to this day, the stubborn rumor persists. It has even turned into the story that I was the one who had an accident at that time. In that case, too, many people couldn't distinguish between reality and fiction, and thought I played myself. And so amusing situations repeatedly ensued.

Once, I was driving north from Lima with Alwin Rahmel, and on the way we gave a lift to a natural scientist whose car had stalled. As chance would have it, he knew my mother. I sat in the back of the car, and Alwin carried on the conversation. The man said: "That was such a tragedy, when Maria Koepcke lost her life. But what makes me especially sad is that her daughter, who so miraculously survived the crash, later had an accident in the United States!"

Then Alwin, who has a mischievous sense of humor, asked: "You mean Juliane? Would you like to speak to her?"

The scientist gave him a dismayed sidelong glance.

"Yes," Alwin insisted, "you're really in luck today! If you would like to, you can speak to Juliane. For she's sitting right behind you."

The man was thunderstruck and could scarcely believe that I was really still alive and actually sitting with him in a car.

I often had such encounters. Once, I even had to show my passport, because the people I met at a reception simply would not believe that I'm really Juliane Koepcke. Just recently a relative of Moro's asked me to give her a current photo of myself to convince her teacher that I'm very much alive. As is typically the case with rumors, the wildest versions of my supposed accident in the United States ultimately went around. In one, I had a car accident; in another, it was a bike. And it's incredible how stubbornly people cling to these stories. Even when I'm standing in front of them, they sometimes believe the media reports more than the evidence of their eyes.

Even the people in Puerto Inca can hardly believe that after several years I've once again found my way to them. Even though I don't find anyone in the city hall to help me in the matter of Panguana, all the secretaries and employees converge, and every single one wants to have a photograph taken with me. Meanwhile, lunch hour has come, and we are happy to take a tip from a young woman who sends us to her mother's restaurant.

I'm not at all surprised that I actually know this woman from earlier days—indeed, from the time before my accident. For she once ran a hotel, the name of which was easy for me to remember. It was called La Lámpara de Aladino, Aladdin's magic lamp, after the woman's husband, who was named Aladino. Here my mother often stopped, and a few times I had accompanied her. The restaurant owner beams from ear to ear; and, of course, we not only receive an excellent lunch, but also are soon engaged in an animated conversation.

We talk—how could it be otherwise—about those days. The time my mother spent the night here and supposedly had a snake in her luggage— which I take to be another rumor, but I don't argue with the woman. Naturally, we soon come to the subject of that Christmas Day, when during a terrible storm the airplane circled over the forest and finally disappeared. Once again I listen to how strangers tell my story as if it were their own.

I can't help thinking of Werner Herzog's remark: "Your story no longer belongs to you alone. It belongs to the public." Whether I like it or not—he is undoubtedly right.

Back then, *Stern* acquired not only the film rights, but also the book rights to my story. Fortunately, all the formalities were handled by my aunt, who was an expert and whom I completely trusted. A book was actually written too. However, when I got to read the manuscript, I wasn't particularly happy with it. So it didn't bother me at all when I learned that no publisher could be found who wanted to bring out the book. At that time I already had a feeling that this is something you should actually do yourself, or in collaboration with someone you trust.

Meanwhile, complete strangers have joined us at our table, talking to me as if I were an old friend. For people here, where the search operation made so many feelings run high, it's still something like a divine sign that I alone simply fell from the sky and remained in one piece.

"You know," says a woman, only a little older than I, "that you have a home here in Puerto Inca."

I thank her. And think of our home in Munich and how long it took before I found a true home of my own after my forced departure out of Peru.

My very first home was the Humboldt House, and when that was gone, Panguana. Isn't it strange that a few Indian huts without walls could be a home? Then I realize that it's not a matter of the place: For me, home was where my parents were. But then, my mother was suddenly dead, and my father, at least for the time being, didn't want me around and found a thousand reasons to keep me away.

Instead of Panguana, I went to visit my other grandmother during that summer break in 1973, my mother's mother, in Sibichhausen on Lake Starnberg. And here I gradually got to know my mother's extended family. For me as an only child, that was something very special.

My grandmother was a lovable, cheerful and extremely gregarious person. She liked having people around, and as long as her husband, a reputable gynecologist, was alive, her house was the center of many social gatherings. In her old age it brought her immense joy in summer when as many relatives and friends as possible filled the house with life. She had a wirehaired dachshund, Anka, who unfortunately died a short time after I met her. But my aunt Hilde, my mother's sister, who was an actress in

Düsseldorf, also had a dog, named Amor, with whom I loved to play.

That was also something I missed in Germany, the fact that I got outdoors so rarely. In Peru, especially in the jungle, I had been outside constantly. Our houses didn't even have walls. Everything happened under the open sky; and here in Germany, I was always sitting indoors. Since I had so much to do for school, I didn't have many hobbies either. I didn't play a sport or get much exercise. That's why I enjoyed taking Amor for a walk to one of the bog lakes or hiking through glorious gorges to Lake Starnberg, collecting mushrooms or blueberries, or watching a little at the horse pasture just behind the house. Once, we found especially beautiful porcini mushrooms, and my grandmother went completely silent. That evening she brought me a framed picture. It was a pretty watercolor of a porcini mushroom.

"Here," she said, "I'm giving you this as a gift. Your mother made it, back before she followed your father to Peru. We were collecting mushrooms, just like you were today. And in the evening Maria said: 'Mommy, this one here you can't cut up. First I have to draw it!'"

My grandmother had tears in her eyes and turned away quickly. I looked at the study. It really had turned out particularly well. A few days after my arrival, we had visited the grave. But only now, in the face of the drawing, did I grasp how much my grandmother, too, suffered from my mother's death.

"Your grandfather wasn't thrilled at all about letting her go all by herself on that long journey. But Maria said: 'I'll follow this man anywhere. If necessary, to the end of the world.'"

My grandmother was silent. She was far away in her thoughts—I could feel that.

"To the end of the world," she repeated softly. Then she pulled herself together. She looked at me, smiling.

"Actually, I would have liked for you to live here with me," she went on. "But I recognized that it's easier for you in Kiel. It's a long way from here to the nearest school."

Then my aunt Hilde entered the room and asked cheerfully whether we didn't want to cook a mushroom dish together and invite Grandmother's friend from next door to eat with us. And that broke the spell of that moment.

It wouldn't be the last time that I visited Sibichhausen. I liked spending time with my grandmother and enjoyed the glorious weeks in the foothills of the Alps. At birthday celebrations or other occasions, I now met my eleven cousins too. I also took pleasure in visiting the family of my father's uncle, who lived in Hanover and later in Lahr, Germany.

I found it wonderful to have so many relatives, and they all warmly accepted me into the family. There were so many new things for me to experience and discover, and I postponed my plans to see Panguana again.

Thus time passed. During the day I studied diligently for my Abitur, and now and then did something with my new schoolmates. And at night I dreamed I was hurtling with insane speed, as if equipped with an engine, in a dark space, always along the wall. Or I dreamed of a deep, roaring sound, and I know that it's the turbines and we're plummeting into the abyss. For a long time these dreams were a part of me like the scars I retained from the crash. Often I'm plagued by headaches, but I accept this. What do I have to complain about? All the others are dead, so shouldn't I be able to bear a little bit of head pain? For my birthday my father sent me preserved rain forest butterflies. Another time he sent me a camera, a Minolta, which I was extremely happy about. We wrote to each other, and both of us ended most of our letters with the request: *Write back soon!*

The two years up to my Abitur went fast. I passed it with a good grade. My father could be proud of me. And as a reward he came himself. Two years and six days after my departure from Peru, I saw my father again. . . .

It's time to try our luck again with the authorities. After a long-winded good-bye, we smile one last time at the various cameras and are allowed to move on.

And lo and behold, we get lucky. We're able to take care of all our affairs. We even find in his general store the neighbor who lets his cattle graze on one of the new properties. He and Moro settle the matter, and then we can head home.

That evening we don't make it back to the village of Yuyapichis before dark. Under a sky that looks as if all you have to do is reach out your hand to grasp the stars, we cross the Río Pachitea. On the other side, below the Módena farm, the faithful Chano waits for us. Is it the exhaustion or the successful day? Is it the many memories or the warmth of the kind people? On this evening I feel almost weightless as I walk behind Moro across the pasture. The many times I walked along this path in the past merge with the present, with the future. For I know I will continue to return to Panguana countless times. Every step I take seems to me like one of those long steps that are required to fulfill my parents' legacy. But I also know that, just as I always come back, no matter what happens, just as at the end of the journey the lupuna tree is waiting for us and under it the huts of Panguana, so I will succeed in protecting this place, once and for all, and preserving it for succeeding generations.

I wonder how my father might have felt when he walked along this path for the last time back then. Was he relieved to finally leave this place, where he had been indescribably happy and later unspeakably lonely and isolated in his grief? Or did he think he would come back soon, perceiving the parting as only temporary, far too preoccupied with the preparations for the long journey? I don't know. And I think, how strange it is, and also sad, that after my stay here in Panguana directly after my accident, I was never again here with my father.

17 A Reunion and a Return

Rainforest jewel: a large Morpho butterfly, 2008.
(Photo courtesy of Juliane (Koepcke) Diller)

On April 12, 1974, I picked up my father at the airport in Hamburg-Fuhlsbüttel. We weren't alone, and maybe that's why the reunion went rather uneventfully. My aunt was there, of course, and my father's friends who had received me two years ago in Frankfurt.

Unfortunately, I have no particularly detailed memories of this reunion. I recall only that I had wanted him to bring me a fresh avocado and a mango. My father came with us to my grandmother's home in Kiel and spent one or two nights with us. Then he went to Hamburg, where he, in accordance with the agreement he had made when he received his professorship, assumed an academic post. There he initially lived in the guest room of the institute, until before long he bought a small row house on the outskirts of Hamburg.

At first he said that his presence in Germany was only temporary, and he would definitely return to Panguana. Later I learned from colleagues at the natural history museum in Lima that he had not said good-bye to anyone there. One day he was simply gone. Before anyone really knew what was going on, his post at the university was occupied by a younger colleague. Today I know that my father was at that time already working on the transformation of Panguana into a nature reserve, and even had a promising statement from the ministry of agriculture. In the early 1970s, Panguana was already supposed to be expanded about four square miles. But then, the whole matter stagnated. Reports were written and disappeared into a file, which gradually grew thicker. From Germany, my father could not really press ahead with the matter, and so it all came to nothing.

Why my father never returned to Peru—I don't know. I suspect that once in Germany, he no longer had the strength for it. Peru was the country where he had been happy with my mother. Without her it wasn't the same anymore. And everything there reminded him of her. In a letter

181

from Panguana during my first year in Germany, he had written: . . . *and in 1975 I would take a trip to Peru, mainly to visit Panguana. I cannot make any promises yet at this point, of course, but I could imagine that it would be nice if we came here together and also left again together.*

But that never came up again later, and I didn't press him about it either.

However, a different journey was coming up, a real trip across the globe. From August 12 to 19, 1974, the Sixteenth International Ornithological Congress was being held in Canberra, Australia. Anticipation for the event had already been building years before. For this long-standing conference, so important for ornithologists, has existed since 1884 and takes place once every four years (however, it was irregular in the beginning and there were missed meetings during the Second World War and its immediate aftermath, which is why this was only the sixteenth). Today I suspect that probably it was originally my mother who was planning to attend it. (After all, she was the ornithologist in the family.) But after her death it somehow went without saying that my father would travel to Australia—and I would accompany him. My Abitur over and done with, full of excitement and with a considerable amount of wanderlust in my heart, I set off on August 5, 1974, with my father. We flew via Frankfurt, Bombay and Singapore to Sydney. From there we went on to Canberra—of course, not without first taking a few excursions to the marine sandy beach and the environs of Sydney. Above all, we visited, as in all places we traveled to, the zoological and botanical gardens.

For me, Canberra was an impressive experience—and not only because of the congress, where I enthusiastically attended events and met many foreign colleagues of my mother's, but also because of the exciting, architecturally interesting city and the glorious surroundings. My father gave a talk at the conference about the birdcalls of the Peruvian rain forest. In other ways, too, this whole trip was not a vacation for him, but rather served a precise plan for his research work. For that purpose we later continued northward along the East Coast, spending five days, for example, on the forested and uninhabited Hinchinbrook Island, located east of the town of Cardwell, where we camped and recorded birdcalls. My father had in his luggage what was then a state-of-the-art tape recorder—though today it is, of course, extremely outdated and cumbersome—the Nagra III, along with a reflector. The Thyssen Foundation provided it for him, and he and my mother had used it to compile their birdcall archive in Peru. In my father's view, only in this way, recorded with the same device, could the recordings really be compared. For that is precisely what he intended to do: We were systematically seeking out rain forests in northeastern Australia, New Guinea and on various islands of Hawaii that had certain similarities with that of Panguana, in order to find or rule out parallels in the world of birdcalls. My father, who had always kept his eye on the big picture, did not want to run the risk of becoming limited as a scientist exclusively to Panguana and the form of rain forest found there.

Hinchinbrook Island has remained memorable to me, for the kind gentleman from Cardwell who arranged our supplies and provisions for the stay on the island forgot the silverware. So we carved primitive spoons with our pocketknives out of the husks of the numerous coconuts lying around. My father had always been a master at improvising. Besides that, on the very first day I sat down on my glasses and broke a lens. To top it all off, it was pouring rain, our tent wasn't leakproof, and the mosquitoes loved us.

We spent a month altogether in Australia, traveled on to New Guinea, tirelessly collected birdcalls and other data there for four weeks, until we continued via the Fiji Islands to Hawaii. Because we crossed the international date line, we experienced the day of this journey twice.

Here, on the gorgeous island of Kauai, I spent my twentieth birthday. My father surprised me with a lovingly arranged gift table, decorated with flowers and candles. He must have crept out of our shared room at night when I was already asleep to get all this. It was a really special birthday, which I will never forget. We took a taxi around the island to gain an overview, and then hiked through a subtropical forest area. It was wonderful to be traveling together. We had the same interests, and maybe my father felt during those weeks a little bit the way he used to, when he had been traveling with my mother.

This time spent so intensively together brought us close to each other again. On a trip it becomes clear whether people do well together or not, and we got along splendidly.

When we landed in Frankfurt in mid-October, I was once again on the brink of a new stage in my life: my university studies. Even though I had still been vacillating the previous year as to whether I shouldn't perhaps study literature and art instead of biology, I had decided to remain with what had been my desire from an early age: to become a zoologist like my parents. My father was really happy about that. He hoped that I would continue his work and that of my mother. And indeed, there was nothing I longed for more than to finally return to Panguana. My love for all living things, my curiosity and my astonishment in the face of the endless diversity of nature—I had felt this again distinctly during our trip—were still just as strong as they were when I was a child and had explored the mysteries of the forest with my parents. I had adjusted well to life in Germany; however, when I began my studies, it was a foregone conclusion for me that I would one day return to Peru and live there.

My first opportunity to do so was in 1977, when I had to get started on my thesis work. I needed a topic, something that had not yet been studied. What could have served this purpose better than one I could work on in Panguana?

Of course, I spoke about it with my father. My interest pleased him. The exploration of life in Panguana remained very close to his heart. My mother and he had set off in those days with the plan of developing a systematic ecological survey and as complete an inventory of species as possible. So many years later that had been accomplished only partially, so diverse is the life in this area of rain forest. Among other things, he mentioned that there had not yet been a scientific study of the camouflage coloring of the carrion- and dung-feeding butterflies, though there were most likely publications on the warning-colored moth. And I thought: *Yes, this could be something for me.* My father and other scientists had already collected a lot of butterflies in Panguana, so I wouldn't have to start from scratch. And these insects are also relatively easy to observe and attract, so that I could manage the topic within the scope of my thesis work. And so in this way, another part of the fauna at our station was explored and illuminated.

For me it was the first and very welcome opportunity to finally return to Panguana. I didn't travel alone, but set off in early August 1977 with four other students. We were a motley crew: Accompanying me were a thesis student of my father's with her husband, who were both interested in reptiles and amphibians. One of my father's doctoral students also came with us, Andreas, who today works at the Stuttgart natural history museum as a herpetologist, a specialist in amphibians and reptiles. He wrote his dissertation on the biological community of frogs in a forest pond and remained there for about a year. And finally we were accompanied by another student, who wanted to get to know the life in the Amazon Rain Forest and also to keep Andreas company.

When we arrived in Lima, there was once again a crowd of journalists waiting for me. I could hardly believe it. After all, I'd be gone for over five years and had been hoping I was long forgotten in Peru. I constantly received requests for interviews, and that really got on my nerves. For that reason I was glad when my companions and I set off toward the jungle, where I could pursue my work in peace.

How happy I was to see Panguana again. At that time we could still stay in the old main house that I had lived in with my parents, which, unfortunately, no longer exists today. It was surrounded by a work hut and a kitchen hut, and somewhat farther away there was another guesthouse. Though this house didn't have any walls, it directly abutted the jungle on one side, and here, where you were really well sheltered from wind and weather, we spent the night—on the floor, of course. There was enough space for all of us. At that time Moro and his family were still living downriver on the other side of the Yuyapichis on his farm, La Ponderosa, named after the ranch in the television series *Bonanza*. Only later did he build the house on the grounds of Panguana directly opposite the present-day guesthouses.

I spent three months altogether in Peru, one of those in Panguana. There I caught and photographed numerous butterflies, which I attracted with various types of bait. There were at that time many wild rats and mice near the houses and at the edge of the forest, above all spiny rats. Moro helped me catch them, and when animals were slaughtered, I got other meat too. These often fist-sized pieces I put out to attract the butterflies. The bait was most attractive to them when it began to rot, above all for the magnificent morphos and the mysterious, palm-sized owl butterflies, with their beautiful eyespots on the underside of their wings. Many species also liked fermenting fruits and fruit juices or dung. The most beautiful species I saw and caught in our toilet, a real outhouse. There I was unfortunately stung in the thigh one night by one of the giant ants, a one-and-a-half-inch *isula*, or bullet ant. A sting like that is extremely painful, and you feel the puncture site for several days. That's why the species is also known as "24 *horas*" ("24 hours") for that's how long you will definitely suffer.

At first my meat bait would mysteriously disappear, and I found out that it was being eaten by turtles, armadillos and other animals. Rotting meat is a genuine delicacy for turtles. What could I do about that? I wrapped the pieces of meat in wire mesh and bound them to a tree or post. Though this put a stop to the feast of the turtles, I could better observe "my" butterflies. On the riverbank I found whole clouds of glorious, richly colored yellow, white and orange butterflies, sitting on tapir dung and urine or on the excretions of spectacled caimans—always a gorgeous sight.

I still remember well how my father's thesis student and I were assailed by masses of tiny ticks one day in the forest. We had grazed a bush on which these beasts were sitting, and they completely inundated us. Nothing helped. We rushed home, tore off our clothes and removed the tiny little pests from each other with tweezers, which we plunged afterward into a candle flame to burn up the ticks.

Once the thesis student and her husband caught a forest crocodile, which she was eager to photograph. But she was bothered by her husband's hands, which were holding on to the crocodile and shouldn't be in the picture. So her husband let go of the snout and tail of the two-and-a-half-foot-long animal, and was holding on to it only by the legs. Of course, it bit deep into his arm. Luckily, the wound didn't become inflamed.

At that time there were many snakes around the houses of Panguana, and one of the neighbors was once bitten by a lance-headed viper. The thesis student gave him a large amount of snake serum so that there was a huge bump. That probably would not even have been necessary, but better safe than sorry. It was important, however, to be careful with the serum, for it could lead to anaphylactic shock if someone is allergic to it—and that can be deadly too.

In those years Yuyapichis was not yet a real village, but rather a cluster of huts on the high bank of the Río Pachitea, and during the week nothing was going on there after sundown. But on Saturdays, there was a fiesta with dancing and eating, and we liked to go there. It was a fun time, which passed too quickly, unfortunately. We girls naturally attracted attention as *gringas* and were simply idolized by the men in the village.

When I was in Lima, I stayed with my friend Edith's parents. They had a small, one-story annex in the garden, in which a room with a bathroom was always available to me. That was, of course, really pleasant. In Lima, I had also been invited to a special event during that visit to Peru, a ceremony at Ricardo Palma University. They had named the biology students' final semester "*Promoción 76B María Koepcke*" after my mother, and I was invited there as a guest of honor, which was, of course, once again all over the press. I was still constantly being asked for interviews, and my stay in Peru was intently followed and commented on in the newspaper. Above all, when I passed through Pucallpa on my journey between Lima and Panguana, my past caught up to me. The head of the local radio station had been friendly with my parents, and so I couldn't refuse to give greetings and such repeatedly on one of his programs.

On those occasions I liked to visit the kind missionaries in Yarinacocha who let me recover in their houses after my rescue. I once had a memorable experience there.

I was invited privately by one of the families of linguists to their house. It was a really nice evening, and I once again felt really secure with these people. I was struck by the way a woman I knew by sight, as I did so many others there, asked me again and again: "Are you doing well, Juliane? I mean: really well?"

"Yes," I said, now starting to get a bit irritated, "yes, I'm doing well!" Why, I wondered, was this woman insisting on this question?

When it was time to get going, she drove me to my hotel. In parting she pressed a letter into my hand.

"Please don't read it until later, when you're in your room," she said. "And don't feel obligated to answer."

I was surprised, of course. I couldn't imagine what this woman had to write to me. But as I'd promised her, I read the letter that same evening.

She was the mother of one of the boys who had stood directly in front of us in line at check-in for the LANSA plane on December 24, 1971, with whom I had joked and laughed. Like all the others, he had died. She wrote that she had long wrestled with her God over why I was allowed to survive and not her son. This question had plunged her—who, like everyone else in the mission community in Yarinacocha, had devoted her life to spreading Christianity—into a deep crisis. She had struggled until she had finally made her peace with this fate.

That night I couldn't sleep for a long time. My past had caught up to me after all the years in Kiel. Why did he have to die and not I? Why did my mother have to die, and I was allowed to live? At the natural history museum, a former colleague of my mother's, who had been close friends with her, had only recently said to me with tears in her eyes: "When we heard the news of the crash, we all said: 'If anyone survives, it will be the *doctora*. For she knows exactly how to handle herself in the jungle.' Oh well. And then it was the daughter." I know she didn't mean it that way, but her tears and that so resigned-sounding "Oh well" reawakened in me what I had felt back then with my father—the feeling that there had been some sort of mistake. That the wrong one had died. Actually, my mother should have survived the disaster. Or perhaps that boy, instead. But not I, of all people.

At that time I was twenty-three years old. The crash had been six years earlier. I was overjoyed to have returned. But for the first time, I thought about whether my father might have been right to send me to Germany. There I had gained a certain distance from the disaster. Here I was reminded of it at every turn. Still, I would come back again and again, for the rest of my life. Deep in my heart I knew that even then.

Back in Kiel, I set to work on the analysis of my investigations. My thesis work was great fun for me, and I finished my studies successfully. There was no question that I would go on to pursue a doctorate—another good opportunity to spend time in Panguana. Though I didn't know yet what I was going to work on this time, there was no better research field for me than Panguana. Despite all the sad memories associated with the place, I was always drawn back to it.

I was, incidentally, not the only one who visited my parents' research station on the bank of the Yuyapichis during those years. My father repeatedly sent thesis and doctoral students to our jungle station with topics that they could work on there. As in earlier days other scientists traveled there with my father's consent as well to complete studies already under way or to begin new ones. Moro was the one who attended to the visitors on-site, when necessary. Thus my father continued to control the fate of this spot while he found his feet in Hamburg and, to everyone's astonishment, never left. Still, he continued, of course, to take numerous excursions. Most of the time, I would then look after his small Hamburg row house. But he never went to Peru again.

188

I, however, was already looking forward to my next chance to go there. Just a year after I finished my thesis, with the title "Species-Specific Patterns of Camouflage Coloring in Carrion- and Dung-Eating Butterflies of the Peruvian Tropical Rain Forest," I traveled for four months with a few friends through the country of my birth, and had a few adventures. A trip over the Andes turned out to be particularly eventful. In a secluded area an off-road truck came toward us. One of the passengers had a handkerchief tied around his head. We stopped, and then I saw that the cloth was blood-soaked. They told us that they were Germans and had been attacked that night. It had happened near one of the copper, silver or bismuth and wolfram mines, when someone knocked on the car in the middle of the night. At first the travelers didn't want to open the doors, of course, and then machine-gun fire began pounding the car. A bullet hit the man and went straight through his neck without tearing a vein or his throat, but the blood was pouring out, nonetheless. Despite his injury, the man immediately flung himself at the wheel and drove away under continued fire.

Who the attackers had been, we didn't know at the time. Only after the terrorist movement around Abimael Guzmán Reynoso, called the *"Sendero Luminoso"*–the "Shining Path"–spread more widely and turned Peru for years into a country to which one was better off not traveling was I able to place this incident in a larger context. At the time we faced the problem that we still had to go through the exact area where the attack had occurred. I remember clearly how tense we all were, for we were driving via Tingo María to Pucallpa, a route that was especially dangerous, and were coming at night as well. The driver remarked: "If the car dies now, God have mercy on us." At the time it was strongly discouraged to pass through those inaccessible areas by car, especially traveling at night. Luckily, our vehicle did us the favor of holding out, and we made it successfully over this perilous stretch without one of the feared encounters.

It was an ominous time in Peru. In 1980, during the election year following the end of the military dictatorship, Abimael Guzmán declared an armed war on the state. In the spring his followers burned ballot boxes in a small village near Ayacucho, where the movement originated. There followed attacks on police stations and villages. Finally, at the end of 1982, the government declared a state of emergency and sent military units into the area. The ensuing violence was of a previously unknown brutality, even for Latin America. The leader of the movement, whose followers called him Presidente Gonzalo or the "Fourth Sword of the World Revolution," demanded absolute submission. He and his followers had absolutely no regard for indigenous traditions or any property or human rights. If the peasants were not willing to support the movement, then there were bloody revenge campaigns. Thus forced to support them, the peasants had to suffer as well from punishments imposed by the military, a cycle that would persist for many years.

We only perceived a distant echo of all this on our journey, for the movement initially spread across the country only slowly, but steadily. There had always been attacks in remote areas. My parents too, during a trip in the late 1950s—I was only three years old and stayed behind in the care of my aunt and grandmother in Lima—had experienced an almost deadly encounter. This one wasn't political in nature, though, but was due to a widespread superstition among the inhabitants of the Andes. My parents were backpacking by themselves in the Andes and would pitch their tent in secluded places, which usually didn't cause any problems. One day they came to a village where no one seemed to speak Spanish and apparently no European had ever passed through before. There were only women in the village. The men worked in the fields. These women thought my parents were *pishtacos*. According to folklore, those are supernatural evil spirits that appear in human form, have blond hair and carry backpacks on their backs. They come to kill people surreptitiously at night and suck out their body fat. The terrified women in the secluded village believed that my parents were such creatures. They didn't let on anything, invited the unwelcome guests into the schoolhouse and locked them in. When the men came home that evening, they appeared with pickaxes and machetes to kill my parents.

Luckily, there was also a teacher in the village who had studied in Lima and knew very well that my parents were definitely not *pishtacos*, and also meant no harm. She was just barely able to persuade the inhabitants to let them live. They were allowed to spend the night in the schoolhouse and leave the village at once, the next morning, under the suspicious glances of the people.

It wasn't so long ago, Moro confided to me, that some of the people in the area around Panguana still believed that we and our scientist guests were *pishtacos* too. To put an end to this mistaken belief, once and for all, he suggested composing a broadcast for the local radio station *"La Voz del Pachitea"* in which we would explain exactly what Panguana is and what goals we are pursuing. So I wrote a text that was read repeatedly on the radio over several weeks, and that generated a great deal of understanding for our cause. In the meantime everyone in the area knows all about our work, and Moro, who in younger days had himself been skeptical and saw the forest more as a supplier of resources, is today the best advocate for the preservation of the rain forest. From the surrounding villages school classes regularly visit, which Moro leads through the forest with contagious enthusiasm. There he explains to the children as if they were adults the peculiarities of the flora and fauna—and how important it is for them and their country to preserve them.

When I returned to Kiel in November 1980, I was greeted with sad news: My grandmother, with whom I had lived together with my aunt for so long, had died. We buried her a day after my return.

It wasn't long before I was already planning another stay in Panguana, this time lasting more than a year. I only needed a suitable topic for my dissertation, one that would allow me to return again to Panguana and that was so fascinating that I would enjoy spending several years of my life working on it.

And that's when my father came up with a suggestion that completely surprised me.

18 The Secret Soul of the Forest

Scary spirit of the night: a vampire bat in the Amazon Rain Forest.
(Photo courtesy of Juliane (Koepcke) Diller)

"What?" I ask indignantly. "Bats? You can't be serious!"

I had always wanted to work on mammals or birds, but definitely not on bats, for I found these nocturnal spirits somewhat ugly. What was appealing or interesting about them?

"Don't underestimate the bats," my father replied, smiling slightly. "They're fascinating animals, possibly even the most interesting mammals of all. And in Panguana, there's an abundance of them."

I rolled my eyes. I remembered the bats in Panguana all too well. Just thinking of the vampire bats, which drank blood from the cattle at night, made me shudder. One even bit me in my big toe once while I was sleeping, and I didn't find that funny at all.

"True," my father conceded, "they definitely aren't among the cutest animals. But just consider: You would be the first person to write about them in Panguana. And what a fascinating life-form that actually is: They're mammals and fly; they're nocturnal and orient themselves by echolocation; and their behavior patterns and ecology are really special. Just think about it."

I did so. And the longer I thought about it, the more persuasive I found my father's arguments. In particular, the diversity of their feeding habits and their choice of roosts had not been studied at all in Amazonian Peru, let alone in Panguana. And in comparison to other mammals, they could be caught relatively easily with nets or observed in their roosts.

And so I entered unknown territory and have never regretted it. There were only a few works I could consult for comparison, and they came from remote areas of Peru's neighboring countries. But who in Germany could adequately advise such a dissertation?

In Munich, there was a professor, a South America specialist, who was recommended to me from all sides: Professor Ernst Josef Fittkau. So I went there and presented my project proposal to him, and he accepted me as a doctoral student. The next years of my life were now predetermined: I would go to Panguana for at least a year and devote myself to the fluttering nocturnal spirits, and would then write my dissertation in Munich.

So it happened that almost nine years after my arrival in Kiel, I pulled up stakes at my aunt's place, packed my things in boxes and put them in temporary storage. For after my return from Peru, I wanted to move directly to Munich. Sitting in the plane to Lima in August 1981, I felt a great euphoria. I had finished my Abitur and thesis. Now I would write my dissertation, and then I would be free to decide what to make of my life and where to live.

The first weeks in Panguana, I had company. An assistant professor at the university in Kiel, named Michael, was researching leaf-miner flies and had already gone to Peru a month earlier to get to know the country and people. Unfortunately, Michael was one of those people who seem to attract bad luck irresistibly. During his journey through Peru, he was robbed three times, and a bus he was on suffered an axle fracture. While he was spending the night in an Indian hut in the High Andes, he was actually peed on by a rat. On top of that, he got dysentery, which gave him horrible diarrhea, and he lost at least thirty pounds. When I met Michael in Lima, I scarcely recognized him: He was terribly emaciated and had grown a full beard. While I was flying to Yuyapichis on the plane, he had set off from Pucallpa a few days earlier by boat, taking along our luggage and a tank of kerosene for our new refrigerator, during the acquisition of which he had almost driven me crazy. For it had to be sealed absolutely tight, which is an enormous demand in Peru. But with much patience he had actually found the "perfect tank" and was very happy—and I was too, of course.

Before his departure he also bought eight gigantic watermelons. I smiled at that, because I found this rather excessive for the two-day boat trip. There wasn't unlimited space on those boats. You had to somehow make yourself comfortable on the cargo consisting of cartons, barrels, boxes and possibly various machines too, and that was mostly an uncomfortable undertaking. But it's true that there was nothing to eat. A day after the departure, Michael's boat had engine trouble, and he had to spend several days with the other passengers on the bank of the Río Pachitea until the boat could get going again. Then, of course, the melons were right on cue, and his fellow passengers also benefited from Michael's foresight.

In Panguana, he once fell down a slope, and another time he got a huge load of bird droppings on his head. That time he had been investigating particularly interesting flies on a large glob, and hadn't been aware that its source was nearby—to be precise, directly above him. It was a boatbill, a large heron. Luckily, none of this led to anything worse. It was just a funny series of mishaps, and we laughed a lot together. Incidentally, Michael baked excellent bread in a cooking pot in the ashes of our fireplace, and he was, like many others, excited by the immense diversity of species in Panguana, especially among the grass flies he specialized in. Unfortunately, he soon left. And I devoted myself entirely to my bats. That meant that I had to adapt my rhythm to theirs. During the day I looked for sleeping quarters, climbed into hollow trees or under banks, and night after night I went into the forest in order to set up and check my traps in the proper places. On one of those dark nights, I saw an ocelot. People encounter these nocturnal loners extremely rarely, and I consider myself lucky that our paths didn't cross.

Another time I heard approaching footsteps, indicating that a larger animal was moving toward me. I stayed completely still and waited. Then a tapir suddenly came out of the bushes and stopped directly in front of me. With its snout it sniffed me, apparently just as astonished as I was. It was probably wondering what sort of strange animal I was. For a long time I didn't dare to move, for I knew that these animals can become unpleasant, especially when they have young. Finally I cleared my throat—and the tapir turned around and disappeared again. And the next night, returning to Panguana from a party in Yuyapichis, I had a still more incredible encounter. I was carrying a carton on my head and feeling my way more than I could see it, for my flashlight battery was almost dead. I deviated a bit from the path in the darkness and ended up at the slope leading down to the river. And there something suddenly growled very deeply and resonantly next to me, like a very large dog and yet somehow different. I shone my flashlight into a small hollow below me, but couldn't make anything out in the dim light. Then there was that sound again, deep and rolling, so that I thought: *I have to get out of here.* The next day I found out that it must have been a jaguar, for a torn-open calf was found in that spot. Apparently, I had disturbed it while eating. If my flashlight had been stronger, I might well have shone it directly into its face.

I grew accustomed to being out mainly at night. Before dawn I was again on my feet, for I had to fold up the bat nets before the birds awoke and could get caught in them. The woodcreepers are awake especially early, and I didn't want the poor animals with their arrow-shaped tongues to get tangled in a net. In those early-morning hours, the ground fog creates a unique atmosphere, for it lies like a white sheet over Moro's pastures and fields. It can get pretty cold and the moisture can get unpleasant. At 100 percent air humidity, the dew falls like rain on the trees.

I could observe many bats at particular clay licks, or *colpas*. These are areas at forest springs or on riverbanks that contain especially mineral-rich earth, an important food supplement for numerous birds and mammals. I had found one of these *colpas*, where bats flocked to drink. I asked Moro to build me a sort of raised platform there so that I could better observe the animals. There were also swarms of mosquitoes, however, and I had to think of my mother, who had such discipline. She managed not to move, even if the sweat was running into her eyes.

On especially dark and soundless nights, I could sometimes hear deep inside the jungle a series of thin, high, almost disembodied whistles, which wafted through the silence as if they were not of this world. They came from the Tunshi, which frightened me as a child in Lima, until Alida came and calmed me down. The fact that I was now hearing those distinctive sounds in the middle of the jungle, all by myself, able to see something only in the beam of my flashlight, was also eerie for me as an adult. No wonder the Tunshi is regarded in Amazonian Peru and in the neighboring countries as a jungle spirit that can be heard only on the darkest, grimmest nights. According to folklore, it is a sad, wandering soul that finds no peace. According to other legends, however, the Tunshi is also a guardian of the forest, for it will do something only to those who harm the forest, chop it down or kill its animals. It can make people deaf or blind and also bring madness or even death. But in reality, it's a perfectly harmless little cuckoo that can almost never be glimpsed. Still, due to its soundlessness and the especially dark nights when it calls, it always affected me strangely.

Most of what I learned about bats was through personal experience on countless nights. To begin with, I learned that though there are especially ugly species with senile grimaces and protruding eyes or, among the vampires, with tiny eyes and sharp fangs, there are also strikingly pretty ones, with colorfully marked fox faces or interesting fur coloring. As a small child I already approached all kinds of animals and wanted to touch them, whether they were small or large, dangerous or safe, pretty or ugly. I once pet a black jaguar through the bars in a zoo. My mother was terribly frightened when she noticed that.

In the case of the bats, the wonderfully soft fur was a completely new and pleasant experience for me. I liked to pet them, which the little guys, of course, couldn't stand. In the beginning they were constantly biting me, but I learned how to let the animals out of the special bird and bat nets, which were known as Japan nets, without making the acquaintance of their powerful fangs all too often. Large nocturnal wasps got caught in the nets too, whose stings were incredibly painful, and sometimes birds of prey that wanted to eat the bats. Once a tapir even marched literally through the net, without regard to losses. There wasn't much left of my Japan net after that. Incidentally, with their sharp fangs and powerful jaws, bats penetrate even the thickest gloves. And once they've sunk their teeth in, that's when they really hold on tight and bite down even more forcefully. So I learned how I had to hold them so that they couldn't get me: I put my middle finger on their back and pressed the two wings back with index finger and thumb. Since bats have a rather thick neck musculature, they cannot turn their heads far enough to snap behind them.

Once, I was bitten by a vampire bat. I learned some things from that, such as the fact that Dracula is always portrayed falsely: It is their incisors, and not the canines, that are so razor-sharp that they pierce the skin without causing pain. The secret is that their saliva contains a painkilling substance, as well as another one that prevents blood clotting, so that the blood flows heavily and can be licked off by them, without the victim waking up. There are three vampire bat species. One is the "common vampire bat," which feeds on the blood of various mammals. The two others, however, drink only the blood of birds. These species also invade chicken coops and bite the fowl in the soft skin at the start of the thigh plumage above the legs, which are horny. Unlike their colleagues that don't drink blood, vampires stalk their prey by walking on the ground. That works because they can fold their wing skin in such a way that the arm bones are like sticks. Then they walk, as it were, on the base of their palms, where the thumb sticks out.

I have never been able to observe this, for vampires are very shy and only active in the darkest hours of the night, but there are excellent films about it.

It didn't take long before I was completely fascinated with the bats that I had originally found so repulsive. And my fascination persists to this day. There are so many aspects of these secret nocturnal animals that are extremely exciting. For example, the vampires are especially social animals. They live in close-knit family groups, engage in mutual grooming and have nursery roosts in which the mothers look after the young of other vampire females when these go foraging. But dealing with them is not without its dangers, for vampire bats transmit rabies and other viruses. For that reason I had myself vaccinated against rabies in Germany beforehand. The third booster dose I had to give myself in the behind. It's a strange feeling when you have to give yourself an injection. But after the doctor explained it to me, it was quite easy.

The calls of bats are largely in the ultrasonic region and are inaudible to our ears. With a special device, the "bat detector," you can record them and learn to tell them apart. But these animals also have communication calls that are audible to us, and over time I got to know this spectrum quite well. It was a really special experience to hear the calls of the large leaf-nosed bats on the flowers of the balsa trees near the river during the dry season and to observe them eating the pollen from the gigantic cream-colored calyces. Other bats flocked around the large fig trees, of which there were several species in Panguana. Along with cecropia fruits, the figs of these trees, unpalatable for people, are an important source of nutrition for many fruit-eating bat species. I was really impressed by the social behavior of a bat species whose males maintain the mood of their harems with songs, dances and scent signals, which they emit from pockets in the skin on the arm bone. What lengths they will go to for the lovely female!

Ultimately I counted fifty-two different bat species. Today we know that there is a total of at least fifty-three. That is quite a lot for the area of Panguana, which was then less than one square mile, if you consider that there are only twenty-seven species in all of Europe.

Later my bat detector was stolen directly from my suitcase at the Lima airport, when I was standing in line to fly back to Germany. The suitcase was too full and slightly open on one side – that had been enough for the thief. Undoubtedly, he wasn't too pleased with the device, for it produced only static, and he surely had no use for bat calls. So it was tough luck for both of us, the thief and me.

After Michael's departure I soon had company again. Manfred, an Austrian doctoral student who had found out about Panguana from my father, was studying aspects of the reproductive biology of the frog species at the large forest pond on which Andreas had already worked, and stayed for a whole year. I got along well with him too. We shared the house—it was a new one by then, for my parents' house had unfortunately collapsed, as had our former work hut and the original kitchen hut. The new house had no walls, and we slept on the floor on mattresses with mosquito nets, each in one of the corners facing the forest, so that we didn't get wet even during storms, which mostly come from the river-facing side. I made myself comfortable all the way in the back, screened by two bookshelves. Later I moved into the attic of our palm-branch-thatched house, where it was especially cozy when it rained and I could fall asleep wonderfully to the regular rushing sound directly above me. Most of the time I came out of the forest after midnight or around two in the morning, bathed in the river and then went to bed, but never without first reading something by candlelight.

Manfred, too, was out in the dark, for most of the frogs at the pond are nocturnal as well. But Manfred and I went our separate ways in accordance with our work. During the day we reviewed what we had observed and collected at night, kept diaries and compiled data. I caught bats, which I carefully placed individually in cloth bags and mostly released where I had captured them. I also collected their excrement, to determine their diet, as well as the louse flies from their fur. For bat louse flies are special parasites, which I wanted to take into account in my dissertation as well.

Cooking was also among our daily tasks. I always had to start on that in the morning, for it took a long time on the log fire before everything was ready. In the evening we contributed the leftovers from our lunch to the shared dinner in a cozy circle at the home of Moro's mother Doña Lida, a strong-willed, capable and warm woman who to this day remains an institution in the Módena family. She supported us energetically, welcomed me with open arms and took care of the people in Panguana when we weren't there. She and Panguana are inseparably bound to each other, and I fondly call her my "aunt" to this day. At that time she was living with parts of Moro's family close to our station house, while Moro still dwelled on the Ponderosa on the other side of the Yuyapichis.

At that time I found Panguana particularly beautiful, more beautiful than ever. There were many animals, bats too, that can be seen only rarely nowadays. I loved the moonlit nights filled with an extraordinary, ivory-colored light, and the glorious starry sky, which can be admired in all its magnificence only in areas where there is no electric light. Especially impressive in Panguana still today is the bright, broad band of the Milky Way, which we often cannot even vaguely discern in Germany due to the illumination of cities.

Soon I moved on those bright moonlit nights as confidently as during the day. And once that was almost my undoing. I was returning home from one of my expeditions and turned off the flashlight when I emerged from the forest, so bright did I find the moonlight. Suddenly something reared up before me. It was a lance-headed viper, so close that it could have bitten me. I froze, and that was instinctively exactly the right reaction during such a confrontation. You have to stand completely still, and then the snake won't perceive any movement. I had been careless. We actually knew that it was there, for lance-headed vipers are faithful to one place, and I hadn't thought of that due to the moonlight. Now it was angry. Once I pulled myself together, I retreated slowly and deliberately. Then it disappeared without a sound into the forest.

That was, incidentally, not my first encounter with a lance-headed viper. In 1969, when I was living with my parents in the jungle, it had already almost happened. Back then, I wanted to catch a frog for my terrarium. On my knees I was following it slowly around a small understory palm when I suddenly saw a movement out of the corner of my eye—it was a lance-headed viper, about six inches away from my nose. It was already darting its tongue aggressively and could almost have bitten me in the face. That could have had a deadly outcome.

Of course, life in Panguana—and this was true back then, still more than today—is a life with great restrictions. We did our laundry by hand in the river, which was rather difficult, especially during the rainy season. Then everything stayed damp and clammy, the laundry began to get moldy, and Manfred and I got fungal infections between our toes, because we almost always had to wear rubber boots in the completely sodden and flooded forest. The Yuyapichis was often swollen and became cold and muddy. Then the daily bath was often hard or sometimes impossible. And lo and behold, things worked out nonetheless.

In Yuyapichis, Manfred and I were soon acquainted with everyone and felt at home. In the jungle, birthdays are lavishly celebrated, and we attended most of them. In Yuyapichis and the neighboring villages there would be a *pachamanca*, which is always a festive occasion. The word *"pachamanca"* comes from Quechua and means "earthen pot meal." You dig a hole, cover the ground with stones heated over the fire, pile on them various types of marinated meat, herbs and vegetables, with banana leaves between them, and then close the pit again. Depending on the size of the *pachamanca*, it then takes one or two hours before the whole thing is done and opened with the participation of everyone present. Moro was a great *pachamanquero* and had mastered cooking in the earthen hole perfectly. Thus he was always being asked to prepare a *pachamanca* at large festivities. When my birthday was approaching, we decided to celebrate it in the village of Yanayaquillo with Moro's parents-in-law. Moro and his two families prepared a raucous party for me with a gigantic *pachamanca* and dancing until five in the morning, to which people came not only from Yuyapichis and Yanayaquillo, but also from the whole surrounding area, emptying over one hundred crates of beer. One of the pilots from the bush airline stopped by, too, and replenished the beer supply. Since the birthday girl or boy is traditionally responsible for food and drink, this tore a deep hole in my student funds, but that didn't bother me. Everyone was happy, especially me.

Since that time the Módenas have treated me as a member of the family. From all of them I learned a great deal about the inhabitants of the jungle and how they live. I was already familiar with the rain forest and had, after all, held out for eleven days in it on my own, and yet only now did my knowledge deepen. I learned how to cook Peruvian cuisine in the native fashion with the products of the forest and fields. That was not only extremely exciting, but also practical and cheaper than bringing things from Pucallpa all the time. Of course, that was still necessary too, now and then, and I enjoyed the required trips to the city. In those days Pucallpa was not yet the roaring inferno that it is today, for there weren't any *motocars*. On the other hand, the roads had not been asphalted yet either, and in the rainy season they became so muddy that you were constantly slipping and your shoes became a couple pounds heavier due to lumps of mud sticking to them. Here I stayed with Moro's oldest sister, Luz, whose husband worked at the petroleum company Petroperú and had a beautiful house, which even had air-conditioning. On later occasions friends of my parents took me in. They were the Escalante sisters, whose brother is a cloth merchant and used to own an airplane for flights in the jungle. To this day I visit the sisters when I come to Pucallpa.

Most of the time I went by myself to Pucallpa and a few times to Lima. My friend Edith got married and, obviously, I couldn't miss that. To extend my stay in Peru after six months, I even had to travel to Tumbes on the Ecuadorian border. Here I briefly crossed the border and then came right back—for I needed only the entry stamp on my passport. But I was always glad to return to the jungle.

Considering how difficult it is still today to reach Panguana, it is easy to imagine the patience and adventurousness it required in those days to travel from there to Pucallpa or even Lima. At that time there was a great number of small airlines, some private, which offered connecting flights in the jungle, often under the most adventurous circumstances. Today I am full of amazement about how undauntedly I boarded these rattletraps after my crash experience. I was seemingly fearless. There was a fifty-minute flight, with a single-engine Cessna, between Pucallpa and the village of Yuyapichis; without batting an eyelash, I got on it.

I still remember well a return flight that was so bumpy that the pilot was constantly crossing himself. He had not yet landed in Yuyapichis and asked his small crew—that is, us—whether we really had to land there or might not rather land in Puerto Inca. There was a real runway there; whereas in Yuyapichis, he had to land on a pasture. It had happened before that a Cessna collided while landing with a cow or a horse that had not gotten out of the way in time. As a result the pilot was sweating blood. But we all insisted on Yuyapichis, for no one wanted to spend an eternity in Puerto Inca, waiting for a lift. During the entire flight a woman was clinging with both hands to my pants, and a little girl was continually vomiting on the floor. When the airplane was finally on solid ground, and only just came to a stop at the end of the pasture, the pilot was such a nervous wreck that he threw us out right where we were and said he was not going another inch—all he wanted was to go home. I couldn't help laughing, even though I was the one who would have had the most reason to be afraid.

Another time I flew on a Spanish plane, an Aviocar, a very strange, broad propeller plane in which about twenty people fit. Inside we sat on wooden benches with our backs to the outer wall. In the center aisle were pigs, which immediately got sick, even before the flight really got under way. The passengers threw bundles of living chickens bound together at the legs onto the open overhead compartments. There were no seat belts, of course. During the flight a sort of airplane conductor went around, collected the fare and, as in a streetcar, pressed a stub into our hands. Next to me sat a woman who told me: "You know, I prefer flying to taking a boat. Because I can't swim." I thought that was a really funny thing to say, because she couldn't fly either, after all, if something were to go wrong. It was better not to tell her what had happened to me.

Why all that amused me at the time more than it frightened me, while today flying is never so easy for me—I have no idea. Maybe in your twenties you're simply more carefree than in later years. In any case, during this so intensive time in the Peruvian jungle, I adjusted completely to life there. Though I already had learned the Spanish language as a child, I perfected it only now and even dreamed in Spanish. My love of Peru and the rain forest, which had always existed, now grew deeper and fuller. In the past I had always been in Panguana only with my parents. Our small family formed a perfect unit. Though our contact with our neighbors was extremely friendly, it remained sporadic. And I had been only fourteen years old back then and had seen my environment with the eyes of an adolescent.

As far as our cuisine was concerned, it was quite simple and far from as varied as what I now learned from Doña Lida. When it came time for the slaughter, Manfred and I were always present and helped the neighbors, and I learned fast how to carve the animals and make use of them and which delicacies could be conjured in the Peruvian fashion from different parts of pigs and calves, as well as chickens, ducks and the fish of the river. There was also a lot of game and native fruits from palms and various forest trees. Now and then Doña Lida even prepared for us the great bullfrogs, turtles and beetle grubs in the style of the natives. Here I learned how to cook or smoke caiman tails, armadillos and possums, and I was astonished that ultimately even marsupials can actually be eaten, even though they stink so terrible. From her and Moro, I also learned about what natural medicines the jungle provides, which tree saps could be used for what. There are lianas, for example, that you cut when you have a toothache, for they contain clove oil, a bloodred resin that heals wounds and much more. In this way I became familiar with the customs of the country and tried everything that I would never have eaten otherwise. Of course, today I would strictly refuse to eat many of those meals for nature conservation reasons, but at that time everything was fascinating for me. I wanted to live just as the neighbors did, and often I was simply curious.

Moro's mother trained me not only in the cuisine of the Indians, but also in that of the people of German origin from the mountain forests of Pozuzo, where she was from. There was, for example, a strudel made of bananas and raisins, a *sopa de knédales*, a *Knödel*—or dumpling—soup, with manioc, corn and all sorts of other ingredients. But such meals were only prepared when Moro's sisters came to visit from Lima. Then Doña Lida cooked still more elaborately than usual. Of course, very special occasions were Christmas and Easter and also the Nativity of St. John the Baptist, San Juán, on June 24, for the solstice has its own tradition in the jungle. Then every self-respecting housewife prepares *juanes*—small pouches of banana leaves with a mixture of turmeric rice, with braised pieces of chicken, black olives and hard-boiled eggs. This is a typical jungle meal that is not even known on the coast. In Germany, I later had to readjust to the electric stove, for I found cooking on the woodstove or on an open flame much simpler.

I still remember well how my dissertation adviser, Professor Fittkau, visited me in Panguana, accompanied by two German colleagues. That was very exciting for me, of course, but also enormously important. I had realized, meanwhile, that with the manifold material I had gathered, I could not only fill a dissertation, but also spend my whole life. He not only helped me sensibly narrow down my topic, but he also made himself tremendously useful getting fires started, for the wood was sometimes damp and hard to get burning. Here Professor Fittkau turned out to be a person with extraordinary endurance. Standing in the middle of the acrid smoke, he fanned the smoldering embers with the lid of a pot without complaint until finally a decent fire emerged. He also impressed me by going into the forest without hesitation in the pouring rain to search in the streams for the midge larvae he was working on. To get hold of a tree cactus—he collected and grew cacti at home—he didn't shy away from climbing around on dangerously rotten branches over streams and ponds. That was something he had in common with my parents: When he wanted to achieve something, there was no going back. On such trips he was game for anything.

Alongside his teaching, Ernst Josef Fittkau was also director of the Bavarian State Collection of Zoology in Munich. And so it happened that a small team of researchers from there visited us in our seclusion a few months later. Apart from that, and from the surprise ambush by a group of English journalists who simply showed up, stayed with us for a week and annoyed me with their questions, it was very quiet all year. And I enjoyed the contact with the locals—Moro's family most of all, of course. Over time I even took on the singsong of the jungle Spanish, without realizing it. On the coast I was teased for it and sometimes called *"charapita,"* an affectionate colloquial term for little indigenous Amazonian girls.

I wouldn't have wanted to miss any of these experiences. Sometimes I even think with a certain wistfulness of those months, which count among the most wonderful of my life to this day.

And my awe of the rain forest habitat truly developed only then, during my studies for my dissertation. Previously I had found all that interesting, new and beautiful, but now I realized that I had still lacked a deeper access to this world. As an adolescent I had marveled at everything with great pleasure, and yet in those days I was a mere observer and "appendage" of my parents. I accompanied them all the time, but remained passive myself. Only during my dissertation work did I put all my soul and energy into the exploration of nature around Panguana. Here I found time to reflect on the rain forest and its structure. And gradually I had the peculiar feeling that the green cosmos was only now truly allowing me to penetrate its secrets. And it really is a phenomenon: For at first glance you think you cannot see anything at all in this forest—many people experience that when they first set foot in the jungle. All around you are countless thriving green plants, nothing more, for the numerous animals have adapted perfectly to their surroundings. There are fingernail-sized frogs sitting on a leaf from which their coloring scarcely differs, and you can stare at this leaf for a long time without noticing them at all. Many grasshoppers, bugs or spiders seem to virtually merge with the bark of a tree or with the branches. Snakes lying motionlessly in tree branches can easily be mistaken for a twig or "disappear" perfectly in the leaves on the ground. Anyone who is unfamiliar with the jungle simply doesn't see such subtleties. But once you get into this world, it is like gradually learning a whole new way of seeing. It is as if a veil has been lifted from your eyes, and you realize that you are surrounded by multitudinous life. This abundance can definitely be overpowering, in the truest sense of the word.

Today I know that my parents, too, especially my mother, felt this intensely. For now I, too, took in the forest with all my senses, the endless diversity of the vegetation and wildlife and their adaptations, nature's incredible play of colors, which often lies in tiny details and nuances, the sounds that sometimes enveloped me like a cloak and that always give me pleasure to this day, the smells, the green and yellow twilight, the warm dampness of the forest. And then I feel as if I were plunging into the energy of a powerful, all-embracing living thing, so intimate by now, and yet always unfamiliar in new ways. And it is precisely this constant rediscovery that we scientists find so extremely fascinating about the tropical rain forest habitat—and this is especially true in Panguana, which we have been exploring for forty years and still do not fully grasp.

It is this secret soul of the jungle, the same forest that helped me return to human life after my accident, which only now, during my one-and-a-half-year research project, reveals itself to me. Only then did I truly understand the life task I decided to take on in the distraught and so boundlessly lonely rainy jungle nights after my crash. Back then, I had resolved that if I could keep my life, I would devote it to a meaningful cause, a task serving nature and humanity. Now, having returned to the station as an adult and fulfilling a research assignment of my own, which I assigned to myself without my parents, everything was suddenly completely clear: My task has a name. And it is Panguana.

19 Keeping an Eye Fixed on the Future

Symbol of a dream: the majestic, sacred lupuna tree of Panguana watches over the field station in the Amazon, 2008. (Photo courtesy of Juliane (Koepcke) Diller)

In February 1983, one and a half years after I had set off, I returned to Germany. I had spent most of that time in the jungle. Those months were enormously important for me. I had returned as an adult to the place where my life had taken such a decisive turn. I had worked as a researcher myself and discovered in my own, personal way the Amazon Rain Forest habitat. More than a decade after my miraculous struggle for survival in the jungle, I had gained a still deeper connection to it. If my eleven-day trek after the crash had been some sort of initiation, during which I already had an intimation that my life was bound to that of the jungle in a mysterious way, those eighteen months during my studies of the bats offered me conscious, adult insight into some of its secrets.

In Germany, a move and a new beginning were waiting for me. My time in Kiel was over, my belongings packed in boxes, and now I took them and my newly gathered experiences and moved to Munich, where my dissertation adviser taught. At first I lived with my grandmother in Sibichhausen, where I had already spent so many wonderful vacation weeks. But the distance from the Munich city center was too far, and so I soon looked for a small apartment of my own in Neuhausen.

I took the necessary subjects at the Ludwig Maximilian University for my doctorate. Parallel to that, I was able to work part-time at the State Collection of Zoology, as well as analyze the wealth of material I had gathered in Panguana.

Here I met many colleagues, and among them was one who courted me especially charmingly. He was working on parasitic ichneumon wasps, always had advice when I needed him, and best of all: He always made me laugh. He liked to treat me to meals, we discovered that we had a lot in common, and before we knew it, we had fallen in love.

The year after my return, I realized that I had to go to Panguana again to complete my observations, and during those three months in the summer of 1984, Erich sent me wonderful letters in Peru. When I was in Munich in September, right on time for the beginning of the lectures, we saw each other even more frequently—due to my work at the State Collection of Zoology, often even daily.

It would take another three years before my dissertation, entitled "Ecological Separation of Bat Species in the Tropical Lowland Rain Forest of Peru," and its oral defense were finished. As chance would have it, there was an opening for a library director at the State Collection of Zoology. Since this position corresponded to my interests and qualifications, I applied for it. As a great lover of books, I work to this day in that unique zoological library, which ranks among the largest of its type in Europe, and here find the perfect balance to my commitment to Panguana.

In 1989, Erich and I got married in Aufkirchen, where my mother officially lies buried. My husband was interested from the beginning in Peru, and above all, of course, in Panguana, but he had not yet had an opportunity to travel there himself. And now, of all times, it became difficult, if not impossible. For in recent years the terror of the *Sendero Luminoso*, whose first excesses I had already encountered during my 1980 trip, had turned Peru into a country full of chaos and violence. Though it was relatively safe in Lima, traveling into the heart of the country was emphatically discouraged. Too many locals, but also foreigners, tourists as well as scientists, had been brutally massacred.

In those years we would without question have lost Panguana, if Moro had not worked in an extraordinary way for the preservation of the research station. Just as I did, he saw in it a sort of legacy that had been entrusted to him and felt the desire and the duty to maintain what my parents had begun there so many years ago. Meanwhile, with my father's consent, he had moved onto the grounds of Panguana. In this way he could better lend his support when necessary to the scientific guests my father permitted to visit and use the research station. After my father had returned to Germany, he stayed in regular contact with Moro, gave him orders by letter and remunerated him for his work. But now, difficult times were beginning for people in Peru and for Panguana as well.

210

The *Sendero Luminoso* itself did not come as far as the Yuyapichis, but a different movement did, which took its name from an Inca successor executed by the Spanish occupiers: *"Movimiento Revolucionario Túpac Amaru."* Though this movement distanced itself emphatically from the *Sendero Luminoso* and officially supported the rights of the indigenous population, it nonetheless did not shy away from bloody revenge campaigns against the tribe of the Asháninka Indians, who were supposedly traitors to the cause. And since Panguana was in the traditional area of the Asháninka, it was, of course, also affected by those confrontations. The members of *Túpac Amaru* collected dues from the inhabitants of the rain forest, east of the Andes, and threatened many people, also in Puerto Inca and the other small surrounding jungle towns. There were many deaths, and for one and a half years their representatives were also based in the village of Yuyapichis, where they made life hard for the locals. That Moro managed in those difficult times to protect the forest area of Panguana and to prevent anyone else from taking possession of it—for that, I will always be grateful to him and his family.

During my stay in Peru for my dissertation work, I had tried to resume my father's efforts to declare Panguana a nature reserve, but without success. Still, I managed at that time to obtain from the local authorities a first option on the site. My parents had actually purchased the land lawfully from the previous owner, even though it was without official papers. But no one else in the region could produce official documents about this area either. And now suddenly it was said that all properties belonged to the state, and one could only acquire them if one used them for agriculture.

So Moro and I considered whether it would make sense to plant cocoa in a small section of the secondary forest. Fortunately, it didn't come to that. Toward the end of the 1980s, it reached the point where the whole area was parceled, and state surveying engineers newly divided the land. I couldn't come to Peru at the time, for the journey was too dangerous due to the *Sendero Luminoso.* On top of that, I was in the middle of my dissertation. What could we do now to ensure Panguana's survival?

In this critical situation Moro's wife, Nery, declared herself willing to have grounds of Panguana temporarily signed over to her name so that they would be secure. For some neighbors had already been casting covetous glances at the forest, knowing as they did what a rich stock of precious timber Panguana boasts. But our friends defended the valuable trees, above all our glorious lupuna tree, if necessary even "with tooth and nail." At the time Moro got a lot of trouble from the neighbors, who didn't understand why this guy was guarding a forest in this way for faraway Germans, instead of chopping it down, selling the valuable wood and turning the land into pastures. But Moro had meanwhile grasped what Panguana is about. Today it is certain: Without him and his whole family, Panguana would no longer exist.

The years passed, a trip to Peru was out of the question, and so Munich became the center of my and my husband's life. We took vacations such as I had scarcely known before then: to Italy, Greece and Spain. I discovered Europe, so to speak, only now, and enjoyed that very much. At that time, during which I increasingly shied away from press inquiries and gave no interviews, when there was nothing I wanted less than to tell the story of my plane crash, over and over again, I was often overcome with a great longing for the country of my birth, but I put that off until later. I was doing well. I finally had a home, which was fundamentally different from the one I had once had in the jungle. Only the exuberant abundance of plants on our roof terrace hinted at where my heart still secretly belonged. A Polish handyman, who once had something to repair on the roof, was amazed by the lush greenery and spoke to the landlord about it. Afterward, he said extremely sympathetically to my husband: "I know, I know: wife crashed—needs jungle."

It was ultimately the phone call from Werner Herzog that prompted me, after a fourteen-year interval, to return to the rain forest and Panguana. I have already described the significant role this trip played in working through my accident. A second, no less important aspect was that I finally saw Panguana, Moro and his family again. It became clear to me that the time had come for me to assume responsibility for the research station, the forest and its inhabitants. That had remained first and foremost the cause of my father, who had meanwhile reached the ripe old age of eighty-four. He still attended to all matters, wrote detailed letters to Moro in which he addressed him, as he had over all the previous years, as "señor"–in the end, at some point, as "estimado amigo," meaning "esteemed friend." My father continued to advise students and doctoral candidates when they were interested in a topic that had to do with Panguana. And he still had research results to review and analyze from his time in Peru. During his retirement he still visited once a week the institute of zoology in Hamburg, where he offered his services to the reptile section.

He still had so many plans. Alongside a book about the forms of human life, about which he had already been speaking when I was still a teenager, he had also begun to write his life story. Unfortunately, he only got to the first chapters, and the unfinished manuscript breaks off, of all places, shortly before his departure for Peru. In the middle of these various projects, he was surprised by a severe illness, which would lead to his death in the year 2000.

After that, I decided to take up my parents' legacy and enable the studies that had been begun such a long time ago to be carried on. It was a great help that my husband supported me in this from the beginning. Ever since he had come for the first time during the filming of Werner Herzog's documentary to the place that had so decisively shaped my life, and was also responsible for my survival after the crash, he, too, had been seized by enthusiasm for this spot.

As a first step we officially appointed Moro as administrator and my local representative and put that in writing. In this way he has an entirely different status with neighbors and authorities and can represent Panguana's cause still better than he already did, anyhow, all those years without an official mandate. For my parents' motivation for exploring the forest without exploiting it was still completely foreign to many locals. Meanwhile, Moro's work has borne fruit. And of course a rethinking has taken place in Peru as well over the past thirty years. Nowadays the schools offer the subject *educación ambiental* (environmental education) and in this connection teachers often visit us with their classes. Slowly, but surely, the thought is beginning to catch on that it is perhaps not such a good idea to chop down the rain forest so as to raise cattle on pastures, which don't even thrive there. Meanwhile, there are already even reforestation programs and environmental specialists to ensure that not everything is destroyed.

The village council of Yuyapichis visited us too and wanted to become informed on-site about what we do there. They were really taken with what they saw and also learned what Moro is accomplishing there. Meanwhile, Moro has turned out to be an outstanding guide in the jungle. He has not only been acquainted since his early childhood with all the animals and plants, but in the meantime he has also embraced the idea of nature conservation. How delighted I am when I witness for the first time how enthusiastically and thrillingly he is able to explain the forest to the children. Meanwhile, it has also become a tradition that every time a group of scientists comes to Panguana, the schools send a class to learn about what the people from Europe and other parts of the world are actually doing here.

This understanding among the local population and the acceptance of our neighbors are enormously important for our work. For what good does it do if we create a tiny idyllic spot in Panguana, but all around it the rain forest is destroyed?

To truly stop this development, I realized quite early on, we require allies—and in Peru as much as in Europe. We need resources that far exceed my private possibilities. That became clear to me at the latest when I got to see the long-since mothballed files at the ministry of agriculture. They had been created in the 1970s when my father had already begun pursuing this goal.

A main argument of the assessment against a nature reserve was that Panguana was too small, so we had to enlarge it, acquire land, expand the research station. For that, we needed money that I could not muster privately. There seemed to be no solution in sight.

Then, as often in my life, a wonderful chance opened up as if on its own. Through an article on Panguana that I wrote for the Munich academic journal *Aviso*, in collaboration with my colleague Professor Ernst-Gerhard Burmeister, the married couple Margaretha and Siegfried Stocker, who are the owners of the Hofpfisterei, the biggest medium-sized ecologically producing bakery business in Germany, became aware of Panguana. When we happened to meet personally by chance in the State Collection of Zoology at an opening for the artist Rita Mühlbauer, who regularly creates art postcards for the Hofpfisterei and had also painted in Panguana, Siegfried Stocker told me that while reading the article he had spontaneously thought: "I would like to get involved in this!"

It was a long time before we truly developed our working relationship, which we cultivate today and about which I am really pleased. First we got to know each other over time, and the Stockers thoroughly weighed all the pros and cons of sponsoring Panguana. But in the end a dream came true for me: In 2008, Siegfried and Margaretha Stocker decided to support Panguana through the additional purchase of areas threatened by slash and burn, and to make a vital, long-term contribution to the expansion of the research station.

It is a partnership that is well matched. As my parents were pioneers, the Stockers were no less so. To bet on a purely ecological bakery business in the early 1970s was widely regarded at the time as quite risky. With their self-commitment to sustainability in their business model, the ecological cultivation of ingredients for the breads and the renunciation of all chemical supplements, they were far ahead of their time, very much like my father, who was already reflecting on ecological contexts at a time when ecology still didn't mean anything to the broader consciousness of our society. When the Stockers decided to support Panguana, it finally became possible to take a decisive step forward.

In Peruvian environmental policy too, some things have changed for the better. Nature conservation used to be under the jurisdiction of the ministry of agriculture. However, since 2009, there is a newly created ministry of the environment. With this restructuring, it became possible to classify private and smaller tracts of land as protected areas. Though this meant starting over from scratch once again—after all, I had already filed an application with the original nature conservation authorities—I saw that it paid to redo all the work and in even greater detail. For meanwhile, thanks to our sponsors, we could expand the previously 460-acre land to 1,730 acres. We had it surveyed again and hope to be able to turn it as soon as possible into a private nature reserve. For then, our efforts for the conservation of the land will have a new, official status, in the eyes of the surrounding population as well as the authorities. It will be still more respected; for, unfortunately, there are still today far too many people who seek only short-term profit. A lot of animals live in Panguana, and there are also people who, unfortunately, see in them nothing but game to be hunted. But for us, of course, that is out of the question. On top of that, our forest contains a great deal of precious timber, and there are prospectors who move through the rain forests in search of mahogany trees. When they find one, they try to wheedle it out of the owner for fifty dollars or less, only to resell it at a profit many times that amount. Such a tree requires more than one hundred years to reach a size that makes it interesting to timber merchants, and then it ends up in Europe as window crosspieces. The wonderful lupuna trees, to which the Indians ascribed magic powers, are manufactured into plywood.

With his commitment Moro has managed to protect our animals and plants all these years. There is no question that it will be simpler for him when Panguana receives the official status of a nature reserve. Our Indian neighbors living at a distance of a few miles have also come to understand our aims and have promised to respect the land. We involve them in our plans too, and in return we support them in their concerns, so that the whole thing becomes a common effort, which can only be advantageous for all parties in the long run. For many people have meanwhile grasped that: Once the forest is destroyed, it will require centuries for it to grow back—if that happens at all.

Meanwhile, the climate is changing, and the rivers are drying out. The younger people might see that more than their elders. But I am certain that we can influence a great deal there. Today, Panguana already serves as a model research station. It can definitely achieve the same as a nature reserve. It doesn't always have to be gigantic national parks—small areas, too, have their significance, and, of course, we will try to steadily expand the grounds.

Once again we are packing our suitcases. Our time in Panguana—for this visit—is approaching its end. Now it is time to head back to Pucallpa, and from there over the Andes to Lima. Here some pivotal meetings at the ministry await me, and I am already looking forward to being able to take another step toward our goal.

Everything began here in the jungle. During my odyssey, between death and life, I gained a completely new relationship to things. I learned that nothing, above all not life, can be taken for granted. Since then, I live every day as if it were my last. That also means never taking quarrels with me into the night, following my parents' example. And the awe of nature—that was burned into my heart already when I was a child. I realized later that not all biologists think this way. My parents never instructed me; they imparted to me the respect for nature as a matter of course. Today I regard that as their most important legacy.

Those days are gone, and yet they shape the present. And the present, likewise, shapes the future. The rain forest is so indescribably manifold, and even though people have been working on it for decades, we understand only a fraction of what makes it up. In Panguana, too, after about half a century of scientific work, there remain endless things for us to discover. There are colleagues of ours who study a single fallen tree trunk for weeks and find hundreds of new insect species. To have Panguana declared a nature reserve—for me that's only the beginning. I have many more dreams; one of them, for example, is someday to be able to perform canopy research at our station.

I often cannot help thinking about how wonderful it would be if my parents could see what we have achieved today. The fact that Panguana still exists after such a long time. How the area has grown and will continue to grow. The fact that so many scientists come here every year from all over the world and do their part to constantly improve our understanding of the rain forest's wonders. I am sure it would make them happy. I have taken up their legacy on every level, keeping an eye fixed on the future. The future of the rain forest over which I crashed, which received me and saved me and gave me so much, is also the future of humanity, our climate and our planet Earth. Someone as deeply bound to it as I am will never stop working for its survival.

Acknowledgments

Panguana remains an inexhaustible Shangri-la for naturalist investigators and scientists. My colleague and I study the rain forest of Panguana, 2006. (Photo courtesy of Juliane (Koepcke) Diller)

My parents taught me to love the boundless diversity of the rain forest and ultimately made it possible for me to survive in it.

My new life I owe with certainty to the five woodcutters who found and rescued me after almost eleven days in the jungle. In particular I would like to mention Marcio Rivera and Amado Pereira, who brought me back to civilization.

The doctors at the Instituto Lingüístico de Verano in Yarinacocha and their families, who so compassionately took me in, were responsible for my swift recovery. I will never forget their selfless dedication.

Without the families of Edith Noeding and Gaby Hennig, as well as many other friends who supported me in Lima, I would not have been able to reintegrate so quickly into my life after the crash.

In Kiel, my aunt Cordula Koepcke took me in and helped me find my way quickly and successfully in Germany and especially in school. She played a decisive role in ensuring that I could soon find a new, appealing home.

The whole Módena family in Peru—but first and foremost Moro, his mother, Doña Lida, his wife, Nery, as well as his sisters, Luz, Pola and Gina, were constantly ready to help and took me into their families as if it went without saying. The fact that Panguana still exists today after over forty years is due solely to them.

Since my childhood our family's good friend Alwin Rahmel in Lima has stood by me and helped me without hesitation. He rescued me from many difficult situations and led me through the labyrinth of the bureaucracy.

Professor Dr. Ernst Josef Fittkau advised me in Munich on my dissertation on bats and made it possible for me to return in such an intensive way to the rain forest of Panguana.

The director Werner Herzog led me back to the site of my memories, and it is thanks to his scrupulous film work that today I can deal much more calmly and openly with my fate and the reactions of the public.

I am extraordinarily grateful to Siegfried and Margaretha Stocker for their generous support of Panguana. Without their long-term commitment, our goal of turning the research station into a nature reserve would still be unattainable.

My agent, Christine Proske, from Ariadne-Buch, in Munich, as well as Bettina Feldweg and her colleagues at Malik-Verlag encouraged and reinforced my decision to publish my experiences in detail after such a long time. But without the excellent, sensitive work of Beate Rygiert, this book would never have come into being. Our editor, Gabriele Ernst, put the finishing touches on the German manuscript.

Tracy Ertl, of TitleTown Publishing, worked with great dedication to make this book available to English-speaking readers. My story has been served excellently by Ross Benjamin's meticulous translation. Stephanie Finnegan's attention to detail as the editor of the English version was also indispensable.

My husband, Erich, shares my enthusiasm for the rain forest and is my source of strength. Many a time, his energetic encouragement and his endurance have kept me from giving up.

Index

My parents at their workplace in the Natural History Museum of Lima, Peru, 1960.
(Photo courtesy of Juliane (Koepcke) Diller)

Index of People, Family & Key Places

Note: Family members are listed individually with their given names in the Index of People and are listed by their familial names under the heading "Family."

PEOPLE

KEY PLACES

Germany
3, 8-11, 13-19, 24-27, 33-35, 41, 43, 45, 48-49, 52, 54-57, 94, 111, 127-129, 136-139, 143, 147-148, 150-153, 162-167, 173-174, 177-178, 181-182, 184, 188-189, 193, 198, 200, 204, 209-210, 212, 214, 219-220

Humboldt House
8, 12, 14-15, 18, 44, 56, 176

Lima
xi, 4-5, 7-10, 12-14, 16-17, 24, 26-27, 29-31, 33-35, 37-38, 41,41, 45, 47, 49, 52-58, 62-63, 69, 79, 85-86, 93, 108, 112, 122, 137, 139, 141, 143, 146-151, 153, 57-158, 162-164, 174, 181, 185, 187, 190, 194, 196, 198, 202, 204, 210, 216-217, 219, 222

Panguana
4, 5, 13, 30, 37, 40, 46-58, 65, 73-77, 84-86, 89, 91, 97, 104, 107-108, 110, 141, 143, 145-147, 150, 155, 157-163, 167-169, 173, 175-176, 178, 179, 181-188, 191, 193-195, 198-200, 202-206, 209-217, 219-220

Peru   vi, vii, 3-4, 7-11, 14-19, 24, 27-30, 33-34, 36-37, 39-40, 47, 54-56, 62-63, 66, 72, 75, 78, 108, 117, 119-121, 127-128, 133, 137-139, 150, 152-153, 155, 159, 164-168, 172, 174, 176-178, 181-185, 187, 189, 193-194, 196, 201, 203, 210-215, 219

Pucallpa
xi, 37, 45, 48-50, 53, 56-58, 61, 63, 66, 69, 80, 82, 84-87, 95, 101, 108-109, 112, 117, 119, 122-124, 132-133, 137, 139-146, 149-158, 160-161, 172, 187, 189, 194, 202, 216

Río Pachitea
11-12, 37, 46-47, 49, 103, 143, 159-160, 172, 178, 186, 191, 194

Tournavista
37, 46-48, 78, 83, 103-104, 110, 117, 144, 172

Ucayali
37, 84 ,87

Yuyapichis
37-38, 46-47, 49-51, 59, 75-77, 86, 143, 155-156, 160-161, 169, 171, 178, 185-186, 188, 194-195, 200-202, 211, 213